PERSPECTIVES OF ARCHAEOLOGY, ART AND CULTURE IN EARLY ANDHRA DESA

PERSPECTIVES OF ARCHAEOLOGY, ART AND CULTURE IN EARLY ANDHRA DESA

K. RAMAMOHAN RAO

ADITYA PRAKASHAN
NEW DELHI

First published: 1992

ISBN. 81-85689-01-6

Published by Pradeep Kumar Goel for Aditya Prakashan
F-14/65, Model Town II, Delhi-110 009.
and printed at Crescent Printing Works (Pvt.) Ltd.,
P-14, Cannaught Circus, New Delhi-110 001.

DEDICATED TO THE
LOTUS FEET OF
MY BELOVED PARENTS

Contents

List of Figures and Plates

Figures:

Plates:

List of Abbreviations

AI	: Ancient India. Bulletin of Archaeological Survey of India.
APGAS	: Andhra Pradesh Government Archaeological Series
APGMS	: Andhra Pradesh Government Museum Series
AR	: Annual Report of the Archaeological Survey of India
ARE	: Annual Report of Indian Epigraphy or South Indian Epigraphy
ASB	: Asiatic Society of Bengal, Calcutta
ASI	: Archaeological Survey of India
ASSI	: Archaeological Survey of South India
CII	: Corpus Inscriptionum Indicarum, Calcutta
EA	: Epigraphia Andhrica, Hyderabad
EI	: Epigraphia Indica, Calcutta/Bombay/Delhi
IA	: Indian Antiquary, Bombay
JNSI	: Journal of the Numismatic Society of India, Varanasi
JAAP	: Journal Archaeology in Andhra Pradesh, Hyderabad
JAH & C	: Journal of Andhra History and Culture, Guntur
JAHRS	: Journal of Andhra Historical Research Society, Rajahmundry and Hyderabad.
JAU	: Journal of Annamalai University, Chidambaram
JIH	: Journal of Indian History, Madras
JISOA	: Journal of the Indian Society of Oriental Arts
JRAS	: Journal of Royal Asiatic Society, London
KSS	: Kashi Sanskrit Series, Varanasi
NSP	: Nirnayasagar Press Edition, Bombay
SBE	: Sacred Books of the East Series, Delhi
SGP	: Superintendent of Govt. Printing, India, Calcutta
TSS	: Trivendrum Sanskrit Series

Foreword

Andhra forms a distinct territorial and cultural unit in our country. It has made rich contributions to the streams of Indian History. The fertility of its soil, its vast mineral resources, the skill of its artisans and the adventurous spirit of its merchants have always made it one of the richest tracts of the country. The Andhras have left some glorious monuments which are cherished with reverence and pride by the people of the country. It will be in fitness of things if the cultural, religious and socio-economic ideals of their founders are studied in a more scientific manner and greater details. Our heritage, and in particular that of the Andhras are rich enough in vitality.

Several scholars have devoted themselves to study the historical, cultural and antiquarian research of the Andhras; the early history of Andhra has been the subject of study by a number of historians. The studies of K. Gopalachari, D.C. Sircar, B.V. Krishna Rao to name only a few are well known. The present work aims to add to our understanding of this period by interpreting the fresh data from the archaeological sources. Even though the political history of the Vishnukundins is portrayed by other scholars, there is no systematic work on the cultural achievement of the dynasty. The author has attempted to fill the gap and has shown the skill in correlating the evidence from different sources. The author has utilised systematically and skilfully the numismatic and field archaeological materials judiciously to produce a clear and cogent narrative of the history and culture of the region from 3rd century AD to 6th century AD.

This book is divided into three unequal chapters besides a comprehensive bibliography and index. The book deserves considerable attention as it is devoted to a study in depth of material culture under the Vishnukundins based on the archaeological evidence, most of which is exposed for the first time by the Department of Archaeology and Museums, Andhra Pradesh from its excavations. It elaborately describes and evaluates the settlement pattern, the structural remains of the contributions in the field of art and architecture, summarises accomplishments in the field of religion and finally examines the details of the material life. In this part of the book the author has attempted to analyse the formative features of the Andhra culture. He has tapped the source material from the excavations mainly from Keesaragutta, Yeleswaram besides various other early historical sites and has presented a convincing picture of the contemporary society in early Andhra Desa.

This well-knit and convincingly argued work proves the ability of the author to exploit the available evidences to the best advantage and his grasp over the research methodology. This is a difinite contribution to the study of early Andhra history and to our knowledge on the history and culture of this part of the country in the period under consideration.

The present study is a welcome addition to the existing knowledge on the subject and as such would be read with interest by researchers.

I greet this venture of K. Ramamohan Rao and have great pleasure in recommending it to students of early Andhra culture.

Mysore,
Mahashivaratri (February 12, 1991) B.K. GURURAJA RAO

Preface

The present work embodies in my main Ph. D thesis for approval by the Karnataka University, Dharwad. In this work, a sincere effort has been made to present a complete survey of archaeology, art and culture in early Andhra Desa, and in doing so both the literary and the archaeological sources, have as far as practicable, been thoroughly utilised. This work is mainly based on archaeology rather than other traditional historical evidences, and an attempt has been made to give a clear understanding to the readers and also to distinguish how archaeology contributes to history in bridging up the lacunae.

In the preparation of this work I have been benefited much by many scholarly works. It would, therefore, be unfair not to record my deep sense of gratitude to the scholars whose works I have thoroughly utilised. I would be failing in my duty if I do not record my profound regards and indebtedness to my revered guide Dr. B. K. Guru Raja Rao, Professor, Ancient History and Archaeology, Mysore University, under whose scholarly shade this work was prepared. As a supervisor, he was always ready to discuss problems connected with my research work. I am ever grateful to him for this and encouragements, besides, valuable guidance, I received from him. Inspite of his busy schedule he was kind enough to write a foreword to this book.

My profound thanks are due to Dr. S. H. Ritti, Professor and Head of the Department, Ancient Indian History and Epigraphy, Karnataka Universty, Dharwad for the encouragement and assistance at every stage without which this thesis would not have been materialised.

My sincere thanks are also due to Dr. V. V. Krishna Sastry, Director of Archaeology and Museums, A. P. Hyderabad from whom I always received encouragement and valuable suggestions. Dr. G. Jawaharlal deserves my profound thanks for his whole hearted co-operation in carrying out my field work.

I am very much grateful to the Department of Archaeology and Museums, Andhra Pradesh for the financial assistance which I received from it in the form of part-time fellowship for a period of two years during the period of research.

My thanks are also due to Smt. M. Varalakshmi, Librarian for supplying books from the Departmental Library with utmost patience and forbearance which enabled me to carry out this part of my thesis work.

Sri Dh. U. Venkateswarlu, Typist also deserves my thanks for typing the thesis.

I am thankful to the Karnataka University for awarding Ph. D. degree to me and also for permitting me to publish it.

I will be failing in my duty if I do not express my thanks to M/s. Aditya Prakashan, New Delhi for publishing this book.

Last but not the least, my wife Maruthi gave me constant encouragement to complete my work.

Sri Laxmi Narasimha Nilayam,
Hyderabad. K. RAMAMOHAN RAO

Introduction

History begins with the written record, Archaeology is believed to be pre-eminently concerned with pre-history. No doubt the archaeologist produces the facts and interprets them for the reconstruction of the lives and stories of those who have left no written records. But very recently it has come to be realised that archaeological methods of recovering data from the past can greatly increase our knowledge of what occured in strictly historical periods. The evidence of the archaeological excavations can vastly increase our knowledge of societies and places which we have previously known only from written records.

Archaeology will also be possible to apply to illuminate the history of many places, in elucidating the lives and the life ways of the people.

Archaeology provides primary evidence for precisely material setting and physical evolution. The evidence which showed that man had a very long history was archaeological in the sense that it was dug out of the ground. The facts that made the findings into evidence about what occurred in the past were the relative positions and depths of the various items that were found.

Archaeology began as a part of Science. Excavation is supplementing our knowledge and adding new vistas to our outlook over man's past due to the fact that antique objects have been dug of the ground scientifically. The achievements of the science of archaeology is given to civilization and history.

The archaeologist, in fact has to keep his eyes open for evidence of all sorts. Archaeology illustrates the history of man and his cultures. In this sense archaeology is a study of man. Archaeology deals with all the material remains of man, the objects he used and made, his dwelling places and defensive structures, his tools and weapons, the remains of his food, his own bones and burial places and from these, deduces how he lived. Archaeology provides the information for the history before the beginnings of written records.

The study of Indian Archaeology has tended to be divided into two main fields, the pre-historic with most attention paid to the great Indus Valley civilisation and work on the art and literature of the much later Hindu, Buddhist and other cultures of the present. Recently brilliant use has been made of contacts with the Roman world through trade in the 1st century A.D. The other branch of Indian Archaeology, the study of Hindu, Buddhist and other cultures has mainly concentrated on the artistic, historical and epigraphical aspects. Almost every area in which archaeology is studied leads on to others, either linking us with another field which is well known, or fringed by areas as yet largely unknown.

The Andhras have left some glorious monuments which are cherished with reverence and pride by the people of the country and it will be in the fitness of things if the history and religions and cultural ideals of their founders are studied in a more scientific manner and in greater detail. The pre-Chalukyan history of the Andhra Desa since the disappearance of the Satavahanas is a period of fragmentary events of royal dynasties. The Vishnukundins played an important part in the political, cultural and art history of the Andhra Desa. The credit of placing them in the map of Indian art goes to the talented French scholar G. J. Dubreuil who first brought to the notice of the scholarly world the importance of the Vishnukundin art, especially architecture.

Excavations carried out in Andhra Pradesh in recent years have opened up enormous new horizons for further co-operation and mutual enrichment between archaeology and history.

Archaeological investigations carried out on the top of the hill-Keesaragutta revealed fortification wall with gates, secondary fortification wall, palace complex, square brick shrines, rows of Siva-lingas, etc., besides valuable antiquities including red-ware pottery, beautiful terracottas, stuccos, beads, etc., all belonging to the Vishnukundin period. This is the only fortification wall that has been brought to light by the spade of archaeologist next to the fortification traced at Nagarjunakonda.[1] The fortification wall, now in ruins on the top of the hill at Keesaragutta, encompassing the huge brick structure of religious as well as secular buildings show that it was a hill-fort (Giri-Durga) constructed in the post-Satavahana period by the Vishnukundin rulers following the cannons of Hindu Science of architecture as enunciated by the ancient writers viz., Kautilya, etc.

Archaeological excavations brought to light clear evidences of habitation belonging to the Vishnukundin period at Nelakondapalli of Khammam District, and Yeleswaram of Nalgonda district on the northern bank of the river Krishna. About ten Buddhist sculptures were discovered at Nelakondapalli in a private land while digging for pati earth. The pit where the idols were discovered was extended and exposed the brick structure constructed with 50 cm. × 25 cm. × 8 cm. size bricks nicely lime plastered to a thickness of over an inch. In course of the operation, hidden and visible sculptural wealth consisting of a number of broken fragments essential for moulding the broken idols were collected. Very interesting brick-structures relating to the manufacture and preservation of the marble Buddhist idols were traced out. A trough measuring 4.45 m. × 1.96 m. × 0.80 m. appears to have intended for preserving the idols under lime plaster and that they were subsequently given high polish. Similar trough-like structures, three in alignment separated by a drain were also brought to light. A thick deposit of lime is noticed in the tubs. The stratigraphy of the trial trenches dug in the mound has shown two brick structures one over the other separated by a layer containing morrum and fine sand. The first phase of the construction was made with brick mud and mortar. The brick wall in the second phase was constructed with lime mortar. The flooring and the walls were thickly plastered with lime. A Vishnukundin coin with lion on the obverse and a kalasa flanked by a lamp stand on either side inside a rayed circle on the reverse was recovered from this layer. Fragments of pottery met with at the site include decorated and designed storage jars, water jars and vessels, of red polished ware and fabric varying from coarse to fine. A beautiful terracotta human figurine with two horns on either side of the head is found which resembles the horned *dvarapalakas* in the cave and other structural temples of the Vishnukundin period.

The excavations carried out at Rajahmundry have brought to light a brick wall, on the bank of the Godavari near the old stair case intended for the bathing ghat. The wall was constructed with brick of the size of 50 cm. × 25 cm. × 8 cm. The structural activity of the earliest period consists of the remains of a wall like structure encompassing a circular structure in brick which is superimposed by the square cellas. The inner length and breadth of the cella is 2.3 m. × 1.7 m. There is a wall running east to west, a few metres away on the north from the above cella. This wall must be an enclosure wall but it's construction was abruptly stopped for reasons unknown. This incomplete wall is seen in bits in the same alignment, each bit having ends with successively receding courses. Mud has been used as binding material.

Yeleswaram a village located in a valley on the bank of the river Krishna contiguous to Nagarjunakonda valley, caught the attention of the pre-historic man who settled down here before the dawn of civilisation and it remained a cradle of culture in historical period. Once it was a flourishing city at the time of Ikshvakus. The excavations carried out at Yeleswaram yielded a hoard of Vishnukundin coins right over the post-Ikshvaku period and it can be inferred that this valley came under the suzerainty of Vishnukundins after the Ikshvakus. An enclosure wall was brought to light pertaining to this period. A brick structure appeared to have been intended for some ritualistic import as sockets were made at regular intervals around a raised pedestal for the erection of wooden columns to support a canopy. A brick structure, something like a chamber, was discovered which functioned probably as a votive shrine for installing a *Banalinga*. Another brick structure of the nature of votive shrine installed with a *Banalinga* was found. The enclosure wall was renovated during this period ın the same alignment and the stratum was full of fallen debris. The brick structure referred to above continued in this period and was installed with *Banalinga* connected by an abhisheka drain. The most noteworthy finds of the period are the five miniature votive shrines found near the temple complex at Yeleswaram. These shrines have a low *adhistana*, flat *kapota* and *vimans* of two steps surmounted by a semi-circular *Sikhara* incised with an inscription, the characters of which resemble some of the characters of the inscriptions of the Vishnukundin period datable to circa 4th century AD. It has a linga on the vedi inside.

During the period of Vishnukundins the constructional activities were on the increase as is evidenced from their copper plate grants viz., Tummalagudem Set I and II. The Vishnukundins inherited the artistic traditions of both the Ikshvakus, whom they succeeded and the Vakatakas with whom they came into contact. The cave temples of Vijayawada, the structural temples such as Satyavolu, Kadamalakalava, Mukhalingam go back to the Vishnukundin period. The palace complex with massive enclosure walls, brick shrines etc., all constructed with bricks measuring 50 cm. × 25 cm. × 8 cm. at Keesaragutta, show that the building architecture flourished during that period and that the ancient Silpa Sastras were followed in all respects. To cite an example, the shape of the palace complex is like the "MAULIKA" mansion described in MANASARA.[2] The Maulika mansion is shaped like a winnowing basket and consists of three rows of buildings. It is likely that two more building complex consisting number of mansions inside, existed continuous to the above palace complex as evidenced from the two compound walls exposed outside the enclosure wall, in the recent excavations. Such constructional activities have also been noticed at Yeleswaram, Nelakondapalli Rajahmundry, Gummadam, Gollathagudi, etc. in Andhra Pradesh.

The Vishnukundin contribution to art and architecture hardly won the recognition it deserves at the hands of scholars who devoted themselves to the study of Indian art and architecture.

The Vishnukundin period witnessed all round progress in the field of fine arts. The votive shrines with or without Bana lingas inside these shrines found in the Yeleswaram excavations,[3] a beautiful sculpture of Vishnu[4] whose head and feet are mutilated found at Yeleswaram, the early sculpture of Narasimha[5] showing Vishnu in anthromorphic form and also in animal form, discovered over a hillock at Kondamotu, a stone-plaque of Mother Goddess[6] and the decorated globular pot[7] recovered from Keesaragutta are the best examples of Vishnukundin's art. Beautifully modelled human and animal stucco figurines used for decorating the walls of the buildings were exhumed at Keesaragutta. A terracotta figure finely depicting a mother holding a child in her left hand has been found. The head of the figure is broken. The collection of the stuccos include a stucco with floral designs, head of a lion, head of a swan-like bird, animal face with circular eyes and a head of a tiger with nose, mouth and two incisors prominent. Some stuccos are painted in ochre, yellow and green.

Chiselled or carved semi-circular, rectangular bricks, some of them plastered with lime, one painted in ochre, yellow and green have been met with.

The age of the Vishnukundins is a trasitional period in the religious history of the country. Though the early kings of the Vishnukundin dynasty like Govindavarman I and Vikramendrabhattaraka followed Buddhism, the later rulers of the family were staunch followers of Brahmanic Hindu Dharma; they styled themselves as 'Parama-maheswaras'[8] and their family deity was "SRI PARVATA SWAMIN". They also worshipped Ganapati, Siva, Vishnu, Devi (Durga) as evidenced from the carvings of the Vijayawada group of cave temples, with special reference to Siva. They built a number of temples, throughout their kingdom in honour of Siva which includes innumerable miniature votive shrines found at Yeleswaram and the row of lingas at Keesaragutta. All the Vishnukundins appear to be staunch followers of Pasupata sect influenced by Agamas, and also patronised the doctrine of "*Panchayatana*". The worship of Vishnu, the cult of Mother Goddess, along with Buddhism and Jainism were also popular during the Vishnukundin period as the kings were known for their religious tolerance.

Buddhism which appears to have been dominant during the time of the Satavahanas began to show signs of decay under the Ikshvakus, who succeeded them as rulers of the coastal Andhra. Though the stupas and viharas were still built for the Buddha by the ladies of the royal family, several of the kings and their officials followed the Brahmanic Hindu Dharma, under the Vishnukundins. Buddhism continued to lose ground steadily until it became practically extinct by the end of the Vishnukundin period.

The Vishnukundins strove hard to uphold the dharma, and spent much of their wealth in promoting goodness. They built stupas, viharas, temples, etc., and made gifts, of land and money for their upkeep.

The art of working in metals during the Vishnukundin period was excellent. A flat iron piece with rivet measuring eleven centimetres in length and three centimetres in breadth, probably used as hinges for the doors and an iron spearhead or a similar weapon, 12.5 cm. in length and one centimetre in breadth have been recovered from the excavations at Keesaragutta. Another iron object 5.5 cm. long, slightly bulging in the middle has also been met with.

The emergence of the historical period marked the maximum usage of iron particularly during the Ikshvaku and the Vishnukundin periods.[9]

The iron objects recovered from Yeleswaram during the excavations throw abundant light on the well flourishing iron industry.[10]

Large number of Vishnukundin coins have been reported from several ancient sites in Andhra Desa and Maharashtra as well. A. M. Shastri has stated that the coins recovered in Maharashtra, at first glance, give an appearance of being copper coins and look rather heavy in proportion to their size and that a recent metallurgical analysis has revealed a peculiarity of their metallic composition in as much as they comprise an iron core with the coating of a thin sheet of copper on the surface.[11]

REFERENCES

1. ________, 1957-58; Indian Archaeology, A Review, p. 5
2. Manasara; 1934; Ch.XXXV.
3. Abdul Waheed Khan, M. D. 1963; A Monograph on Yeleswaram Excavations, A.P G.A.S.No.14
4. *Ibid.*, plate XXVII.
5. Abdul Waheed Khan, Md. 1964; An early Sculpture of Narasimha, A.P.G.A.S. No.16
6. Vide II, ART, pp. 92-93 ff.
7. Vide IV, Material Culture-Pottery; p. 118-119 ff.
8. Epigraphia Indica IV, pp. 193-198.
9. Abdul Waheed Khan, Md.; 1963; *op.cit*; p. 21.
10. *Ibid.*, p. 48.
11. Ajay Mitra Shastri; 1973; Vishnukundins in Maharashtra p. 96.

CHAPTER 1

Settlement Pattern

Land and the man are the true foundation of the history of any country. The actions of many have their first cause in the nature of the land in which he lives, and history is the record of his attempts to satisfy his evergrowing needs, both on the material and spiritual plane. The physical features of Andhra Desa, its mountains, rivers, climate and forests have a great influence on human character and largely determine human action.

Andhra Desa covers a wide expanse of territory which presents infinite varieties of soil and scenery. Wide downs, rolling plains smiling with harvest, fantastic tors and logans, luxuriant forests, rivers tumbling over precipices and leaping in wild water falls, and streams foaming in wild torrents along with rugged rocky beds, combine in one superb panorama the varying aspects of awe and beauty. Alluvial tracts added to the natural wealth of the country.

Walls and rocks that crown many of the hill-tops were easily turned into impregnable fortresses.

Archaeological excavations and explorations conducted by the Department of Archaeology, Andhra Pradesh in the recent years have revealed evidence of human habitation belonging to the early historical period particularly of the Vishnukundin period at (1) Yeleswaram in Nalgonda district (2) Keesaragutta in Rangareddy district (3) Tummalagudem in Nalgonda district (4) Gollathagudi (5) Gummadam in Mahaboobnagar district (6) Rajahmundry in East Godavari district; (7) Vijayawada in Krishna district and (8) Veerapuram in Kurnool District.

Yeleswaram

Yeleswaram is situated on the bank of the river Krishna in Devarakonda taluk of Nalgonda district. The village is located in a valley, covering an area of 13 square kilometres and is contiguous to the Nagarjunakonda valley. These two valleys form a ring of hills cut into two halves by the river Krishna.

This valley is relieved by small-hillocks with precipitous hills surrounded on all sides and the swift flowing river Krishna serving as a means of both defence and transport. The picturesque landscape and the natural setting of the valley caught the attention of the pre-historic man who settled down here before the dawn of civilisation as evidenced by stone tools left by him and it remained a cradle of culture in the early and mediaeval historical periods. Vast and varied remains have been encountered belonging to the late Satavahanas, Pallavas, Vishnukundins, Chalukyas and many other dynasties that followed in succession right upto the late mediaeval period or even modern times. Large scale excavations were undertaken during the period 1960-1965 as this valley was threatened with submergence under the waters of Nagarjunasagar Dam across the river Krishna.

Excavations laid bare several distinct occupation levels lying one above the other and exposed a whole phase of human society teeming with life.

The first civilised people who settled here were megalithic folk whose burials were encountered nearly 3.09 m. to 3.68 m. below the surface.[1] The historical period witnessed building construction activity. The excavation yielded a rich crop of minor antiquities such as terracottas, iron implements, potsherds both designed and decorated, chaitya shaped sprinklers, high-necked vases, bangles, stucco, coins etc., which shed enough light on the culture milieu of different periods.

In a small pot, a hoard of 49 coins of Vishnukundin dynasty was found which had on the obverse a rampant lion and on the reverse two hanging lamps etc. This clearly proved that the direct successors of the Ikshvakus in this valley were the Vishnukundins.[2]

During the early part of this period dull red-ware of Ikshvaku period continued but the grey ware emerged and pre-dominated this pottery. The important finds of this period consisted of beads, terracotta, figurines, stuccos and glass bangles, iron slags, iron nails, stapplers, finials, stone pots, etc. Some votive Saivite shrines were found associated with layer 4 which is assigned to Vishnukundin period. Layer 4 cutting I consisted of ritty earth mixed with white pellets and brick bats, layer 4-cutting II-contained rubbles, brick bats and gravel mixed with sand. In this period an enclosure wall was brought to light. Brick structures continued in this period and was installed with *Banalinga* connected by an abhisheka drain.

The spade of the archaeologists brought out a good number of implements, representing various activities of the people in agriculture, building construction, warfare and other household objects. The emergence of the historical period marked the maximum use of iron and the Vishnukundin period particularly yielded a large quantity. The iron implements could be classified broadly under four categories namely (1) building materials (2) agricultural implements (3) implements of war and chase (4) household objects.[3]

Keesaragutta

Keesaragutta is about 40 kilometres away from Hyderabad which is a great Saivite centre from times immemorial. The name Keesaragutta might have derived from Kesarigiri a hill of lions or lion hill.[4]

Physical features of Keesaragutta and its surroundings[5]

The district is mostly hilly, and thickly wooded, known as the Rajkonda range and the Anantagiri range of hills which is composed of high-level laterite across the district. Isolated granite hills are seen everywhere. The slope of the land is from west to east and south-east. The geological formation is of the Archaean greiss. Tors and boulders of fantastic shapes are seen everywhere, composed of basalt and granite piled up in picturesque confusion.

The most important river of the district is Musi which rises from Anantagiri hills near Sivareddipet and flows almost due east; it joins the Krishna river near Vadapalli in Nalgonda district.

FLORA AND FAUNA

There are two protected forest tracts in the district where certain kinds of good timber viz., teak, ebony, and nallamaddi are available. Unprotected forest tracts exist in all parts, consisting of ghairi or common wood used as fuel and also for thatching and wattling. Low scrubby jungles give cover to leopards, bears, hyenas and occasionally tigers, while in the more open plains antelopes abound. Partridges, quail and wild pigeons are very common, and in the tanks and rice fields wild duck, teal and snipa are plentiful in the winter.

Climate and Rain fall

The climate is salubrious and equable, exempt from the fierce heat and severe cold of the north and the depressing influences of the coast. However, the numerous tanks and streams make the climate some-what damp especially during the rainy season. The temparature during the winter and summer seasons stands at 13° 9° and 39.8° centigrade respectively. The average rainfall of the district is about 90.68 cm. or 35.7 in. The district recieves rains both from the south-west and north-east monsoons mostly from the month of June to August but occasionally in September, October and November also.

Geological Setting[6] Archaeans

The prevalent rock belonging to this group is known as "The Peninsular Granite Complex" which includes a variety of granites polyphiritic, equigranular, massive, banded and streaky. Depending on the colour of felspar two types of granites are recognised one pink and the other grey, but there is gradation from one to the other. Rocks are usually coarse to medium grained and wide variation is seen regarding their textural features. The most common minerals are quartz, felspar ferromagnessian minerals which include biotite, hornblends and epidote, where as magnetite, apacite, zircon, sphene, allanite and pyrite, occur as accessories. The granites are traversed by numerous quartz and pegmatite veins and basic dykes, which vary in size considerably from small veinlots to large roofs. The basic dykes stand out prominently as ridges trending in east-north-east, west-south-west or north-north-east, south-south-west directions and range from 30 metres to several kilometres in length. These are either deleritic or basaltic in composition, consisting of plagioclass felspar and antige.

Bhimas

Rocks younger than the Archaeans but older than the Deccan traps are represented by the sedimentary rocks known as the Bhimas. These include grits, sandstones, shale and lime stones. These overlie the granites unconformbly with coarse gritty and pebby sandstones at the base, succeeded by shales, lime stones. The shales are olive green, drab or purplish in colour and the limestones are grey, cream coloured and flaggy.

Deccan Trap

Lava flows known as Deccan traps cover a considerable portion of the district, concealing part of the Bhimas as well as the Archaeans. These traps are formed by the solidification of lava extruded through fissure like eruptions in the older rocks. As the flow of lava was intermittent, there are several layers of flows of the rock, the individual layers differing slightly in texture and thickness. They are mostly fine to medium grained, dark grey to almost black in colour and consist of plagioclase felspar and angite. Some of the layers of the traps are scoriaceous due to escape of gases through the lava before it was fully consolidated. The scoriae or cavities in such rocks were later partly or wholly filled by secondary minerals, like zeolites, calcite and various forms of crypto crystalline sillica, such as chalcedomy agate, onyx, jasper etc.

Laterite

Laterite is a product of tropical alternations suffered by some rocks and is developed typically in the tropics. It is a porous, pitted, clay like rock with red, yellow, brown, grey or mottled columnes depending on some measure on the composition.

Mineral Resources

The district is gifted with deposits of clays, felspar, quartz, kankar, laterite, ochre,. Granite is quarried extensively for use as building and constructional material. The granites of the district provide excellent building stones. The granites in the pink and grey shades are capable of taking high polish.

Keesaragutta about 90 m. high from the planes with a flat and undulated area over the top of the hills extending from 3 to 4 Sq Km. was enclosed by a fort wall now defunct. The fort was provided with four main gates to stop direct onslaughts of the enemy forces. Some water gates were also provided near the water pools for fetching water into the fort. As there are no perennial sources of water such as a river or streams in the vicinity, the natural depressions at the gradients were cross-bunded during the Vishnukundin period to store rain water. There is a huge tank at the foot of the fort on the west which must have served both as a source of drinking water and as a deep water hurdle for the protection of the fort. Entire fort is studded with remains of brick structures.

In the course of excavations at the palace complex many Vishnukundin coins of a squatting lion with a spiralled tail and raised fore-paw on the obverse, a poornaghata flanked by two lamp-stands all enclosed in rayed circle on the reverse were found. Besides, beautifully modelled human and animal stucco figurines used for decorating the walls of the building were also recovered. The pottery was red polished, brown polished and dull red-wares. The collection also included a few necks of sprinklers and spouts of red polished vases. The other antiquities were shell bangles, beads of semi-precious stones, a stone plaque of Mother Goddess, and a decorated globular pot, and a human skeleton in inverted position found under the fallen bricks.

The massive style of architecture of the multi-storied secular buildings and the decorative features indicate that it was the palace complex of Vishnukundin period, protected by a secondary fortification wall of rubble which encompasses an approximate area of 1 Sq. Km. The outer and the inner defensive fortification walls, the numerous religious and secular structures inside the fort, the coins, the pottery and other finds, all datable to the Vishnukundin period are evidences enough to prove that Keesaragutta was a centre of human activity in the early Christian era. It can also be deduced that the people settled in and around Keesaragutta during the times of Vishnukundins in view of the historical, political and religious importance of the region in those days.

More details regarding the finds of Keesaragutta excavations are given in the following chapters.

Tummalagudem

Tummalagudem is a village in Ramannapet taluk of Nalgonda district, eight kilometers away from Ramannapet, on Bhuvangiri-Nalgonda road. There is a big tank near the village. The length of the tank bund is about 4 Km. There are reminiscenes of an ancient city on the banks of river 'Musi' extending upto the tank-bund near Tummalagudem. This extensive area is surrounded by fields. Ruined temples, votive shrines, brick structures, basements, show that it was a great city which flourished by the name Indrapalanagaram during the Vishnukundin period. North of Tummalagudem and adjacent to the river Musi there is a hillock called 'Indrapalagutta' extending one Km. in length and half a Km. in breadth. There is an ancient fort on this hillock belonging to the Vishnukundin period.[7] This fort has twelve turrets. On the top of the hill there is a deep tank which is locally known as 'Enugula Bavi'. Big sized bricks, stones, basements, walls and ruined rooms are seen near this tank. The fortification has gates and towers. A figure of priest carrying material for the worship of Lord Siva is carved on a huge boulder. At the back of this hill there is a spacious mandapa supported by twelve pillars. There exists another Siva temple on the eastern side of the hillock. The linga is made of black granite the height of which is 60 cm.

In the vicinity of this temple towards east, there are ruined buildings; adjoining these ruins there is another Siva temple, with a tank to its north, flight of steps leading down to the Musi river. About 200 m. away from Indrapalagutta one hundred and one Sivalingas are seen, carved on flat rock in the Musi river bed.

The people of those times might have preferred the area for their habitation in view of the availability of natural water resources, cultivable fertile lands in the vicinity, abundant rain fall for agricultural operations, natural rocks, and other material required for building activity for secular, religious and defensive purposes.

Gollathagudi

Gollathagudi is situated about 10 Km. from Jadcharla railway station on Secunderabad-Dronachalam metre guage line within the precincts of Alwanpalli village of Jadcharla taluk. Alwanpalli is situated about 100 Km. from Hyderabad.

Excavations at this place, brought to light an early temple of Mahavira with a sanctum, antarala and Mukhamandapa foundations of two more temples with its lime plastered brick walls and the Mukhamandapa. Excavations were continued in order to expose the brick temples situated on the southern flank of the mound IV (Padalagadda) and to clarify their chronological position in the general structural sequence of the site.

The details of the temples were completely obliterated for they were entirely ruined leaving the foundations in position. Three temple plans, all oriented east-west, were brought to light during the excavations. Temple I was built on a plan containing the Garbhagriha, a pillared mandapa and an entrance porch on the east. Temple III consists of a Garbhagriha and an entrance constructed in between these two temples. Temple II originally stood on a simple plan having a Garbhagriha facing east and a pillared mandapa with a northern entrance.

The excavations also yielded large number of stucco figurines which include human and mythical animals.

In the temple south-west of Padalagadda a Nandi carved in granite with its head mutilated and decorated with band of beads with hanging bell around the neck, is found. The size of the bricks used in construction of this temple is 41 cm. × 21 cm. × 7 cm. This must be a Saivite temple of Vishnukundin period.

Red-ware pottery found here consists of storage jars, vases, vessels etc.

Though the entire area, where excavations were conducted, revealed only the temple complex, there are evidences of extensive habitation, half a kilometre away from the temple complex towards Alwanpalli village, where pottery like storage jars of coarse dull red-ware, vases, etc., were found from a deposit of two metres on the road side. On the other side of the Jadcharla-Devarakonda road towards south, pieces of red-ware pottery of early historical period are visible on the surface itself. The land is under cultivation of dry crops like Jawar etc. The area extends upto two kilometres towards south touching the western bank of the Dindi river, a tributory of the Krishna which supplies water both for drinking and agricultural purposes. The river takes a curve near the outskirts of Alwanpalli village giving a picturesque view.

The climate is generally hot with moderate rainfall.

The soils of the area are (1) black cotton soil derived from Deccan traps; (2) Calcurious loamy soils covering the purana sedimentaries; (3) red loamy soil derived from the Dharwar schists and (4) sandy gneissic soil occurring in the granite country. The soils of Mahboobnagar mostly consist of stiff black 'ragur'.[8] Stony red soils are observed in a few parts.

Ancient workings of copper are found in the neighbouring taluks like Mukthal. Quartz viens with malachite stains were also observed in the vicinity.

The pink and grey granites of the area supply any amount of building material for heavy construction. The porphyritic granites take excellent polish and produce decorative stones in pleasing colours. The massive Narji and flaggy limestones yield good material for construction and pavement. The extensive quartzites of Amarabad plateau afford suitable material for construction and also for making grinding stones.

Gummadam

Gummadam ia a small village on Wanaparthy-Kolhapur road in Mahaboobnagar district, a few kilometres away from the river Krishna. This is one of the villages which comes under the submergeable area of Srisailam Project.

Excavations were conducted on the mound situated 1 Km. away from Gummadam towards east which brought to light a Saiva shrine constructed with bricks measuring 40 cm. × 20 cm. × 6 cm. datable to the Vishnukundin period. Linga and Panavatta are partly broken, and uprooted.

Pottery consisting of vases, lids, jars of coarse pale red-ware some of them washed with deep red, were recovered.

Animal bone fragments and terracotta figurines were also found. Evidences of early settlements are noticed in this region. The region enjoys fairly good weather throughout the year. The bulk of the rain fall is received during the later part of the south-west monsoon period.

The main soils of the region are the chalk and the sandy soil. Black cotton soils are also found.

Rajahmundry

Excavations were conducted by the Department of Archaeology and Museums, A. P., at Rajahmundry on the eastern banks of the river Godavari near Chandrika mini-theatre to glean the vertical cultural development at the site. The archaeological site is situated on the banks of the river Godavari bounded by Chandrika theatre on the east and the river

Godavari on the west, an elevated area on the north and a Katcha Municipal road on the south. The site is actually located in the area of Chagalnadu pumping scheme.

The excavations brought to light very interesting stratigraphical and structural evidence from the site. The deposit exhibited 7 layers above the gravel. Layer 7 is the earliest occupational deposit. It indicates structural activity datable on the basis of pottery to 4th century AD. A wall of bricks of the size of 51 cm. × 23 cm. × 7 cm. and 46 cm. × 23 cm. × 7 cm. exposed in the slopes of Godavari bund near the old steps intended for the bathing also belongs to this layer.

The foundations of a brick temple of two rectangular cells was discovered. The temple was badly ruined and no superstructure was extant. No presiding deity is found in the cella. The bricks used in the construction measure 30 cm. × 20 cm. × 7 cm. The bricks of this size were also used in the construction of contemporaneous wall running east-west, a few metres away from the temple on the north. Layer 6 is the earliest layer of the site. Conspicuous change of pottery fabric is of some significance. A structure probably apsidal or round was found below the foundation of the brick cellas. The plan of the structure could not be exposed to view, since it was thoroughly super imposed by the cellas. The bricks are about 46 cm. × 23 cm. × 7 cm. in size. The size of the bricks are generally assigned to the Vishnukundin period in Andhra Desa.

The fabric of black and red ware is profusely prevalent in the early historical period in A.P. The earliest layer which contains fragments of sprinkler necks, arrettine ware and the other dominant red-ware sherds suggest a date that ranges between 2nd and 4th century AD.

The layer that overlies the earliest one is associated with the remains of the temple complex that contains the brick of 46 cm. × 23 cm. × 7 cm. size which again suggests continuity upto a later date.

The earliest mention of Rajahmundry in any literature is in the introduction to the Telugu translation of the Mahabharata which was composed by Nannayabhatta in the reign of the Eastern Chalukyan king Raja Raja Narendra. In this the town is called Rajamahendrapatnam and is referred to as the capital of the Eastern Chalukyan kingdom and the central gem of the Vengi country.

Geology

Rajahmundry and its surroundings (hinterland) form one of the most interesting regions geologically, because of the variety of its formation. Trap rocks which are evidently the south-eastern most extension of the Deccan traps, occur on both sides of the

Godavari near Rajahmundry. The traps are greenish basalts containing amygdales with chalcodomy and agate. The main interest lies in their showing a set of intercalated limestone beds.

There are in addition some limestones beneath the traps. The traps are overlain unconformably by reddish sandstone and conglomerates which in other places rest directly on the gneisses and Gondwanas. They vary from shaly sandstones to conglomerates; the prevalent colours are reddish, purplish and yellowish-brown.

Climate

The climate is comparatively equitable and although it is very warm in April, May and June, it is never too oppresive during the rest of the year. More than half of the annual rainfall is brought by the south-west monsoon while a greater part of the rest occurs in October and November.

Forests

The forest near Rajahmundry contains timber and bamboos. Some of the beds are highly ferruginous and have been used as sources of iron ore when an indigenous smelting industry was in existence.

Graphite is an essential but sparsely distributed constituent of some of the members of the gneissic series. The different sandstones of the area yield good building stones. The limestones associated with the traps are used for lime making.

Vijayawada

"Egypt is the gift of Nile" wrote Herodotus centuries ago. It can be said in a like manner that the hinterland of Andhra Desa, from Rajahmundry to Vijayawada is the gift of the Godavari and the Krishna figuratively the white and the blue Niles of the Deccan. These two rivers have exercised, from times immemorial, a profound influence on the economic and the political life of the Deccan and the two eastern Deltas.[9]

The period of Vishnukundin rule was a period of great building activity. A number of temples were excavated on the hill sides for the accommodation of the deities of the Brahmanical pantheon. There is a group of Brahmanical cave temples in and around Vijayawada situated on the northern banks of the river Krishna. There are two caves in Vijayawada, five in the neighbouring village of Mogulrajapuram and five more in the village of Undavalli, about two miles (3 Km.) away on the opposite bank of the river.

Vijayawada, Vijayavata, Vijayawatika, modern Bezwada, seems to have risen to great importance from the 9th century AD onwards. Its antiquity would be carried much further back if future discoveries should prove its identity with the Vijayapura of an early Amaravati inscription.[10] "Bezawada" is mentioned in the inscription of 'Yudhamalla' found on a stone pillar in Malleswaram temple at Vijayawada. This inscription belongs to Saka 820 (898 AD)

In the inscription of Pandranga of Addanki datable to S.770 (848 AD); it was stated that 'Kandukur' was made as great as Bezawada city. So it can be taken that Bezwada was a flourishing city even prior to the 9th Century. Cave temples of Bezwada, Mogulrajapuram, and Undavalli further prove that people had their early settlements in these parts.

Besides the above monuments, the recent archaeological excavations conducted on the top of the hillock Mogalrajapuram brought to light, a Brahmanical shrine built in brick belonging to Vishnukundin period. Vestiges of brick structures in complete ruins are also seen. A square plinth with large bricks before a votive stupa is also visible. Votive stupas were neatly carved over the surface of the living rock in bas relief are observed.

The 'U' shaped hill was found quite convenient to the builders to have a series of rock-cut shrines from end to end. Exploration of the surrounding area has brought to view carvings of early Buddhistic faith in the form of chaitya representations executed on the vertically cut ridges. Cave no. V which faces west is at the turn of northern end; it has a flight of steps at its extreme right leading to the terrace. Right from this point to the hill top the ridges were found cut down vertically for facilitating easy ascent and sometimes steps were carved out within the bed rock to make the access easier. The flat hill top at one place was found scooped out to a depth of 1 m. in square and circular shapes, which in all probability was meant for conserving water. Some heaps of brickbats scattered here and there deserve further examination.

A Vishnukundin coin, partially cut, bearing double 'ya' ' ' symbol in addition to a few red-ware potsherds were collected from the surface.

The climatic condition of the region is of extreme kind with hot summers and cold winters and may be classified as tropical. At Vijayawada the heat is excessive and unbearable owing to radiation that develops in the crest of Indrakeela mountains nearby. The rainfall of the region is unevenly spread and it is determined by the two monsoons it receives i.e. the south-west and the north-east.

The soils consist of three main varieties namely, the alluvial, the black-regur and the red-ferruginous types. Endowed with a rich variety of soils, the region occupied an important place in agriculture. Enormous mass of silt, which the river Krishna carries has in course of ages, been deposited in the form of wide alluvial delta and every bit of the alluvial soil must have been put to agricultural use by the early settlements in and around the river near Vijayawada.

Mineral Resources

The gneissose granite and dolerite serve as a good material for building construction.

Veerapuram

Veerapuram village is situated on the right bank of the river Krishna in Nandikotkur taluk of Kurnool district. Early temples and living floors of early historic times have been brought to light during the excavations conducted by the Birla Archaeological and Cultural Research Institute, Hyderabad. Cultural succession from about 18th century back to 4th-5th century AD has been established. An addition to the known pottery fabrics of the early historical period at the site consists sherds of the Russet coated ware. The crowning part of the mound consists of temples which are among the early brick built shrines in South India and the oldest known in Andhra Pradesh. There is continuity of occupation here.

The climate of the region is on the whole quite healthy. The first three months of the years are usually pleasant and the wind blows with moderate force from the south-east. Very heavy rain usually falls over the region, the heaviest showers usually coming from the north-west.

Geology

Mostly shales, limestones and quartzites are found here. In places around the right bank of the Krishna owing to denudation, these lime-stones have come up to the surface. They are of a red purple colour, generally purple and are at times seemed with pale turquoise green calcareous layers or thin bands of limestone. The actual limestones lie below the shales.

Flora and Fauna

The region is covered with very thick forests. There are extensive grassy level lands which afford pastures to the numerous herds of cattle.

Wild animals are also found in this region.

Soil

The region is rich in regur, a soil of a superior kind. Inspite of inadequate rainfall this soil responds very well to jawar and cotton. Minerals like barytes clay, iron-ore, ochre and steatite are found in the area. It is well endowed with regard to building material etc.

Tellakunta

Tellakunta is on the motorable road from Sultanabad to Dharmapuri in Peddapalli taluk of Karimnagar district. The importance of the place lies in the fact that a hoard of Vishnukundin coins have been recovered in the past which have been examined and published by M. Rama Rao.[11]

To the east of the village lies a series of low lying hills, consisting of large quantities of iron-ore. A huge tank is situated on one of the hills. Surface exploration over the hills revealed some circular structures made of bricks which are apparently remains of blast furnaces. Human habitation is not found on the top of the hills but for these furnaces. It is quite likely that iron ore was smelted in situ and exported as pig iron. As such, the place must have been a commercial town of considerable importance during the early historical period. Exploration over the neighbouring mounds revealed red-polished and dull-redware potteries.

The range of hills around Dongathurthi, Nandimedaram and Tellakunta consists of magnetite quartz rock. Iron ore in the form of banded magnetite heamatite quartizite occurs in this area.

The climatic conditions are moderate. Red sandy loamy soil, familiarly known as Chalka soil, forms the main type although large patches of black clay loamy soil are found scattered.

The sources of irrigation are tanks and wells.

The epidiorites form low hillocks and occur as sheets and dykes invariably covered by residual soils. By far the major portion of the region is composed of the peninsular granite complex, comprising the pink and the grey granites. Limestones are also available which are high in calcium carbonate and low in magnesium carbonate. These can be used for the production of magnesia used in the preparation of refractory linings in mettallurgical furnaces.

Nelakondapalli

Nelakondapalli is situated on the Khammam-Kodad road some 26 Km. from Khammam. At a distance of one and half kilometres from the village there are places known as *Viratrajudibba* and *Kichakagundam* claiming importance in the days of Mahabharata.[12]

The old relics and coins unearthed in an area within a radius of 16 kilometres and the supposed relics of the cowsheds of *Sahadeva* strengthen the belief that the place was noted as far back as the days of Mahabharata. Some Buddhist stupas also existed around this village.

Physical features

The village is lying between 17° of the North Latitude and 8° of the Eastern Longitude. The climate of the taluk is moderate. The average annual rainfall is about 40 inches. The soils in this region are of four varieties viz., (1) sandy soil (2) red chalka, (3) black cotton soil and (4) choudu. Agriculture is the main occupation of the people here. The two important rivers that flow through this taluk are the river Muner and the river Palair both of which ultimately fall into the river Krishna.

Khammam district is very rich in mineral resources, forest wealth and power potentialities.[13] This district forms part of the Indian peninsula which is quiet stable, composed of geologically older rocks. The oldest rocks are the archaeans comprising schists, amphibolites, dolerites, nepheline, syenites, gneisses and granites. The Gondwanas of this district were represented mostly by lower Gondwana rocks and partly by upper Gondwanas. Lower Gondwanas are represented by Talchir Boulderabad followed by Barakar sand stones, shales and coal seams and by younger Kamthi felspathic sand stones and grits of light brown colour with red clay bands and few limestone beds.

Slates and slaty phyllites, argallaceous group of end rocks is best developed and are the most wide spread rocks in the area. Sericite, biotite, chlorite and quartz form the essential minerals where tourmaline is an important accessory. Quartzites are of massive, fine grained recrystallised rocks, white, cream or purplish in colour. Occasionally iron oxide forms the cementing material. Dolomites and dolomitic limestones are fine grained, dark or cream coloured, of highly siliceous variety. These are economically important, since they contain deposits of Barytes in them.

There are vast reserves of dolomitic lime stones within the pakhals. The district possesses various other mineral deposits though in minor quantities such as iron ore, graphite, garnet, kyanite, dolomites, corundum, slate, mica, soapstone, chronite etc., apart from the vast sources of building materials.

Limestone and marble deposits are occurring in this region. The reserves are not estimated but it is clear that they will run into enormous quantities.[14] These marbles are found to give low porosity and absorption values and suitable for interior and exterior decoration and also building purposes.

Forests[15]

The forests in the Khammam division lie mostly on flat and undulating ground. The hills are low rising to a maximum height of 1,300 feet above mean sea level. The forests consist of mixed decideous species, characteristic of the Deccan peninsula. The main types found in the division are teak type, mixed type, satin type, anduk type and bamboos. The quality of bamboos is fairly good.

Archaeology

There is an extensive ancient habitation site very close to Nelakondapalli. Since the mound was dug away for removing pati earth, the strata were thoroughly examined. In the trial trench dug to a depth of half-a-metre, black and red-ware pottery, clay-beads, one terracotta human figurine, etc., were brought to light besides innumerable lead coins of the Ikshvakus and the Vishnukundins. During the course of scooping operations, fragments of broken hands, legs and bronze knobs, terracotta figurines, coins etc., have been brought to light. In the nearby fields, marbles are noticed in abundance, in the course of ploughing. Four trenches were taken here covering the mound where brick walls connected by rubble alignment were noticed. Stumps of columns of white marble and some decorative motifs are also noticed among the fragments collected in the course of exploration. About 2 Km. north-east of Nelakondapalli there is a mound popularly known as Viratraja Gadda or Erradibba. This appears to be a stupa constructed with bricks. Evidences of two phases of habitation in the early historical period are seen at this site.

Nelakondapalli appears to have been a flourishing township of the Ikshvaku and Vishnukundin periods.

REFERENCES

1. Abdul Waheed Khan, Md.; 1963; A Monograph on Yeleswaram Excavations, APGAS No. 14, p. 1-3.
2. *Ibid.*, p. 14.
3. *Ibid.*, p. 48.
4. Krishnasastry, V. V.; 1979; "Keesara-Capital of Vishnukundins", JAAP., Vol. I, No.1, p. 100.

5. __________, 1961; District Census Hand Book; Hyderabad District, chapter 1, pages 1, 2, 3.
6. __________, 1968; District Census Hand Book; Hyderabad District chapter I, pps. A5, A6, A7.
7. Sastry, B.N.; 1975; Andhrula Sanghika Charitra, Hyderabad p. 216.
8. __________, 1966; District Census Hand Book, Mahaboobnagar District, 1961; chapter I, p. iv.
9. __________, 1968; District Census Hand Book, East Godavari District, 1961; p. xxxviii.
10. Hemachandra Raychowduri; 1960; The Early History of the Deccan Part I, p. 60, ed. by Yazdani, G., London.
11. Rama Rao, M.; 1963; Vishnukundin Coins in A.P. Govt. Museum, APGAS No.10.
12. __________, 1961; District Census Hand Book, Khammam District, A.85 A.86.
13. *Ibid.*, page A4, A5.
14. *Ibid.*, page A9.
15. *Ibid.*, page A3, A46,-47.

CHAPTER 2

Structural Pattern

Yeleswaram

The historical period witnessed building construction activity at Yeleswaram. During the excavation, stumps of columns of a *mandapa* were noticed throughout the entire length and breadth of the site. The trenches revealed the terminal point of the *mandapa*.

Below the Madhavaswamy temple, a stupa was revealed at a depth of nearly 1.24 m. from the surface level showing two distinct phases; below this stupa, vestiges of tier of another stupa were noticed. The vestiges of stupa below and above the other structure in the same level could be safely dated to 4th or 5th century AD.

Layer 4 contained rubbles, brick-bats and gravel mixed with sand. An enclosure wall was brought to light in this period. A brick structure appeared to have been intended for some ritualistic purposes as sockets were made at regular intervals around a raised pedestal for the erection of wooden columns to support a canopy. By the side of this ritualistic import, iron nails, iron slags and copper moulds were also recovered. A brick structure, something like a chamber, was discovered in period IV which functioned probably as a votive shrine for installing a *Banalinga*.

Another brick structure of the nature of votive shrine installed with a *Banalinga* was found. The enclosure wall was renovated during this period in the same alignment and the structure referred to above continued in use during this period and was installed with *Banalinga* connected by an *abhisheka* drain.

The most noteworthy finds of the period are the five miniature votive shrines about more than 90 cm. in height found very near the temple complex. These shrines have a low *adhishtana*, flat *kapota* and *vimana* of 2 steps surmounted by a semi-circular *Sikhara* incised with an inscription, the characters of which resemble some of the inscriptions of the Vishnukundin period datable to circa 4th century AD. It has a linga on the vedi inside.

The other miniature shrines have the same architectural features as described above but they contain sculptures of Siva as Ardhanareeswara, Harihara, Umamaheswara and also a linga on a vedi. All these figures are carved in deep niches serving as *Garbhagriha.*

Gollathagudi

The excavations conducted at the site has thrown fresh light on the successive phases of construction, styles and artistic appendices of the temples. The aim of the excavations was to establish the sequence of temple construction and to unearth the profuse art pieces that once adorned the lofty spires and inner apartments of the temples which give expression to the artistic taste and cultural tradition of the age.

An extensive mound rising to an approximate height of 4 m. composed of loose powdery earth, brick-bats and jutted cut stone slabs, etc., was partly excavated bringing to view the plans of two brick temples facing east. The respective plinths constructed in brick and stone besides porches and other related structures were exposed in the next field season.

Phase I — Temple I

An extensive deep trench on a more stable soil that is hard morrum, revealed the large sized baked bricks, having a mud mortar-binding material in between, provided with intermittant footings to bear the dead-weight of the superstructures. The original ground level was then raised outside the temple by spreading morrum to a considerable thickness so as to arrest seepage of rain water into foundation. The walls over the plinth were built in brick with a system of bonding to which was added another layer to give veneering effect. The surface in turn was rubbed down to achieve excellent smoothness, but practically had no purpose behind it except to adhere to the past tradition. The veneered layers being apart from the main core of the wall, began to widen in due course and the glazy finish imparted to it could not retain the lime plaster and the applied stucco moulding for long, and thus exposed the brick work to the vagaries of weather, which finally led to the premature collapse of the temple. The short life of the temple can be inferred from a very thin representative layer that formed while the temple was in use. This thin layer sealed the layer of spread morrum and was superimposed by the actual fallen debris of the temple itself.

This temple being constructed in brick must have given ample scope to the builders for greater constructional possibilities, which is almost lost now due to its total collapse. From the extant details available on plinth and off sets on the exterior wall, in which elegant designs were carried out, it can be seen that the necessary carved and ornamental details were chiselled out of the brick works after the walls were built. Necessary parts were left boosted for this purpose. The carvings were delineated over the joints meticulously to look as if the whole belonged to one piece. However, the builders significantly overcame the disadvantages of small units in bridging spaces by using stone for lintels, jams, sills, perforated screens, pillars, and their bases which received little ornamentation in the hands of brick-carvers. This adaptation of stone was extended to the plinth portion also in the subsequent phase of construction.

The temple was decorated with clean lime plaster applied repeatedly. Friezes of human and animal figurines, floral designs carried out in stucco over the plasters deserve a special mention. The stucco applications were painted frequently in bright colours super-imposed by red, green and yellow. These applique decorations and bright colours catch the imagination of an observer.

No less than the excellence of its elevation was the grandeur of its plan, comprising of *garbhagriha* adjoined by two accessory cellars on either side, a *Mukhamandapa* and a *Mahamandapa*, with its porches. The *Mahamandapa* was flanked by two unidentified structures on either side.

The *Garbhagriha* was roughly square on plan measuring 3.45 m. in length by 3.37 m. in breadth, with the enclosed walls now standing to a height of one metre. The floor paved with burnt brick was found disturbed at several places. The chamber was entered by means of a rectangular door of pale brownish granite stone, which carried a week moulding on the margin. On either side of the *Garbhagriha* were two rectangular cellars measuring 3.35 m. × 1.80 m. each separated from the *Garbhagriha* by a partition wall and entered through the *Mukhamandapa*. The entrances of these cellars were subsequently blocked by small squarish construction of brick blocks. The outer walls which bear the dead load of the lost *Sikhara* were solid and measured 3-20 m. in thickness. The back wall of the sanctum measured 16-15 m. on the outside. These walls of the *Garbhagriha* and that of the whole structure were very badly ruined and stood to a little height over the plinth. The *Mukhamandapa* measured 9 m. × 6.75 m. It retained its northern wall to a little height whereas its southern wall was completely ruined. The remains of 25 moderately carved pillar bases in stone suggest that the roof of the *mandapa* might have rested on stone pillars which are now lost. On the northern and southern remains of the walls were found pieces of perforated screens worked out in the semi-granite stone. These were originally fitted to the windows for admitting light and air besides being ornamental to the pillaster designed walls. In between the *Mukhamandapa* and *Mahamandapa* there stood a partition wall with a door-way of 1.25 m. width for entry.

The remains of the *Mahamandapa* were very few. However, the uniform distribution of the squarish pillar bases resting on the lime floor have given the clue that there in the past the temple had a massive pillared *mandapa* supported by atleast 36 pillars with four centrally arranged pillars, plainly carved, carrying flat vertical bands on each of the four sides, surmounted by a squarish abacus. Again this *mandapa* shows the traces of having perforated screens, carved in stone fixed in the northern and southern walls. The bricks used in the entire construction are of almost uniform size measuring 39 cm. × 22 cm. and 8 cm. on an average.

Temple II

This temple is called by the local people as Gollathagudi. An elaborate pit was dug out to lay the foundation. The foundation was laid in brick and the outer gap in the foundation pit was filled with loosely knitted courses of brick pieces clodded with mud and finally well rammed. The outer ground level was raised to the height of the rammed stump against the foundation and finally paved with brick-bats, just to arrest percolation of water into foundation and to provide a rough flooring over the ground, outside the temple. At a subsequent phase of its history, once again morrum was spread to raise the ground level for the second time and stone slabs were spread over the morrum all along the length of the outer walls to strengthen the foundation. These two phases of its history also proved in the decorative elements of the super-structure.

The wall over the plinth was constructed with a type of bonding to which was added another layer of bricks giving veneering effect. There after the outer surfaces of the wall were rubbed down to a smooth finish to embellish with floral designs, pilasters, plasters and Chaitya arches. The tower is typically of southern order. The plain bricks before the application had linear paintings, gracefully drawn in lime. In the subsequent phase, represented by the second morrum filling, the temple was plastered with lime besides adding stuccos, the traces of which were encountered in the longitudinal trenches laid over the mound.

This temple facing east was built on a plan consisting of *Garbhagriha* and a *mandapa*. The *mandapa* was raised on 12 pillars which are now lost, except three stone pillar bases and the traces of this foundation, constructed in squarish brick stumps overlaid by a stone slab to bear and distribute the weight of the squarish pillar. Morrum was used to raise the level of the *mandapa* to lay lime-concrete floor of about 12 cm. in thickness. A massive retaining wall was constructed all around the mandapa, now traceable only at its foundation level as they were extensively subjected to brick robbery in the past. The gap in the foundation of this wall was filled with brick courses clodded with mud, as found in the foundation of the *Garbhagriha* thus proving to be a contemporary one.

On the eastern side of the *mandapa* at a distance of 4.70 m. was a squarish four pillared *mandapa* each side measuring 1.80 cm. The whole *mandapa* was lost including the pillars and at present, what can be seen is only the four foundation brick stumps. No stone slab was noticed on these stumps and probably the pillars erected over the stumps might have had a weak decoration in the centre.

Towards further east was encountered another similar *mandapa*, with the foundations of brick stumps replaced by stone bases. This might be of a later addition.

Temple III

This one and the temple-I look alike, since no appreciable difference was noticed in their plan and execution. However, the two phases found in the filling of foundations of temple-I of the mound were repeated in this temple.

The foundation was raised in brick giving proper fittings to withhold the dead-load of the structure at a subsequent date, the ground level was once again raised by refilling it with morrum overlaid by stone slabs all along the wall, to further strengthen the foundations.

The *Garbhagriha* flanked by two accessory cellars was entered from the *Mukhamandapa* adjoined by a *Mahamandapa* with a porch to it. The *Garbhagriha* was squarish, measuring 2.80 m. on each side, with a squarish pedestal at the rear and measuring 40 cm. in height and 1.55 m. on each side. The *Mukhamandapa* was raised on pillars, the remains of which is now manifest only in the form of their bases. The *Mukhamandapa* was also raised on stone pillars, the remains of which were noticed in the form of their bases resting on a foundation of squarish brick stumps capped by squarish or sometimes irregular granite slabs. The whole of the temple floor was made up on lime concrete mix. Regarding the pattern of wall execution nothing can be deduced now as they were completely ruined and the bricks ruthlessly robbed even from its ground level. However, the patches of lime plaster found intact at one or two places below the ground level and the stucco pieces collected during excavation speak of the final decorative touches given to the exterior walls of the temple.

Temple IV

Though brick was the dominant material during this phase, the use of stone was restricted to the foundation and plinth. The marked difference in the execution of plan and that of erecting walls point to the change of techniques.

The foundation of this temple was laid in stone slabs which were made to rest on a stone boulder pack mixed with whitish natural morrum. The depth of this foundation is much less when compared to the foundation of the temples 1 to 3 mentioned above. These stone slabs and underlying stone boulders have afforded greater stability and load bearing capacity than the solid brick used in the earlier phase. The foundation pit after laying the stone slabs was filled with natural morrum to raise the ground level and strengthen the foundation.

The wall constructed over this stone foundation were in brick, but the coursing and bonding of the bricks were of the superior quality, in that the outer layer of brick course was also well bonded with the main core of the wall. The wall surfaces were not so smoothly finished as encountered in the other examples, temples 1 to 3. This shows a marked development in techniques of brick constructions adopted in this phase.

On plan also this temple slightly differs from those of the earlier phase. It consists of a small sanctum adjoined by a *Mukhamandapa* and a *Mahamandapa* entered through an elaborate porch. The *Garbhagriha* measured 4.10 m. × 3.30 m. in size and had as its centre, a brick built pedestal sealed by a flat granite slab which might have served as a base to the idol. The *Garbhagriha* was entered from the pillared *mandapa* by means of a rectangular door, the jambs being fitted with massive granite stone, dressed moderately. The over all thickness of the enclosed walls ranged from 2.90 m. to 3 m. On account of the use of bricks the thickness was not always uniform and measured 40 cm. × 20 cm. × 7cm. on the average. The chamber was paved with bricks which did not extend to the centre due to spoilage.

The *Mukhamandapa* enclosed by a dilapidated brick wall of .5 m. high was raised on 16 pillars the bases of which are still intact. The lime plastered floor was made up of lime concrete mix and finally it was plastered to achieve a smooth finish. The granite slabs fixed into the recesses of the external wall had prominent incissions on them for fixation of perforated screens into the grooves. The *Mahamandapa* and the *Mukhamandapa* were separated by a brick wall having a passage for entry.

The *Mahamandapa* was ruined almost totally leaving only the foundation of the plinth on one side and the brick wall to a height of about half a metre over the plinth on the other. This was also raised on stone pillars which is noticed by the presence of the bases. It was floored in lime concrete mix which was finally touched with lime plaster. This *mandapa* was entered through a porch, the vestiges of which now consist of only a part of its plinth and a few stone slabs arranged inside to form a slab floor.

Temple V

This temple was also constructed on stone foundations and plinth. The foundation rests on the second morrum filling thus falling into the second phase, subsequent to the construction of the temples 1 to 3. The lowest slab of the foundation resting over the boulder pack was given dentitions on the under surface to provide grip and stability to the entire edifice. No foundation trench was traceable as it was constructed in between temples 1 and 3 in a spread of debris of the original two temples. A few centimetres gap between this temple and temple 3 at this lowest plinth level was compactly filled with lime concrete so as to check a possible foundation drift. This is more clearly manifested where a roughly hewn stone beam was tightly inserted between the foundation slab of this temple and brick foundations which was actually cut vertically for this purpose. The walls were constructed in brick well bonded. The brick wall of *Garbhagriha* measures 7.35 m. on the western exterior and 5.75 m. on the northern and southern exteriors while the thickness measures 1.75 m. The *Garbhagriha* was slightly rectangular measuring 3.90 m. × 2.30 m. At the rear end of the *Garbhagriha* were seen traces of brick pedestal construction intended to erect the deity.

A notable feature in the development of the plan of this complex of structures was found in this temple i.e. an *antarala* like ante-chamber was roughtly 1.50 m. deep. The two circular pedestal bases on either side of the ante-chamber were probably meant for subsidiary deities. This practice was not unknown in the temples well developed on this plan. The *mandapa* of this temple lies in between the *mandapas* of temple-I and temple-3. It is not known whether this *mandapa* had over it a ceiling like thing since no pillar bases were found erected in this *mandapa*. While the *garbhagriha* and ante-chamber were well floored with the usual lime mix concrete, this *mandapa* had no traces of such lime concrete but was plastered with fine lime over a paved brick base. This flooring might have been added subsequently. The outward decorations of the wall are not known with any certainity since it is in an utterly ruinous condition; only few lime plaster pieces were seen on the wall but the stucco pieces collected in the course of excavation from the debris, points to the lavish decoration made to catch the eye.

Temple VI

This represents the latest phase of construction activity on the site. This phase witnessed complete departure of age old tradition of brick construction and shows a developed plan with regular *antarala* which has been met within an incipient nature in the second phase itself in temple 3. A change to maturity has been reached in stone carving.

A stone temple much restricted in size, had in it, all the necessary parts required for a temple. This was thoroughly ruined and now only the plinth and the foundations are seen in situ. The massive slabs, well carved outwardly on the traditions of stone work, were completely fallen from the plinth. Not even a single slab was in its original position to understand its actual form.

On plan this temple has a *Garbhagriha*, an *antarala,* a *mandapa* and probably a porch. The sanctum measures 8.50 m. × 5.35 m. It was floored with lime but the quality of flooring is much inferior to the floors of the earlier phases. Neither the pedestals were seen in existence nor any traces of them were left behind to glean the religious affinity. The *antarala* measuring 7 m. × 2.67 m. was similarly floored. The *mandapa* measured 11.20 m. × 11.20 m. Only one single pillar base in stone was found in this *mandapa.*

Temples VII

Three temple plans, all oriented east-west, were brought to light during the excavation. Temple (a) was built on a plan containing a *Garbhagriha,* a pillared *mandapa* and an entrance porch on the east.

Temple (c) consists of a *Garbhagriha* and an entrance constructed in between these two temples. Temple (b) originally stood on a simple plan having a *Garbhagriha* facing east and a pillared *mandapa* with a northern entrance. The latter was subsequently added on the eastern side with an east facing *mandapa* raised on a stone plinth. Still later a flight of stone steps were given to the left side of the eastern entrance. Adjoining the added *mandapa* on its northern side was constructed a chamber on a stone foundation probably for housing temple properties.

The development of plans shows a unilinear pattern starting from a single cell and an entrance, passing through an intermediary stage having a *Garbhagriha* and *mandapa,* and an entrance porch, and finally culminating in complex plan initially containing a *Garbhagriha* and *mandapa* and later added with an additional *mandapa* adjoined by a chamber and a flight of stone steps.

Keesaragutta

An early Saivite temple of brick was brought to light during the minor excavations conducted by the Department of Archaeology and Museums some years ago. The temple is square in plan with a square brick pedestal in the middle to insert possibly a square based linga. Now, the linga is missing, but on the evidence of a covered drain on the north-east corner for conducting out the water of ablution and the floor inside the temple being paved with brick it must be a shrine dedicated to linga worship. This shrine is situated just opposite the western gate-way of the fort. Post-holes were noticed over the corners of the square pedestals, possibly to support wooden pillars. A running verandah possibly existed on all the sides outside the shrine, supported by wooden pillars based on granite pedestals. The granite slabs with grooves in the middle are found outside the temple along the walls at regular intervals of 2.01 m.

A thorough exploration over the top of the hill revealed extensive fortification walls all around the hills encompassing an approximate area of 3 to 4 Sq. Km. The fort wall was constructed of rubble and the superstructure was raised with bricks measuring 50 cm.× 25 cm. × 8 cm. Evidently the brick and the fortification wall with which it was constructed belong to the early historical period.

There are many brick temples scattered all over the area. The transition from brick to stone is clearly discernible in this place.

Structure I

The recent excavations concentrated on the north bank of the tank at the lower gradient of the Keesaragutta hill revealed a huge brick structure with five rooms prefaced by a rectangular hall, a square porch and flight of steps. The external walls are about 2 mts. broad and it is likely that a superstructure with 0.5 m. broad wall, must have been raised. Considering the breadth of the wall it is likely that it must have been a multi-storeyed building. The flat roof made of rectangular terracotta tiles and plastered with lime was laid over horizontal rafters supported by wooden pillars, raised outside the walls.

Structure II

Facing this building on the north was found another elaborate flight of steps with a *chandrasila* leading to another building consisting of five rooms with a central hall. The entire complex was protected by a brick enclosure wall and connected by the flight of steps. This structure consisted of three rooms in two rows probably with a central hall of middle path-way. The building is situated on the extreme left of the steps and it is possible that a similar building must have existed on the right. During further excavations a series of trenches were sunk between structure-I and the compound wall with the aim of connecting structure-I and II and to find out the extension of the enclosure of the compound wall of structure I. The ground level to a length of 20 m. was exposed which is the intervening space between structure I and the flight of steps noticed in the compound wall. The flight of steps, seven inside and four outside, have been provided for the main gate. The top step at the level of the door slab has two granite pedestals with sockets for possibly supporting the door jambs to carry a '*torana*'. The steps are two metres broad and the descent has hand-rails. On either side of the steps are noticed heaps of lime concrete possibly stored for repairing the roofs of some buildings. The flight of steps have ended with *chandrasila* on both the sides. The entrance of the palace complex was raised to a height of 1.22 m. from the ground level. The devise was adopted to make entry into the palace a little difficult.

Inside the enclosure wall and exactly on the north-east of the structure I, another structure with multiple projections and recesses was exposed, a typical architectural feature of some of the buildings of the early historical period.

Rajahmundry

A brick wall on the slopes of the Godavari bund near the old staircase intended for the bathing ghat running from east to west is discernible. The size of the bricks used in construction of the wall is 51 cm. × 23 cm. × 7 cm. and 46 cm. × 23 cm. × 7 cm.

The structural activity of the earliest period consists of the remains of a wall-like structure encompassing a circular construction in brick. The bricks used in this construction measure 46 cm. × 23 cm. × 7 cm. The plan of the structure could not be exposed to view since it was fully superimposed by the cellas of the later structure.

The layer that overlies the earliest one associates with the remains of a temple complex that contain the brick of the size of 46 cm. × 23 cm. × 7 cm. A brick temple of two rectangular cellas was constructed with foundations sunk into the underlying layer. The temple was badly ruined and no superstructure except the foundation is extant. No presiding deity is found in the cellas. The floor of the cellas is devoid of any kind of pavement. Eastern cella measures 2.3 m. × 1.7 m. inside and 4.5 m. × 3.5 m. outside. The bricks used in this construction measure 30 cm. × 20 cm. × 7 cm. Similar bricks were also used in the construction of a contemporaneous wall running east-west a few metres away from the temple on the north. This wall must have been intended to close the temple, but its construction was abruptly stopped for reasons unknown. This incomplete wall is seen in bits in the same alignment, each bit having ends with successively receeding courses. The bricks are bonded with mud in all the periods, use of lime could not be traced. Burnt bricks were used. They vary in size from period to period.

Gummadam

A mound situated about one and half kilometres away from the village towards east has been excavated by the Department of Archaeology and Museums, where a Saiva shrine belonging to 3rd or 4th century AD and a Jaina shrine surrounded by one enclosure wall are found side by side in east-west orientation. The sanctum sanctorum is square in shape which is constructed with bricks of the size of 40 cm. × 20 cm. × 20 cm. × 6 cm. Linga and *Panavatta* are partly broken and uprooted. The linga is made of lime stone and there are no *brahma sutras* on it. *Garbhagriha* is 3.70 m. in length, stone slabs are used at the foundation level and the walls are constructed with bricks. The walls are 75 cm. in width and 30 cm. in height. The outlet is 1.45 cm. in length and 43 cm. in width. The length and width of the *Panavatta* are 1.50 m. and 15 cm. respectively. *Antarala* is 1.45 m. in length and width of the wall is 75 cms. At the entrance of the *antarala*, broken shale slabs are present. The enclosure wall on the northern side of the temple is about 27.5 m. in length. While exposing the structures of the Saiva temple, another brick structure of an earlier phase was found on the top of the mound. The structure and the composite layer are formed and strengthened with loose morrum mixed with small pellets of gravel and sand particles. The underlying deposit associated with the structural level is formed with brick-bats and lime earth. The size of the brick that is used here is 40 cm. × 20 cm. × 6 cm. At a depth of 55 cm. pottery such as vases, lids, jars of coarse pale red-ware, some of them washed in deep red are recovered. The brick structure is built on stone slabs. A deposit of morrum is laid to the height of 15 cm. from bottom. The brick wall is constructed over a single brick projecting on the inner side of the cell; over this projecting single brick a brick wall is constructed to the height of 90 cm. The length of the outer wall is 3.60 m. on all the four sides. Innerside of the wall is 2 m. in length. On each side of the brick wall a brick structure is projecting outside at a distance of 10 cm. and at a length of 1.40 m. on the brick wall in the centre of the wall. In the middle of the brick cell a basement is constructed measuring 1.10 m. in length and 90 cm. in breadth. Over the basement a deposit having morrum is raised to the height of 32 cm. and on this deposit a shale stone slab with a thickness of 5 cm. is placed. Probably, this is intended for installing an idol, but the idol is missing now.

Nelakondapalli

About ten Buddhist sculptures were discovered at Nelakondapalli in a private land while digging for pati earth. The pit where the idols were discovered was extended exposing the brick structures constructed with 46 cm. × 28 cm.× 7 cm. size bricks nicely lime plastered to a thickness of over 2.5 cm. In the course of the operation hidden and visible sculptural wealth consisting a number of broken fragments essential for moulding the broken idols were collected. Very interesting brick structures relating to the manufacture and preservation of the marble Buddhist idols were traced. A number of trough like structures measuring 4.45 m. × 1.96 m. × 0.80 m., three in alignment separated by a drain were also brought to light. A thick deposit of lime is noticed in the tub. It is quite probable that these troughs were intended for preserving the idols under lime plaster and that they were subsequently given high polish.

The stratigraphy of the trial trenches taken in the mound has shown two brick structures one over the other separated by a layer containing morrum and fine sand. The first phase of the construction was made with brick, mud and mortar. An Ikshvaku coin containing the symbol of an elephant with raised trunk is found associated with this brick structure. The brick wall in the second phase was constructed with lime mortar. The flooring and the walls were thickly plastered with lime. A Vishnukundin coin with lion on the obverse and a *Kalasa* flanked by a lamp stand on either side inside a rayed circle on the reverse was recovered from this layer. Fragments of pottery met with at the site include decorated and designed storage jars, water jars, and vessels of red polished ware and the fabric varying from coarse to fine. A beautiful terracotta human figurine with two horns on either side of head is found which resembles the horned *dwarapalakas* in the cave, and other structural temples of the Vishnukundin period. An excellant piece of '*Nandi-pada*' carved on a lime-stone is also recovered in the fields along with other antiquities.

Virataraja-Gadda or Erragadda

After fixing the central point and dividing mound into four quadrants, two trenches were taken on the south-eastern quadrant and dug upto a depth of about 4.80 m. In trench one, the circular end of the *Anda* was traced and exposed to a depth of nearly 5.60 m. and brought to light 52 layers of bricks. Each brick measuring 46 cm. × 23 cm. × 7 cm. In the corner of the trench under the baulk brick alignments in the shape of steps were noticed. About 1.40 m. away from the circular end of the *Anda* an enclosure wall with a thickness of nearly 1.50 m. was noticed. At a depth of 5.60 m. a fine brick flooring was noticed connecting both the structures.

In the second trench regular steps in different stages were noticed buttressing the enclosure wall leading to the foot of the mound.

It appears that the enclosure wall served as a raised platform from where vertical steps leading to the *Harmika* are seen in the baulk. Both burnt and unburnt or half-burnt bricks were used in the construction. The brick noticed in the top-most portion of the mound is red in colour fully burnt where as the *Anda* and enclosure wall were constructed of unburnt or half-burnt bricks. These bricks are very brittle and easily dissolved in water. The average size of the brick also differed in both these categories. Hence, it is quite likely that the *stupa* was conserved at a later date establishing two phases of constructional activity. Except a red-ware pot no other antiquities were noticed in course of trial exploration at this mound.

CHAPTER 3

Architecture

Religious : Cave Temples

The Vishnukundin contribution to art especially architecture has hardly won the recognition it deserves at the hands of the scholars who devoted themselves to the study of Indian art and architecture. The Vishnukundins inherited the artistic traditions of both the Ikshvakus whom they succeeded and the Vakatakas with whom they came into contact and enriched them by their own contribution and transmitted it to posterity.

The Cave temples of Vijayawada

There is a group of interesting Brahmanical cave temples in and around Vijayawada, situated on the northern bank of the river Krishna in Andhra Pradesh. There are two caves in Vijayawada, five in Mogalrajapuram and five more in the village of Undavalli, situated three km. away on the opposite bank of the river.

There is a long lozenge shaped hill at western end of Vijayawada near the barrage recently constructed. There are two sets of caves in the western slope of this hill. Of these, one is excavated at the foot of a projection of the hill and the other is 90 m. higher up and reached by a flight of steps.

Cave I : This cave is rectangular on plan and consists of an open portico with eight pillars in the front with the '*ankana*' or inter-columnal space covered by a low parapet ornamented with sculptures. Behind this there is a *mahamandapa* and an *ardhamandapa*, constituted by two rows of pillars. The back wall of the *ardhamandapa* is in the shape of concave curve and in the curved portion are excavated three cells at varying distances in the interior. These three shrines are separated from each other by two short walls projecting from the back wall of the *ardhamandapa*. The rock itself forms two walls at the southern and northern extremities.

There are four openings in the front part of the cave, two before the first shrine, one before the central shrine and one before the third shrine in the south. The low parapet which is in between these openings is in two sections. The outer side of this wall is sculptured all over. It seems to contain the figures of lions and standing deities. Further identification is not possible because the wall is much worne out.

Beyond the parapet is a row of seven pillars with corresponding pilasters in the northern and southern walls. Only the lower part of these pillars is visible. It is probable that like the pillars of the row beyond these pillars are also cubical pillars without base or capital. The roof above these pillars is gone and there is open space now above these pillars. Beyond these pillars there is another row constituting the intervening space into the *mahamandapa*. In the northern wall of this *mandapa* are four niches, three of them empty and one containing the figure of Ganapati. This deity has four hands and holds *modaka* in the lower right hand on which rests the tip of the trunk. In the next row are one pilaster in the southern wall and three pillars. The space between these pillars and the back wall constitutues the *ardhamandapa* of the first shrine. There is a short projecting wall at right angles to the back wall which contains a *kosta* or niche with the figure of a *dvarapalaka* inside it. This *dvarapalaka* wears a turban-like head-dress with a horn protruding on either side of it. He stands in *tribhanga* leaning to the left. There is a big mace between his legs and on its handle rest his two hands. Above him are three individuals seated in *padmasana*. The short projecting wall on the north also contains a niche with a *dvarapalaka*, standing in *vyatyastapada* leaning to the right with his right hand resting on *gada* and the left in *katihasta*. There are four sitting individuals above him.

The back wall contains the entrance of the shrine in the centre and a *makaratorana* niche on either side of it. The portion beyond these niches is empty. Both the niches contain standing figures inside which are too worne out to be identified. Above these niches is a row of geese and above it the *kapota* or cornice. There are three rafter ends above the *kapota*. The wall beyond the *makaratorana* niches also contain two pilasters, one on each side. The upper beam is decorated with a row of geese. Above this row is the moulded *kapota*. There is a row of lions above the *kapota* of both the entrance and the side niches, four above each niche and six above the entrance, supporting the roof above.

The cell beyond the entrance contains a narrow *antarala* and the *Garbhagriha*. There is a square hole in the centre of the *Garbhagriha* intended for locating a linga or an image.

The second shrine is separated by two short walls projecting from the back wall, from shrines nos.1 and 2. Each of these short walls has a niche containing a *dvarapalaka*. The *dvarapalaka* in the niche in the wall to the south stands leaning to the left, wears a horned head-dress and rests both his hands on a *gada*. The *dvarapalaka* in the niche in the northern wall stands in *vyatyastapada* leaning to the right and rests his right hand on a *gada* and presses his left hand against his stomach. The back wall contains the shrine entrance in the centre and a *makaratorana* niche on either side of it. The niche to the south contains the figure of a deity standing in *dvibhanga* leaning to the left with his left hand resting on the *kati*. The niche on the opposite side contains the figure of a deity standing in *dvibhanga* leaning to the left with his left hand resting on the *kati*. The niche on the oppsite side contains the figure of a deity standing in *vyatyastapada* leaning to the right with his right hand resting on a *gada* and the left pressed against the stomach. The entrance of the shrine is similar to that of shrine no.1. The cell beyond contains an *antarala* and *Garbhagriha* with a hole in the centre of the *Garbhagriha*. There are traces of *nasikas* or gables on the *kapota* of the shrine entrance.

The third shrine which is the north is mostly ruined. It is farther in the interior. The entire rock above this shrine has fallen and disappeared. The shrine entrance is closed by a brick wall.

Annexe Cell: There is a small single-celled shrine to the south of this cave temple reached by a short flight of steps. This is a plain cell with nothing worthy of notice.

Cave II : This cave, locally known as the Akkanna-Madanna cave, is situated about 275 m. higher up and reached by a flight of steps. It is 14.75 m. long and 8.95 m. broad and consists of an *adhistana*, a flight of steps in its centre, three rows of six pillars each with corresponding pilasters forming an open varandah. *Mahamandapa* and *ardhamandapa* and the back wall with three cells excavated into it.

The cave stands on an *adhistana* which consists of *upana, gala, jagati* or moulding, *patta*, another *gala* and a plain *kapota*. The flight of steps in its centre has a *chandrasila* before it.

Among the pillars above the *adhistana* the stumps of three pillars to the right of the steps and three to the left are seen. They seem to have been cubical pillars without base or capital. Like the pilasters at either end, they too must have had an octagonal shaft in between two massive rectangular portions. The pillars of the next two rows are octagonal throughout and have no base or capital.

The back wall contains three shrines with entrances projecting forward. The wall beyond these entrances is empty. The entrance of each of three shrines is on a low *vedi* and flanked by an empty niche on either side. The entrance is surmounted by a *kapota*, plain and undecorated. Above this *kapota* are four beam heads and over them a *patta*, supporting the roof.

There is a fine animal frieze on the beam between the last octagonal pillar in the north and the pilaster next to it in the first row. This frieze contains the figures of a lion running and an elephant walking with the trunk hanging.

The Caves of Mogalrajapuram

The village of Mogalarajapuram is now almost a part of the growing town of Vijayawada. There are several hills and these hills contain five caves which are of great architectural value.

Cave I : This cave is the nearest to the town of Vijayawada and excavated in the eastern face of a hill and faces the east. It is 6.50 m. broad and 2.45 m. high.

It consists of two rock walls in the north and south with open space between them. These walls do not have any *kostas* or niches. Beyond this open space there is a *mandapa* of three rows of two pillars each with corresponding pilasters in the northern and southern walls. It has a plain *adhistana* below. The back wall of the *mandapa* has a projecting part containing an entrance in the centre with a *kosta* on each side. Beyond the entrance is a shrine 1.83 m. long and 91.5 cm. broad.

The facade of the cave consists of a broad flat *patta* or band above the pillars in the front row. Above this band is a row of dwarfs in various poses. There is no *kapota* or cornice above this row of dwarfs.

The pilasters and pillars are cubical with an octagonal shaft in the centre and a curved bracket capital above. The pilaster in the front on the southern side contains at its base a *Purnakumbha* adorned with a cross ribbon. There is a horizontal beam above the pillars of the front row. On the northern part of this beam between the pillar and pilaster is a row of dwarfs in various poses and also a row of geese.

The back wall of the *mandapa* contains empty space at the extremities and a projecting portion in the centre. There is an entrance in its centre flanked by two *kapotas*, one on each side. Each *kosta* has two pillasters containing in the upper half the *kalasa, tadi, padma, idai* and *phalaka*, and capital with the *taranga* or roll ornament on the underside. The northern *kosta* contains a peculiar *dvarapalaka* figure. This *dvarapalaka* stands leaning to the left holding a long sword or spear in his right hand and resting the left hand on a shield. He is in the *vyatyastapada* pose.

The entrance in between the *kostas* is reached by a short flight of steps with a *chandrasila* before it. The upper beam is decorated with a row of lotus petals. There is a *kapota* surmounting the entrance and both the *kostas* on its sides. It contains one *nasika* or gable over each *kosta* and two above the entrance. All the *nasikas* contain human heads inside. Above the *kapota* are three rafter ends. The *garbhagriha* contains part of a *vedi*.

Cave II : This is the largest and most beautiful of all the caves in this place. It is excavated on the northern side of a hill and faces the north.

This cave consists of open space in the front enclosed by rock walls in the east and west with two *kostas* or niches in the west wall. Beyond is a *mandapa* 9.55 m. long, 4.65 m. broad and 2.45 m. high. It contains, in the front, two pillars and two short projections of the rock on either side dividing the front into three openings. Beyond these pillars is another row of four pillars with corresponding pilasters in the north and south walls. Beyond is the back wall into which three shrines, each about 1.83 m. have been excavated.

The *adhistana* of the cave contains *upana, gala, tripatta*, another *gala* divided into compartments by short pilasters and a moulded *kapota* or cornice. Of the four niches in the east wall enclosing the open space, one contains the figure of Ganapati. This deity is seated with his left leg folded and resting on the seat and the right bent at the knee and hand rests on the right knee and the trunk rests on it. The left hand holds *danta*.

The facade of the cave is beautiful. The two rock walls, one on each side of the pillars in the front row, contain figures of *dvarapalakas* in the niches or *kostas*. The *dvarapalaka* on the eastern wall stands leaning to the left with his left hand resting on the top of *gada* and the right resting on the *kati* or waist. He wears a horned head-dress. A long snake starts on his right hand, and stretches across the chest and its hood emerges out of the left shoulder. The *dvarapala* on the western wall stands leaning to the right with his right hand resting on a *gada* and the left resting on the waist. At the end of each of these two short walls there are pilasters. Between these pilasters are two masssive pillars with octagonal shafts in the centre and curved bracket capitals above, whose underside is adorned with the *taranga* or roll ornament with a plain band or *patta* in the centre. Above the pillars the *prastara* is plain. Above the *prastara* is a moulded *kapota* adorned with three *nasikas* or gables surmounted by *simhalalatas*. Each of these gables has a lotus scroll on either side at the bottom. These gables are located above the openings below. The *nasika* on the east contains three heads, representing Brahma; the central and western *nasikas* contain two heads each representing Siva and Vishnu with their consorts. Above the *kapota* there is a broad band containing a row of animals, five lions with tails curled above, one elephant and one bull all in vigorous poses. Above this animal frieze is a fine figure of Siva as Nataraja with the portion below the waist broken. This deity is represented as dancing on the prostrate body of the *apasmarapurusha*. He has eight hands.

There are a few sculptures on the pillars and pilasters of this cave temple. There is fine representation of Siva dancing on the pilaster adjacent to the rock wall on the east. Standing with his legs apart, this deity has two hands, the right stretched to the right side in *katihasta* and the left bent at the elbow and placed on the left side of the chest adjacent to the arm pit. *Jatas* emanate from the head all-round. There is a representation of *Gajendramoksa* on the first pillar in the front row to the east. To the left is the elephant yelling out, with its trunk upraised and the *makara* catching its right hind leg. To the right is Vishnu flying on *Garuda* with two hands, one resting on the head of the elephant and the other upraised in *vismaya*. On the south face of the second pillar of the front row there is a sculpture showing *Putanā* suckling SriKrishna. There is a worn-out female figure on *mandapa* to the west.

In the back wall of the *mandapa* are excavated three shrines each with a projecting entrance. Each entrance is on a raised base on which are two pilasters with the entrances between them. The entrance of the central shrine and the *vedi* below project a foot further. All the three entrances are surmounted by *kapota*, or cornices which are plain. There are two rafter ends above the *kapotas* of the side shrines and four above the *kapota* of the central shrine.

Cave III : This is a single and plain cave temple situated about a hundred metres higher than the road level and reached by a flight of rude steps cut on the side of the hill.

This cave consists of two crude pillars without base or capital in the front with short walls on either side. The *mandapa* beyond is 5.56 m. long and 6.00 m. broad. There is a single cell in the back wall of the *mandapa* 2.31 m. long and 2.23 m. broad.

The facade of the cave consists of a narrow flat *patta* or band above the two pillars. There is no *kapota* above.

Cave IV : This is a small single celled cave facing the south and dedicated to Durga. It consists of two rock walls in the east and west in the front and two pillars beyond with corresponding pilasters. The *mandapa* beyond is 4.6 m. long and 3.9 m. broad. There is a cell 1.8 m. square in the wall.

The pillars are plain and cubical with octagonal shafts in the centre and with no base or capital. Above these pillars are two plain *pattas* or bands. These are surmounted by a moulded *kapota* or cornice and adorned with three empty *nasikas* or gables with spade-head tops. Above the *kapota* are two bands with four rafter ends between them.

The entrance of the cell is reached by a short flight of steps with a *chandrasila* before it. The wall on either side of the entrance is plain. The back wall of the cell contains a shallow niche in which there is a half relief figure of Durga sculptured. This deity stands facing the right with her right foot resting on a small stool and the left stiff and resting on the ground. She has four hands, the upper right holding *trisula*, the lower right resting on the bent knee and the lower left in *katihasta*. The upper left hand is worn-out. There is a low rectangular platform below this niche.

There are two niches to the west of this cave of which one is empty and the other contains the standing figure of Vishnu with four arms. There are five niches in the east wall. These contain the sculptured figures of Siva with four hands dancing on the prostrate body of the *apasmarapurusa*. Brahma with three heads and four hands holding *kamandalu*, *aksamala* and *pustaka*, another standing figure, a representation of Vishnu standing with *samkha* and *chakra* in the two upper hands, *gada* in one lower hand and the other lower hand in *katihasta* and a figure of Ganapati with the head of a real elephant.

Cave V : This is a triple celled cave facing the north. It has two short projecting walls on the east and west, and two cubical pillars without bases or capitals with short projection rock walls on the sides forming three openings. The *mandapa* beyond is 8 m. long and 1.67 m. broad. There are three cells in the back wall each 2.28 Sq. The entrances of these shrines are level with the wall and do not project. The facade above the pillars has a low *kapota* or cornice without any decoration. Above it is a row of swans.

The Caves of Undavalli

There is a big four storeyed cave in this village and four more smaller cave temples.

Cave I : This is the main, four storeyed cave popularly known as the temple of *Anantasayi*.

The ground floor of the cave is irregularly excavated and incomplete. Its ground level is varying and not uniform. It has a *mandapa* of three rows of six pillars each and one pilaster at either end. There are seven openings between these pillars which are all cubical and without base or capital. The facade has a low flat *kapota* or cornice containing an inscription in Telugu characters of the 9th century.

The first storey is in four sections from south to north and reached by a short flight of steps cut in the rock at the right end of the ground floor. At the top of this flight of steps to the left there is a rectangular niche in the rock wall and above it the railing ornament in three sections. Above is a frieze of two lions and one elephant in vigorous poses. The first section is opposite the flight of steps. It has in the front an open space between two rock walls on the north and south. There is a niche in the north wall adorned with the railing ornament. On the south wall opposite there are two long inscriptions.

Beyond the open space is a low *adhistana* with a flight of steps in the centre. Beyond these steps is a *mandapa* of two rows of two pillars each with corresponding pilasters. These are cubical pillars with an octagonal shaft in the middle. They have simple curved bracket capitals. The back wall of the *mandapa* contains the entrance of a cell with a *Kosta* or niche on either side. Each niche has two pilasters and a *makaratorna* above. There is a distended *makaratorana* above the entrance. The beam above the pillars of the front row contains a row of swans with their wings open. Above is the moulded *kapota* decorated with three *nasikas* or gables with a spade head top. Above the *kapota* are seven figures which are too worn-out to be identified. Above these figures is an ornament in three sections containing three horizontal rows of rafter ends with two beam-heads between them.

The second section is to the north of section I and reached through an opening in the north wall. It consists of a *mandapa* with four rows of four pillars each with the corresponding pilasters in the northern and southern walls. All the pillars are cubical and contain the *taranga* or roll ornament on the underside. At the base of the second pilaster to the south there is the figure of a woman standing with the right leg bent and the right hand resting on the right thigh and the left hand held up in *vismaya.* Five pillars and two pilasters in this section contain the full lotus medallion on the rectangular block at the top.

The third section is to the further north and reached from section II through an opening in the northern wall. It contains a *mantapa* of two rows of two pillars each with four corresponding pilasters in the walls. All these pillars and pilasters have on their underside the *taranga* or roll ornament with a *patta* or fillet in the centre. Two pillars contain the lotus medallions.

The fourth section is in the extreme north and at a lower level. It consists of a *mandapa* of two rows of two pillars each and two corresponding pilasters in the walls. These pillars and pilasters are like those in section III. There is an empty cell excavated in the back wall of this *mandapa.* There is an empty niche in the back wall of this cell with a low *vedi* before it. One pilaster contains the lotus medallion and two contain the figures of swans. There is a niche in the south wall at right angles to the back wall of the *mandapa* with a sculpture representing a male being seated with the right leg bent and resting on the seat and the left hanging. The left hand is on the left thigh and the right is bent at the elbow and upraised. There is a woman to the right and two to the left. A boy stands below before a *Purnakalasa.* On the rock wall to the south there is a fine miniature temple of the Nagara order.

The second storey consists of a pillared *mandapa* and an open portico before it. This *mandapa* contains six pillars and a pilaster in the south wall in the front row, a short rock wall projecting behind the first pillar in this row, six pillars and a pilaster in the north wall in the second and third rows and five pillars and a pilaster in the north wall in the fourth row. To the north of these rows of pillars there is a huge figure of Vishnu Anantasayi. There are three niches in the south wall. The outer or eastern side of the short projecting wall behind the first pillar of the first row contains the figure of a *dvarapalaka* standing, leaning to the left with right hand in *katihasta* and the left resting on a *gada*. A snake starts on his right hand, runs across the chest and emerges above the left shoulder. At the end of the south wall there is a fire niche of two pilasters with a flat *kapota* above them and a solid *nasika* or gable surmounting all with a lotus scroll on either side at the bottom. On the beams above the front and second rows of pillars towards the northern and there are two rows of dwarfs opposite each other. The pillars in the front row are surmounted by a *kapota* decorated with ten *nasikas* each with a spade-head top and a human head inside. Above the *kapota* is the series *kuta, sala, kuta, sala, kuta, sala,* and *kuta*. All the pillars of the *mandapa* are cubical and contain on the underside the *taranga* or roll ornament with a patta or fillet in the middle. They are adorned with many sculptures viz., a bearded sage, man playing *mridanga*, *chauri* bearers, *Gajendramoksa*, lion, elephants, Vishnu with Prithvi, Narasimha, Vamana and Bali, Trivikrama and Sita under the *Asoka* tree. The open portico before the *mandapa* contains on its eastern edge the figures of three bearded sages and two lions. The image of Anantasayi found at the northern extremity of the *mandapa* is hewn out of the rock. It represents Vishnu as lying on the seven coiled body of *Sesha* with the hoods spread above his head. The deity keeps the right hand folded at the elbow under the head and holds up the left hand also bent at the elbow in *vismaya*. There is a man at the feet of the god sitting on his knees and keeping his hands in *anjali*. Beyond the feet of the God are two demons, Madhu and Kaitabha. On the wall are to be found the figures of Brahma with four hands seated in *padmasana* on a lotus and of four other flying gods keeping their right hands in *vismaya*. On the back wall of the *mandapa* are the figures of the Vaisnava devotees and a fine figure of Vishnu seated in *padmasana* on *Sesha*. He holds *shamkha* and *chakra* in the two upper hands and keeps the lower hands in *abhaya* and *varada*.

The third storey contains a narrow open space and a wall to its west decorated with ten pilasters. Two simple plain cells are excavated into this wall.

Cave II : This cave temple is to the south of the main cave. It contains two plain empty cells and a frieze of two lions and two elephants above it. There are two niches above this frieze, and one of them contains the figure of Vishnu holding *shamkha* and *Chakra* in the two upper hands, *gada* in one lower hand and keeping the other in *katihasta.*

Cave III : This cave is to the south of cave no. II. It contains a single celled shrine. There is open space in the front, enclosed by two rock walls on the two sides of a *mandapa* on a low *adhistana* containing two rows of two pillars each with corresponding pilasters in the walls and two niches in the walls between the pilasters. The back wall of the *mandapa* contains a central entrance with a *kosta* on either side. There is a moulded *kapota* above the pillars in the facade decorated with three *nasikas*, one containing three heads, and another containing two. The heads in the third are worn-out. The pillars are cubical and without the base or capital.

The *kostas* in the back wall are adorned with a *makaratorana* with dwarfs seated on the necks of the *makaras*. There is a lotus bud above the *torana* in the centre. Inside the *kosta* are the figures of *dvarapalakas* standing in *samabhanga* with the right hand resting on the right hip and the left resting on a *gada*. The pilasters of the *kostas* are fully developed and contain the *kalasa, tadi, padma, idai* and *palaka*. There is a *makaratorana* above the entrance also and two human heads, one on either side of its central projection.

Cave IV : This cave is situated to the north of the main cave and reached by a narrow pathway cut in the hill side. It consists of open space in the front enclosed by rock walls on the sides, a low *adhistana*, a *mandapa* with two rows of two pillars each with corresponding pilasters in the walls and the back wall containing shrine entrance with a *kosta* on either side.

All the four pillars are cubical and have curved bracket capitals. The two pillars and pilasters in the front contain sculptures which are much worn-out. There is the lotus medallion on two pilasters in the interior.

The *kostas* in the back wall have distended *makaratoranas* above them extending to the sides and not hanging below. The *kosta* on the south contains the figure of woman standing with her right hand upraised and the left kept in *katihasta*. To her left is another, woman carrying a basket on her head.

Cave V : This cave is also on the same hill but just behind the village. Its front has fallen.

This cave has in the front a wide open space enclosed by rock walls on the sides each with an empty niche. Beyond is a low *adhistana* on which there is a *mandapa* containing two rows of two pillars each with corresponding pilasters in the walls. Beyond is the back wall with three shrines excavated into it. The pillars are cubical and have curved bracket capitals. In the northern part of the back wall there is a fine shrine with its entrance spanned by a *makaratorana* whose plume like part hangs below. The upper beam is decorated with row of geese. The architrave above the *makaratorana* is adorned with lotus petals. The moulded *kapota* above contains at the ends *nasikas* with human heads inside. There is an elephant at each end above the *kapota* supporting the roof. The shrine to the south has a *kosta* on either side of the entrance containing the figures of *dvarapalakas*, with a snake emerging above the left shoulder. Above the *kapota* of this shrine there is a row of two lions and two elephants supporting the roof.

Miniature Shrines

These shrines are carved on the rock to the farther north of cave No. III. Two of them contain a linga on a *vedi* inside. One is on an *adhistana* having *upana*, *tripatta* another *patta, gala* cut into compartments by short pilasters, and a flat *kapota* above all. One shrine has a single pilaster on the sides of the entrance while the others have double pilasters. Above the pilasters there is a moulded *kapota* without any decorations. Above this is a narrow *patta* or band with four rafter ends above. Then there is a wide *patta* and two narrow bands above. Above these bands there is the *gala* cut into compartments by four pilasters. One shrine has a plain *Nagarasikhara* and stone *kalasa* above. The *sikharas* of the other shrines are decorated with a *nasika* or gable with spade-head top. Inside the *nasika* are two pilasters with a beam head between them.

G. J. Dubreuil[1] has shown that the cave temples at Undavalli and Mogalrajapuram on the banks of the Krishna are Vishnukundin excavations and that the Pallava king Mahendravarman I, was inspired by a study of these to excavate similar shrines in several places in his dominions in the south. After a careful comparative study of the caves at Undavalli with those excavated by the Pallava king Mahendravarman I at Mandagapattu, Mamandur, Pallavaram and other places in the south he had come to the conclusion that the latter bear close resemblance to the former in design and style, and that Mahendra who admired the Vishnukundin caves had similar ones cut on the rock around his capital Kanchipura and other places in his dominions.[2]

It is apparent that the Vishnukundin dynasty, having been contemporary to Vakatakas should have had opportunity of knowing the great achievements of these in the realms of architecture and sculpture. A south-ward flow of Vakataka architectural traditions from Ajanta to the lower Krishna valley due mostly to the intimate dynastic relationship between the Vakatakas and the Vishnukundins is quite possible. The intense devotion to *Brahmanism* of the Vishnukundins is also vouched by many of the kings like Madhavavarman I and III having performed *Aswamedhas* and thousand *Agnishtomas* and also by the entire family having been dedicated to the worship of the God Sriparvathaswami and this would make it appropriate that they be credited with the cave temples of Mogalrajpuram and Undavalli.

It has been suggested by early writers like Longhurst that the nature of the pillar, corbel, the cornice and the panel work in the cells, including the ground plan, and the dedication of the caves jointly to Brahma, Vishnu and Siva although establishing the primacy of the last mentioned in the Mogalrajapuram would imply that the work has the stamp of Pallava rock-cut architecture modes.[3] Longhurst's view was proved to be untenable by some scholars.[4]

According to several writers[5] the Vijayawada group of temples are of Vishnukundin origin and the main argument in favour of this theory rests on the following facts.

i. A number of copper coins found in the coastal districts containing the lion on one side and a vase on the other are attributed to the Vishnukundins.

ii. There is the figure of a vase of *purnakalasa* in one of the caves of Mogalrajapuram and of a lion in the Anantasayi cave of Undavalli.

iii. The seal of Ipuru I plates contains, in the upper half and above a horizontal line, the figure of Lakshmi seated on a pedestal flanked by a lamp stand by the Sun and the crescent Moon. The seal of the *Ramathirtham* plates contains the figure of a lion with mouth open tail looped above the body and the left fore-paw raised. The lion found on the obverse side of the Vishnukundin coins is similar. This lion also resembles the animal found sculptured at the bottom of two pillars in the second storey of the main cave temple at Undavalli.

A fine *purnaghata* is found at the base of one of the pillars in a cave at Mogalrajapuram. It is then clear that the copper plate grants containing the figure of the lion on the seal, the coins containing the figures of the lion and *kalasa* and the caves containing the figures of the lion and the *purnaghata* belong to one and the same family of rulers.

iv. The Mushinikunda grant of the Eastern Chalukyan king Vishnuvardhana III, records the gift of the village of that name to a Jaina temple at Vijayawada by Aryamahadevi, the queen of Vishnuvardhana-I (624-642 AD). The grant was executed by the queen herself and the seal bears the well known epithet, Vishamasidhi, borne by Vishnuvardhana.[6] This is a copy of an earlier grant made in the time of Vishnuvardhana-I.[7] Among the boundaries of the village gifted, mention is made of *layanam* or a cave which obviously refers to one of the cave temples in Mogalrajapuram. This shows beyond doubt that the caves were in existence for sometime before the foundation of Eastern Chalukyan rule and that they were familiarly known by that time. The Vishnukundins preceeded the Eastern Chalukyas as rulers in this region.

v. On the top of the triple celled cave at Mogalrajapuram is a figure of Nataraja with eight hands, tampering *Apasmarapurusha*. It is a unique one and such a figure is found nowhere else including the Pallava cave temples at places like Mandagappattu, Mamandur, Davalanur etc.[8] These caves must therefore be ascribed to the Vishnukundins.[9]

Most of the architectural features found in these cave temples can be traced to the architecture of the Satavahana period or its representations in the sculptures of the period. Massive cubical pillars without base or capital and with octagonal shafts in the middle are to be found in Buddhist caves of Guntupalli in coastal Andhra Desa. Many lime stone pillars of this type have been found at Amaravati, Bhattiprolu etc. Animal friezes are found on the *anda* or dome of the *mahachaitya* of Amaravati and Nagarjunakonda and at the base of the half lotus medallions on pillars. The *purnakalasa* as a decorative device was widely employed by the architects of the Satavahana period.[10]

The frieze of dwarfs found on the beams of some of these cave temples, sometimes carrying a garland, is found on the *mahachaitya* of Amaravati.[11]

The Vijayawada group of cave temples influenced considerably the architecture of the Pallavas and the Eastern Chalukyas.

Influence of Pallava Architecture

i. Ornamentation of the cave facade with the *kapota* containing *nasikas* found in cave temples of the Pallavas.

ii. Most of the southern caves of this period contain pillars and pilasters decorated with the lotus medallion and this feature is found in one cave at Mogalrajapuram and two caves at Undavalli.

iii. The *kosta* adorned with *makaratorana* is found in the Dalavanur cave and many caves of the Vijayawada group.

iv. The Durga temple of the Kotikala-mandapam is suggestive of the Durga temple of Mogalrajapuram.

Influence on Early Chalukyas

Some architectural features of this group of cave temples are seen in the temples of the Eastern Chalukyan period found at Bikkavolu and Chebrolu. The *makaratorana* niches and entrances adorned with the *kapota* above are an instance to the point. The row of geese and dwarfs is also common.[12]

The front towers of the temples like the Huchimalligudi at Aihole and the Virupakasha and Mallikarjuna temples at Pattadakal built by the Chalukyas have representations of Natesa with many arms with a bull behind[13] and reminds us of the figure of Nataraja i.e. dancing Siva, with eight hands, in the *Urdhvajanu* pose and tampering *Apasmarapurusha* found on the top of the triple-celled cave at Mogalrajapuram.

REFERENCES

1. Dubreuil, G. J.; 1917; The Pallavas, Pondicherry
2. *Ibid.*, p. 27-35.
3. Longhurst, A. H.; 1924; Pallava Architecture, Memoirs of ASI No. 17, p. 22-30.
4. Rama Rao, M.; 1963; Vishnukundin Coins in A. P. Govt. Museum, APGAS No.10, Hyderabad p. 28.
5. Somasekhara Sarma, M.; 1959; Telugu Vignanasarvasvamu, Vol. III, Madras, p.119. Sivaramamurthi, C.; 1957; Eastern Chalukyan Sculptures, Madras, p. 26.
6. Annual Report on Indian Epigraphy, 1916-17; p. 116. c.p.9.
7. *Ibid.*, para 21.
8. Srinivasan, K. R.; 1964; Cave Temples of the Pallavas, New Delhi.
9. Rama Rao, M.; 1963; *op.cit.*, p. 30.
10. Longhurst, A. H.; 1938; Memoirs of Archaeological Survey of India No.54, plate xxic.
11. *Ibid.*, pl. xiv, a.
12. Rama Rao, M. 1963; *op.cit.*. p. 32.
13. Cousen, H.; 1926; The Chalukyan Architecture of the Kanerese Districts, pp. 39-40.

Religious : Brick Temples and Structural Temples

The origin of image worship and the construction of temples may be assigned to pre-Buddhist period or pre-Christian era in the absence of any clear evidence. The next phase in constructions goes to the Buddhist period to 3rd to 4th century AD. In both these types of constructions, brick was the main material which could be conveniently fabricated into the desired structure being cemented either with mud or mortar. Further, brick architecture was also an inextricable companion of stucco workmanship which was a clear precursor of stone sculpture.

The Satavahanas and their successors like Ikshvakus adopted the brick medium for the Buddhist *Stupas, Chaityas*, and *Viharas* from their very inception, as at Amaravati, Nagarjunakonda, Goli, Ghantasala, etc. The spurt that was given to brick architecture spread far and wide and became the common pool of Buddhist as well as Hindu Brahmanical architecture. The continued use of brick medium in the lower Deccan by early Hindu architectural pioneers, even with the admitted availability of stone as raw material of the requisite quality shows the influence of age long and customary use of brick by their Buddhistic fore-runners in the same region.[1] Thus the very earliest examples of Brahmical structural architecture are mostly of brick medium.

Brick is the most ancient material for a sacred building. Bricks of large size and of strong texture were made in Andhra Desa from quite early times; the size of the bricks found in the excavations at Yeleswaram on the banks of river Krishna at the Satavahana and Ikshvaku levels was 56 m. × 30.5 cm. × 7.5 cm. During the period extending from the 1st to the 3rd century BC or still going farther back, the use of bricks for walls seems to have been quite common in Andhra Desa for both religious and secular buildings.

The *Matsyapurana* describes the possible forms of the Hindu temple and says that they may be built either of wood or brick or stone.[2] Bricks had formed "the body of sacrifice". Detailed prescriptions are given as to how to make good baked bricks and this practical knowledge gained by experience accompanies a "*Smriti*", a tradition by which the acquired technical skill became perfected.[3] The act itself of offering had gone into the making of the brick. It is a rite of identification. The substance of the brick is its carrier, earth and fire are the elements which take part in it and help the sacrificer to build his sacrificial body.[4]

Bricks and stones are frequently combined in one and the same building.

Essentially the acts and rites in building the temple are sacrificial. One of the main sacrifices being the *vastu-homa*.

"Let him who wishes to enter the worlds that are reached by sacrificial offerings and the performance of religious obligations build a temple to the Gods, by doing which he attains both the results of sacrifice and the performance of religious obligations", says Brihat Samhita.[5] The body of architectural knowledge behind the short compilation of the Brihat Samhita is supported by the traditional science of architecture, *vastusastra* listed in the Matsya Purana.[6]

The structure of a temple is a work of art and science. Their knowledge and practice are conducive towards the same end, the making of a perfect instrument whose sight and ritual use procure release.

The Hindu temple is built with the fervour of devotion as a work of offering and pious liberality, in order to secure for the builder, a place in heaven, which means a high level of inward realisation and to increase the religious merit of his near relatives. The temple is built as a work of supererogation, with the utmost effort in material means and the striving of the spirit so that the *prasada* attains and leads to the Highest point. He who builds a temple of Siva leads his ancestors of 21 generations to the world of *Sambhu.*[7] To the pilgrim and devotee who goes to the temples, it is a *Tirtha* made by art, as others are by nature and often it is both in one. It is the seat, abode and body of divinity. In addition to being an offering and work of pious liberality, the temple has not only its proportionate measurement but also the carvings on its walls, and the total effect of its form.

The temple consists of thick walls and a roof forming a dark square chamber entered through a door with a more or less elaborate frame.

The Brihat Samhita[8] and the Matsya Purana[9] describe twenty types of temples. Amongst them *Meru, Mandara* and *Kailasa* are the first three names, all three are the names of the Mountains. Some inscriptions extoll the temple as the Mountain.[10] In the geography of the *puranas*, the *Mandara* is the mountain to the east of *Meru.*[11] *Kailasa,* the abode of *Siva,* is situated to the north of Mountain *Meru,* or it is said to be one of its three peaks,[12] so that either of these peaks, *Mandara* and *Kailasa,* is a part of *Meru.*

Sculptural Representation

The sculptures from Amaravati, Jaggayyapeta, Nagarjunakonda and Goli include a number of bas-reliefs where a variety of examples of architecture, both religious and secular occur. The types of religious shrines amongst them may be taken to give us clues to the fact that there actually existed then shrines of similar types in the open air. In certain cases secular buildings, shown in the bas-reliefs, such as palaces may also be seen to possess some of the details of a religious edifice, a fact which shows that during the early period there was comparatively greater freedom in the practice of the art of building.

The '*Punyasala*' from Jaggayyapeta,[13] the *harmikas* surmounting the stupas and the Budhagharas from Amaravati[14] are examples of shrines built on square plan and there are shrines built on circular plans.[15] A number of structural *chaitya-grihas* have been found amongst the ruins of buildings at Nagarjunakonda.[16] The excavations carried out at Nagarjunakonda brought to light remains of a large apsidal structural shrine devoted to Siva who is called as Pushpabhadraswami in the inscription occurring on its *dhvajastambha.*

A peculiar brick structure of elongated beehive outline and with a *Gavaksa,* carved on its lower part, is represented in a relief from Amaravati. The *Gavaksa* is surmounted by a very tall finial of several components probably *Amalaka* etc.[17]

A lead coin belonging to Satavahana king Yagna Sri of the last quarter of the second century AD shows on the reverse a beautiful design of a bow and arrow and on the obverse a three-stepped pedestal on which is placed a figure resembling a human head. It carries a three-pronged design. To the proper left of this head there is a tall-pillar. To the proper right there is a square, with a small opening at its bottom, suggesting an enclosure; within the enclosure is depicted a tiny little but beautiful bull standing facing proper right. This bull is of the type which occurs in early sculptures from Amaravati etc., as well as the type met with in the seals of copper-plate grants of the Salankayanas. All these figures as well as their arrangement appear to us to suggest clearly that what is meant here is a shrine. The trident head and the bull on the left show that here the deity represented is Siva. It leaves no doubt of the fact that during and earlier than the second century AD, there existed Siva shrines of this type.[18] In fact references to Siva shrines are met within the '*Saptasati*' of Hala who is a ruler of Satavahana dynasty in the first century AD[19]

Examples of rock-cut shrines date from about 5th to the 7th century AD and the non-availability of material proving the existence of structural temples of this period does not suggest that no such temples were built then. Probably, quite a number of them of brick and mortar, were built then. Of these, atleast one or two examples have survived. The famous apsidal temple at Chezarla is one of them.[20]

Brick Temples I : Keesaragutta

An early Saivite temple of brick is situated just opposite to the western gate-way of the fort. The temple is square in plan with a square brick pedestal in the middle to insert possibly a square based linga. There is a covered drain on the north-east corner for conducting out the water of ablution. The floor inside the temple is paved with bricks. The superstructure is in ruins. There are many brick temples scattered all over the area. The transition from brick to stone is clearly discernible here.

In the early phase, all the temples were constructed of brick. There is a Jaina temple with a brick square *Garbhagriha* to which was later adjoined a *Mukhamandapa.* About a hundred metres away from the Jaina temple and on the bank of the tank is another small temple dedicated to a linga constructed entirely of granite but for the brick *yoni*. This may belong to the last phase.

About four hundred metres away from the present excavation site towards west, one square brick structure with a hole and a linga was brought to light. The linga has a square at *Brahmabhaga*, octognal shaft at the *Vishnubhaga* and *Rudrabhaga.* The shrine is in east-west orientation. This structure is unique because there is no *panavatta* and also in view of the fact that the plan of this Saivite structure is similar to that of Saivite open shrines noticed at Yeleswaram on the banks of the river Krishna. Now, let us study each shrine in greater detail.

Square Brick Shrine

This is a single celled square shrine constructed in west-east orientation. The main cell was constructed with brick including walls and flooring. The outer length of the cell is 7.50 m. × 7.50 m., the inner length of it being 6 m. × 6 m. The walls of the cell are of 0.75 m. thickness.

There is a square pedestal in the centre of the shrine. The distance from the inner side of the wall to the pedestal is 2 mts. It is 40 cm. high from the floor, outer and inner lengths being 2.10 m. × 2.10 m. and 52 cm. × 52 cm. respectively. There is a cavity in the centre for installing the linga, which is missing. There are five courses of brick from floor level.

A covered drain of 22 cm. width was provided from inside on the north-east corner of the shrine. The total length of this drain from inside the shrine to the other end which opens on the other side of the outer wall is 4.80 m. The water with which linga or image is bathed in the daily rites passes from the image to the drain which is also known as *Pranala*, on the floor which traverses the middle of the north wall of the *Garbhagriha* and leaves through a spout. The water in which the linga or image has been bathed is sanctified and therefore is made to flow to the north.[21]

Outside the *Garbhagriha* there are twenty stone slabs with hollow round cuttings in the middle probably for holding the wooden pillars. These base stones are of various sizes and their shape also is irregular. The distance from stone to stone is 2.25 m. which is equally maintained. There are six stones on each side at equal distance and in all, there are 20 stones. This might be an open *mandapa* or *pradakshanapatha.* The floor level of the cell is 60 cm. below the pillared *mandapa* outside the cell. Leaving a space of 4.40 m. on all sides, a wall of 0.95 m. was constructed around the shrine. The length of this enclosure wall from outside is 17.70 m. and the inner length is 15-80 m. Superstructure is completely ruined and only the ground plan of the structure is visible. The size of the brick used in the construction of the shrine is 50 cm. × 25 cm. × 8 cm.

The square plan, being associated with the divine beings in the Vedic rituals, became sacred and shrines built on this plan and on the plans derived from it began to assume a special sanctity. Hence, such shrines in Buddhist context are seen to enclose Bodhi-tree.[22] (e.g. the Bodhighara from Amaravati) and Buddha-pada[23] (e.g. the *punyasala* from Jaggayyapeta). More important than these are the square *harmikas* which surmount the stupas. Although they are fences, yet from the way they are shown on top of the stupas and from their functions of enclosing sacred objects like the *Chatradanda,* their distinctly sacred character is evident. An objection to the singling out a *harmika* from its context and attributing to it a significance that should strictly go to an independent shrine may be anticipated. The reply to this objection is that during that period, the temple complex was only in its beginnings and its various parts are therefore not met with in one and the same context but are found scattered in a variety of contexts. There is, therefore, no illogicality in recognising in the *harmika,* a shrine, the suffix *ka* being used to denote, diminutive *harmya.* A *harmya* means a structure with terraces and is used to denote shrines also. Thus, a diminutive square shrine on top of a funerary monument naturally gets special significance.[24]

Structure No. 2

This can be called a Jaina shrine, as at present, there is a seated Jaina idol in the open *Garbhagriha,* which is carved of black basalt; the height of the image is 85 cm.

It is rectangular in plan facing towards east. Eleven courses of bricks are visible from the ground level to the basement, over which rectangular stone slabs were placed for giving support to the super-structure. The Jaina idol is placed in the centre of a pillared hall on a rectangular stone slab.

The central cell of the shrine is 2.50 m. in length. There are in all nine granite pillars supporting the ceiling slabs. There is another cell to the north of the present *Garbhagriha* which must be the sanctum-sanctorum of a Saivite shrine belonging to earlier period. The length and width of this cell is 1.80 m. × 2.00 m. Ruins of brick platform in front of the shrine to the east are traceable. The length of this platform is 6.35 m. and its width is 2.25 m. This platform was given offset projection to a width of 2.30 m. and a length of 5.70 m. The thickness of the wall is 75 cm. The total length of the shrine on the northern side including the projection on the east is 6.50 m.

Three lion figures are carved on a granite slab measuring 78 cm. × 70 cm. × 40 cm. one lion in the centre in a sitting position looking front and the other two on proper right and left turning side ways and looking front with mouths opens. At present this panel is lying in the ante-chamber i.e. proper left to Jaina idol.

C. Sivaramamurthi observes that "the basement of *stupa* does not show any mouldings. It, however, shows an interesting detail which has a significant bearing on the development of the mouldings of the basement in the later day temples. It is the continuous series of friezes showing a variety of animals usually the Buddhist quartet namely lion, elephant, horse and bull in different postures".[25] This shrine is the best example for showing the transition from brick to stone. The *mandapa*-shrines etc. the *punyasala* from Jaggayyapet, show that in early times the shrines were unwalled and open.[26]

Structure 3

Remains of another brick structure was traced on the southern side of the western gate (fortification). There is a square enclosure wall constructed with stone slabs, arranged in two rows leaving hollow space in the middle for filling with rubble etc. The length of the side of the enclosure wall is 45.6 m. There is a 1.35 m. wide entrance to this structure on the eastern side and provided with four steps; stone slabs are used for steps. Inside the square enclosure there is a mound of 19 m. × 2 m. × 19.2 m. Two trial trenches taken on the mound revealed four skeletons of infants with associated pottery in four corners of the mound. These skeletons were found in north-south orientation with head placed towards north.

A porch like brick structure facing towards the entrance of the enclosure wall is also traced. On the southern side of the mound, at a distance of 6 m., a dolmenoid cist like structure is found. Three verticle slabs are placed over it, capstone is fallen and displaced from its original position.

While the primeval shape of the dolmen is, architecturally, the prototype of the sanctuary enshrined in the Hindu temple, other closed types of sacred buildings also have preceeded the Hindu temple.[27] The proto type of these shrines is the dolmen with its one large flat slab of stone, supported by three unright slabs set on edge so as to form a small chamber with side open to serve as an entrance.[28]

Dolmens have actually been used as Saivite temples.[29] Old dolmens are set up as Siva shrines for example at Kambaduru, Kalyanadurg in Anantapur district.[30] The Siva temple at Kambaduru is a dolmen converted for this purpose by a careful dressing and fitting of the stone slabs. They are not planted in the ground but are raised on a moulded plinth.[31]

Structure 4

About 400 m. towards west from the site where the present excavations are carried out, one square brick structure with a linga fixed in a hole was exposed. The linga has a square base at *Brahmabhaga*, octoganal shaft at the *Vishnu* and *Rudra Bhagas*. It is in east-west orientation facing east. The structure is unique because there is no *panavatta* here and since this Saivite structure is similar to that of Saivite open shrines found during the excavations at Yeleswaram on the banks of the river Krishna.

Plenty of such square brick pedestals with or without lingas are found scattered on Keesaragutta.

Yeleswaram

Stumps of columns of a *mandapa* were noticed, and an enclosure wall was also brought to light. A brick structure appeared to have been intended for some ritualistic import as sockets were made at regular intervals around a raised pedestal for the creation of wooden columns to support a canopy. A brick structure something like a chamber was discovered, which functioned probably as votive shrine for installing *Banalinga.* Another brick structure of the nature of votive shrine installed with a *Banalinga* connected by an *abhisekha* drain was found.[32]

Gollathagudi

The plans of two brick temples facing east were brought to view. The walls over the plinth were built in brick with a system of bonding to which has added another layer to give veneering effect. Temple I being constructed in brick must have given ample scope to the builders for greater constructional possibilities, which are almost lost now due to its total collapse. The floor paved with burnt bricks was found disturbed at several places.

Gollathagudi temple complex contains a *Garbhagriha*, accessory *Mukhamandapa*, *Mahamandapa* and porch, which are all contemporary. The earlier ones at Gollathagudi were constructed in brick. A notable feature of these temples is the treatment of brick with excellent stucco work. The remains of a Saivite shrine are noticed to the south-west of Padalagadda. Large and small size boulders were raised to a height of 60 cm. at the foundation level. Each stone slab is of 20 cm. in thickness. Superstructure was constructed in brick bonded with mud and mortar. Flooring is covered with rubble and brick.

The structure under study is rectangular in plan facing east with a square *Garbhagriha* on the west. The main entrance of the temple has three steps 1st, 2nd and 3rd steps are 0.06 m., 0.05 m. and 0.25 m. in length respectively. The entrance is 1.30 m. in length and width. The height of the steps is 20 cm., 16 cm. and 0.13 cm. respectively. There is a square cell adjoining the steps to the proper right, raised over a rubble foundation. The length of the cell is 2.10 m. and its width is 2.20 m. Main temple was constructed with granite raised over rubble foundation. Its total length is 16 m. and width is 11 m. There is an *antarala* of 4.35 m. length and 4.50 m. width. The thickness of the wall is 0.85 m. *Mukhamandapa* is 4.00 m. in length and 6.45 m. in width. Brick measuring 41 cm. × 21 cm. × 7 cm. is used in the construction. Parallel to *Mukhamandapa* on the left there is a platform constructed with five courses of bricks. The length and width of the platform is 3.75 m. and 4.00 m. respectively. There is another platform parallel to *antarala* measuring 3.60 m. in length and 4.90 m. in width. In between the *antarala* and *Garbhagriha* there is a cistern like structure 1.50 m. in length and 1.55 m. in width and 1.00 m. deep; fourteen courses of bricks are visible.

The *Garbhagriha* is square in plan measuring 2.20 m. on each side. There is square stone pedestal measuring 0.35 cm. × 35 cm. with a hole in the centre for installing the deity. But the idol is missing. A Nandi carved in granite with mutilated head, and decorated with band of beads and a hanging bell was found in *Mukhamandapa*.

Structural Temples

Lovers of temple architecture are hard put in visualising structural forms of temple in very early times prior to the first known monuments, like the cave art of the Vishnukundins in Andhra Desa. It is, however, clear by both direct evidence as well as indirect stylistic evidence that before temples of durable material were erected, brick, mortar, and timber were the media. One might also presume that no complicated character in layout or elevation could have been feasible then although some variety in presentation was quite likely. The most popular aspect of such a structure might be its open character, by which the major part of the layout of the interior even including the deity fixed in a central spot might be visible to the onlooker. Early northern textual evidence reveals that there were five basic shapes which were exploited for raising of structures and those were square, rectangle, ellipse, circle and octagon. Architectural evidence of the latter day fully corroborates the application of these shapes on plan and elevation, which ultimately got reduced to three-square, octagon, and circle and were at the root of the ternary division of styles in the south into respective Nagara, Dravida and Vesara orders.[33]

It is generally believed that the Brahmanical temple builders borrowed this style from the *chaityas* of the Buddhists.[34] But some scholars[35] believe that the *stupa*, the most important religious foundation of the Buddhist, was itself pre-Buddhistic in origin and that it was a common form of tomb, nothing more or less than a regularly built dome-shaped pile of masonary, which was undoubtedly the oldest form of funeral monuments.[36] The *chaitya* like the *stupa* was also a pre-Buddhist institution adopted by the Buddhists to secure the loyalty of the masses to their own faith. The Arthasastra of Kautilya teems with allusions to the *chaityas*. Certain interesting details regarding the *chaitya* are given in the Arthasastra. On full and new moon days, the worship of the *chaityas* may be performed by placing on a varandah, offerings such as an umbrella, *hasta* flag and a *chhaga* (he-goat).[37] The first point which deserves notice in this context is that the *chaitya* is a building with a varandah. It appears that in the time of the Mauryas, the *chaitya* was still a Hindu religious institution.[38] It is argued that the Buddhists borrowed many good things from the Hindus in giving a definite shape to their religion, and asserted with confidence that the *chaitya* type of temples such as those at Chejarla, Ter and other places were not Buddhist temples in their original condition, but Brahmanical structures built by the Hindu architects, in accordance with the architectural traditions which they inherited from their ancestors.[39]

No specimen of the temple structure of the Vishnukundins period is known to exist at present. The copper plate grants of the Vishnukundin rulers such as Tummalagudem inscription of Govindavarman I and the Chikkulla plates of Vikramendra Varman-II tell us that a number of temples, monasteries etc., were built and the old ones were kept in good repairs. The Velpuru stone inscription of Madhavavarman II gives us indication that the temple of Vinayaka was constructed. It is also likely that the temple of Somagireswaranatha of the Chikkulla plates owed its origin to the workmen of the Vishnukundin period.[40]

Some writers assert with confidence that there is reason to believe that the temples of Ramalingesvara and Bhimalingeswara at Satyavolu in Giddalur taluk of Kurnool district go back to the age of Vishnukundin monarchs.[41] The two temples in the village dedicated respectively to Ramalingesvara and Bhimalingesvara are built of stone from basement to *sikhara*. The *vimanas* of both the shrines rise in tiers, eleven in the Bhimalingeswara and fourteen in Ramalingesvara, they are surmounted by circular *sikhara* capped over by fluted *kalasa*. The shrines consist of a square *Garbhagriha* and a wagon roof *mandapa* attached to it.[42] In front of the *Garbhagriha* on either side of the gateway, stand two horned *dvarapalas* very closely resembling their counterparts in the early Pallava temples of Mahendravarman-I time.

Satyavolu Temples

The horned *dvarapalas* guarding the entrance of the sanctum are peculiar to the Vishnukundin and the Pallava temples. The observations of one writer,[43] who examined the *dvarapalas* from the Vishnukundin, Pallava, Chalukyan and Rashtrakuta temples are noted here. "While the tradition of the horned *dvarapalas* from the Vishnukundin caves is found transported to the Pallava area through Bhairavanikonda further south to Tiruchirapalli caves, it is absent in these Eastern Chalukya figures that follow the traditions of the home land. Even with the lapse of time and the interplay of influences we find the horned *dvarapalakas* as one of a pair just as in Pallava temple, fails to occur in the Chalukyan temples, and normal type continues as in the Mallesvara temple at Vijayawada or the temples at Biccavolu. The significance of the presence of the horns in these *dvarapalakas* appears to have been due to the continuance of the motif of Nagarajas known from Nagarjunakonda and Goli.[44] If the middle three hoods out of the five snake-hoods from these *Nagarajas* are removed they will look exactly like the horned *dvarapalakas* of later times. If the horned *dvarapala* is characteristic of the Vishnukundin and the Pallava temples, and not found in the Chalukyan temples either of Badami or of Vengi, as stated by the above writer, Satyavolu temples could not have been built by the Chalukyas. As all the Pallava temples were built only in the Dravidian style, and no specimen of a Pallava shrine in the Indo-Aryan style is found anywhere, it is not unreasonable to suppose that the Satyavolu temples were built by the Vishnukundins."[45] The Stayavolu group of shrines contains an apsidal or *gajaprishta* structure, a feature datable to pre-Chalukyan period.[46]

Alampur Temples

The Alampur temples are among the most important ancient monuments in Andhra Pradesh. They are the largest temple complex in the state distinguished by the style of their architecture. Temples built in the same style are found in several other places in the state.

There is a fine temple of this type dedicated to Siva at Kadamalakalva in Nandyala taluk of Kurnool district. Another shrine of the same style is at Mahanandi in the same taluk.

Opinion differs regarding the origin and the age of these temples at Alampur. Some draw attention to their resemblence to the Orissan temples and assign them to the 12th century AD[47] whereas others assign them to the western Chalukya kings of Badami who ruled over this part of the country in the 7th-8th centuries of the Christian era. Based on the epigraphical evidences some writers[48] have asserted that these temples are some of the earliest in existence in Andhra Pradesh. Labels in archaic characters found on the walls of other temples in this complex show that they belong to an even earlier period.[49]

These temples constitute a veritable treasure house of architecture, sculpture and iconography and throw valuable light on the evolution of art and architecture in eastern Deccan during the post-Satavahana period.

The existing *Vimanas* of these Alampur temples are exactly like those of the Bhimalingeswara and Ramalingeswara temples of Satyavolu and the Mahanandiswara temple of Mahanandi.[50] These temples in Andhra Desa must be studied together for a correct understanding of this style and the temples of the so called Indo-Aryan style, particularly those belonging to the Mukhalingam and Bhuvaneswara groups on the other.

Speaking of the Ramalingeswara groups at Satyavolu, one writer[51] states that they approach very nearly what is designated as Orissan style. Another writer[52] asserts that the spires of the temple of Alampur are so ingeniously overlaid with decorative detail that they appear to be almost replicas of the Lingaraja temple at Bhuvanesvar in Orissa. At Alampur one notices a marked change in the shape of the spire, which is more akin to the towers in the temples of Orissa than to those in South India.

Percy Brown[53] also noticed the resemblance. "A comparison may be instituted between this (*Parasuramesvara*) temple (at Bhuvanesvar) and the somewhat earlier temples of the Chalukyans at Aihole. It will be seen that the example of the *Parasuramesvara* although inclined to be heavy and crude, is an improvement of the Indo-Aryan type of *sikharas* subsquently added to the Aihole building. Moreover, the incipient form of clerestory introduced into the Orissan temple is also an advance on the double roof of the

Durga and Huchchimalligudi temples of Chalukyan group from which, however it may have been derived". The resemblences between the two groups of temples noticed by the writers cited above, pertains only to the *sikhara* or spire. In this connection the views of one of the modern writers[54] is worth considering.

"The Andhra-Karnataka group differs from the Orissan in one important respect; whereas the spire of the former is built on the roof of the square chambered *garbhagriha* or sanctum, the spire of the latter starts straight away from the ground, a cell inside the ground level forming the *garbhagriha*. Notwithstanding this difference, the close resemblance between the two calls for an explanation. The Orissan architect seems to have derived inspiration from his Andhra-Karnataka compeer. This is not unlikely, for the Orissan style had its origin in the temples of Mukhalingam in Andhra or that part of Andhra which in ancient times had gone by the name of Kalinga. Although the Kalingas, formed a distinct group by themselves from the Andhras, they were racially, linguistically, and culturally one and the same with the Andhras. Apart from this, Kalinga which was at first conquered by the Vishnukundins in the 5th century and subsequently by the Chalukyas in the beginning of 7th century AD remained an integral part of the kingdom of Vengi for several centuries when the peoples of the two countries mingled freely and lived together as common citizens of a single state. The Kalingas must have imbibed during this period, the artistic traditions of their western neighbours and gave a concrete shape to them by erecting the temples at Mukhalingam. The observations of Percy Brown deserve notice in this connection. "There is reason to believe that this (Orissan) style of temple architecture approached the eastern region from its southern extremity, spreading northwards to form the development in Orissa. Although the series at Mukhalingam may not comprise of the earliest examples, that the beginning was made in this locality is not unlikely. It has already been shown that a type of temple in a primitive Indo-Aryan style had begun to appear as far south as in the territory of the Chalukyas as early as the 6th century AD implying that they may have originated in that quarter. That the style of the Mukhalingam temples and of those of Orissa of a later date originated in the south (south-west) may be readily admitted. Whether it had come from the Chalukyas is more than doubtful. It is true that Pulakesin II had conquered Kalinga and together with it Vengi in 616-17 AD but he conferred the sovereignty of the countries on his younger brother Kubja Vishnuvardhana and recognised his right to bequeath them as a heriditary dominion to his descendants. With the appointment of Kubja Vishnuvardhana as the ruler of Vengi, Pulakesin II's connection with the east coast came to an end; and his successors at Badami had nothing to do with it. The style of Mukhalingam temples were popular.

The Eastern Chalukyas, as the descendants of Kubja Vishnuvardha or the E. Chalukyas as they are called, ruled over their Kalinga subjects. They did not however, favour the Indo-Aryan style, they built all their temples in the pyramidal or the Dravidian style. The builders of the Mukhalingam temples could not have adopted the style of their architecture from the Eastern Chalukyas. The recent discoveries of inscriptions in the 6th-7th century Telugu characters and the existence of horned *dvarapalas* in the Mukhalingam temple show that this temple goes back to the Vishnukundin period. It may be remembered that the Vishnukundins, who ruled over Kalinga before the Chalukyas made their appearance on the east coast and favoured the Indo-Aryan type. If the Kalinga architects of Mukhalingam and their predecessors acquired their fondness for the Indo-Aryan style from the south, as it is obvious, it must have been from their Vishnukundin masters of Vengi. The eastern Gangas who were the feaudatories at first of the Vishnukundins and subsequently of their Eastern Chalukya successors carried it later into Orissa in the east when they conquered that country in the 12th century AD.

The resemblance between the Andhra-Karnataka and the Orissan temples noticed above seems to be due to the inheritance of the same type from a common source rather than to conscious adoption. The Chalukyas in the West and the Kalinga Gangas in the east adopted the practice of building temples in the Indo-Aryan style from their Vishnukundin overlords who appear to have been the first among the South Indian dynasties to introduce it in the south"

REFERENCES

1. Soundara Rajan, K.V.; 1964; Architecture of the Early Hindu Temples of Andhra Pradesh, APGAS No.21, p. 2.
2. *Matsya Purana*; 1907; Anandasrama Sanskrit Series, Poona, Part VII, chapter ccl.xix.
3. Krama Risch, Stella; 1946; The Hindu Temples; Calcutta, p.102.
4. *Ibid*., p. 102.
5. Kern; 1895; *Brihatsamhita* of Varahmihira (translated by) Benaras, L.V.2.
6. *Matsya Purana*, *op.cit*., chapter ccl ii.
7. Mallayya, N.V.; 1930; "Studies in Sanskrit Texts on Temple Architecture; JAU, Vol.IV, p.172.
8. *Brihatsamhita*, *op.cit*., L.V. 17 f.
9. *Matsya Purana*, *op.cit*., CCL XIX, 28 f.
10. Fleet, J.F. 1888; CII, III, Calcutta, p.83.
11. *Vishnu Purana*; 1921; S.V. Press, Bombay, II, chapter 17.
12. *Siddhanta Siromani*, of Bhaskaracharya, 1929; Kashi Sanskrit Series, Banaras, 11.111.36.
13. Burgess, J.; Buddhist Sculpture from Amaravati, ASSI, London pl.LV, fig.2.

14. Sivaramamurti, C.; 1976; Amaravati Sculptures in the Madras Museum, pl. XLII, fig.12.
15. Coomaraswamy, A.K., 1927; *op.cit.*, fig.145.
16. Longhurst, A.H., 1938; The Buddhist Antiquities from Nagarjunakonda, Delhi, pl. IV (B), V (a), VI(a).
17. Sivaramamurti, C.; 1976; Amaravati Sculptures in the Madras Museum, pl.xvi.
18. Srinivasan, P.R.; 1959; Bulletin of the Madras Govt. Museum, Vol. VII, No.4, p. 27-28.
19. *Ibid.*, p. 28.
20. *Ibid.*, p. 20.
21. Kram Rische Stella; 1946; *op.cit.*, p. 171.
22. Sivaramamurti, C.; 1976; Amaravathi Sculptures in the Madras Museum, pl.XLII, fig.l e.
23. Burgess, J.; Buddhist Sculptures from Amaravati, ASSI, London pl.VL, fig.2.
24. Srinivasan, P.R.; 1959; *op.cit.*, page 11.
25. Sivaramamurti. C.; *op.cit.*, p;.XVI, fig.4.
26. Srinivasan, P.R.; 1959; *op.cit.*, page 11.
27. Kramrisch Stella; 1946; *op.cit.*, p.156.
28. *Ibid.*, p. 151.
29. Census of India Report, 1931; p. 406.
30. Longhurst, A.H.; 1015-16, Annual Report of the Archaeological Survey of India, Southern Circle, p. 29, pl.111.
31. Kramrisch Stella.; 1946; *op.cit.*, p.152, note.
32. Abdul Waheed Khan, Md.; 1963; A Monograph on Yeleswaram Excavations APGAS No.14, p. 24.
33. Soundara Rajan, K.V.; 1978; The Art of South India, Tamilnadu and Kerala, p. 19.
34. Percy Brown; 1959; Indian Architecture (Buddhist and Hindu periods), Delhi, p. 64
35. Venkataramanayya, N.; 1975; The Vishnukundins, Madras, p. 54.
36. Longhurst, A.H.; 1015-16, Annual Report of Archaelogy, Southern Circle p. 90.
37. Arthasastra of Kautilya, 1924; edited by Shamasastri, Mysore, p. 256.
38. Venkataramanayya, N.; 1975; *op.cit.*, p. 56.
39. *Ibid.*, p. 57.
40. Sankaranarayanan, S.; 1977; The Vishnukundins and their times, p. 147.
41. Venkataramanayya, N.; 1975; *op.cit.*, p. 58.59.
42. Annual Report on Indian Epigraphy; 1939-40 to 1942-43 p. 5.
43. Sivaramamurti, C.; 1957; Early Eastern Chalukya Sculpture, Madras Govt. Museum Bulletin, N.S. Vol.VII, No. 2, pp. 36.
44. Ramachandran, T.N.; 1929; Sculptures from Goli, Madras, pl.1(a) and IV (i).
45. Venkataramanayya, N.; 1975; *op.cit.*, p. 59.
46. Epigraphia Andhrica Vol.IV; 1974 p. 141-142, APGES No.11, Hyderabad.
47. Yazdani, G.; 1960, Early History of the Deccan, p.739-40.
48. Venkataramanayya, N.; 1975; *op.cit.*, p. 60.
49. *Ibid.*, p. 60.
50. Rama Rao, M.; 1965; Early Chalukyan Temples of Andhra Desa, APGAS No.20, pp. 41-42.
51. Krishnamacharyulu, C.R.; 1939-40 to 1942-43; Ramalingeswara and Bhimalingeswara temples at Satyavole; ARE p. 5 ff.

52. Yazdani, G.; 1960; Early History of the Deccan, pp. 736-739.
53. Percy Brown; 1959; *op.cit.*, p. 103.
54. Venkataramanayya, N.; 1975; *op.cit.*, pp. 62-64.

Secular : Fort-fortification walls, Gates etc., at Keesaragutta

Keesaragutta has an extensive fortification wall around the hills encompassing an approximate area of 3 to 4 Sq. Km. Presently there are traces of three metres broad, dressed rubble stone foundation of a very extensive fortification wall. The bricks measuring 50 cm. × 25 cm. × 8 cm., used for raising the super-structure are still visible all along the fortification wall in fragments and at some places intact. In most of the places the rubble wall was divested of the brick superstructure but the fallen brick is visible along the entire length of the wall. The fort was provided with four main gates on the east, west, north and south. Prefaced by strategic secondary walls in the shape of crescentic bulge possibly to stop direct onslaught of the enemy forces. The natural precipices of the hill were utilised as natural barriers and vulnerable points were plugged by constructing the ramparts.

Besides these main gates some water gates were also provided near the water ponds for fetching water into the fort. As there were no perennial sources of water such as rivers or streams in the vicinity, the natural depressions at the gradients were cross-bunded. Such numerous ponds are visible even today.

There is a huge tank at the foot of the fort on the west which must have served as a source of drinking water as well as a deep water hurdle for the protection of the fort. Similarly, there is a big tank on the eastern side below the fortification.

Traces of guard rooms were found near the main gates and the entire fort is studded with brick structures.

Antiquity of the fort

Before taking up a detailed study of the fortification at Keesaragutta it is necessary to examine the antiquity of the word 'fort' and its importance.

The term 'fort' denotes defence; defence from the hazards of nature like rain and sun and attacks from outside.

"Forts are built in times of peace, designed to protect political, industrial, transportation and communication centres".[1]

Their importance is chiefly strategic, erected for the purpose of strengthening a place or position. According to G.T. Data "in times of Yore, the fortress, was a capital means of defence".[2] Defence is the predominant characteristic feature of the fort.

The growth of the fort as a defensive structure depended to a large extent upon the contemporary trends of warfare i.e., the methods of attack and defence, the weapons used and the military organisation of the various kingdom in different periods.

According to B.P. Sinha[3] fort grew as a carrolary to the existing trends of warfare which is one of the oldest aspects of human existance. He remarks that the art of warfare evolved from the earliest times with attention paid to both offensive and defensive weapons and it continued to be the most dominant and persistant features of Indian History.

According to S.D. Singh[4] kingship grew out of warfare which it may be said in turn, gave birth to the system of defences in the form of forts and fortifications. Hence, the nature and character of a fort depend to a large extent upon the contemporary trends of warfare. Kautilya[5] assigned a place of importance and honour to forts in the body politic as a politico-military institution, and included it among the seven constituent elements of sovereignty of the State or the *sapthanga* viz. 1. King (Rajan); 2. Minister (Mantri); 3. Country (Deśa); 4. Fort (Durga); 5. Treasure (Kośa); 6. Army (Bala) and 7. Friend (Mitra) and it became the guiding principle in later times for almost all the kings to follow.

According to Kautilya it is only in a fort, that the army and treasury are secure and it is a powerful defensive instrument to the king in times of danger.[6] He therefore, enjoins upon a king to erect forts not only around his capital but also on all the frontiers of the kingdom, in the four quarters.

The Arthasastra of Kautilya was followed by a number of other works of polity, as Dharma Sastras, Puranas, and Nitisara of Kamandaka, Sukranitisara, and the Nitivakyamrita of Somadeva Suri. The Manusmriti and the Puranas like Matsya, Vayu, Brahmanda, Agni, and Vishnudharmottara, all of which ascribe a place of importance to the institution of fort, and insist upon its possession by a king. For instance, Manusmriti,[7] says that a king should have a fort, equipped with a spacious palace, habitable in every season and well supplied with water, weapons, money, grains and Brahmanas, artisans, and engines, fodder etc. It considers that a bowman placed on a rampart is a match for 100 foes and 100 bowmen for 10,000 foes.

The idea of concept of a fort as a military structure appears to have undergone several changes from time to time in its size, methods of construction, disposition of various structures, additional defensive equipment, etc., depending on the contemporary trends of warfare, methods of attack and defence, and weapons and implements of warfare.

The first criterion that governs the construction of a fort is the selection of the site. The suitability or strength of a site is often determined by its strategical importance and the availability of building materials in close proximity and the availability of water resources in plenty.

The second criterion is the availability of strong building material locally or in close proximity.

The third and the most important criterion is the strategical importance of a site, both from political and military aspects.

The last criterion is the availability of natural potentialities offered by the hills, like water resources in plenty, insurmountable cliffs, and difficult pathways etc.

The principles of fortification enunciated by Kautilya guided the builders and architects of the following ages. Kautilya's Arthasastra, the style and contents of which presuppose its antiquity and which cannot be later than 1st century BC[8] says that defensive fortifications against an enemy in war shall be constructed on grounds best fitted for the purpose; a water fortification, a mountainous fortification such as a rocky tract or a cave; a desert or a forest fortifications.[9] He further stresses that water and mountain fortifications are best suited to defend populous centres. The king may have a fortified capital as the seat of his sovereignty in the centre of his kingom in a locality naturally best fitted for the purpose.

Fort planning in India dates back to the Vedic period. Vedic literature mentions forts made of stone and iron.[10]

The importance of the forts is stated in the Mahabharata also.[11]

The importance of the forts and ramparts increased enormously long before the Christian era as the Indian civilisation progressed and prospered considerably. The importance of forts was appreciated by Manu. The planning formed an essential part of military engineering of the Indo-Aryans from ancient times. All exponents of the *Silpasastras* have stressed the importance of the forts. It was necessary to have the fortress amidst villages and towns for the efficiency of administration and government. Kautilya in his Arthasastra[12] emphasises the distribution of forts throughout the kingdom for the purpose of administration, jurisdiction and supervision.

Classification of forts

There are two broad classification of forts — the natural and artificial. The natural forts are divided into six categories i.e. water fort, mud fort, forest fort, desert fort, mountain fort and cave fort. A natural fort is one which is rendered inaccessible to hostile encroachments by its advantageous situation secured by natural defences, like mountains, rivers, marshy lands, deserts, and forests. The use of the natural forts is evidence of the skill of the ancient town planners in utilising local natural barriers and in turning them into best fortification by slight manipulations and modifications.

When a town is planned, with all its accompaniments such as health residences, devotional places, public halls, common pools and wells as reservoirs of water, public parks, garden - belts etc., it becomes the supreme consideration of the master town planner to have security considerations. Kautilya gives his preference to hill forts and considers them as the most unassailable. A fort on a mountain is of a self-defensive nature, and not easy to besiege or to ascent.[13] A fortified capital might be of any shape, circular, rectangular or square, in consonance with the requirement of the ground.[14]

The ruins of fortification wall on the top of Keesaragutta encompassing the huge brick structures of religious as well secular buildings clearly show that it was a hill fort constructed in the post-Satavahana period by the Vishnukundin kings following the cannons of Hindu science of architecture as enunciated by the ancient writers.

Detailed study of the Fort

Moat : The first place in the technique of construction of fortification goes to the formation of the mound or the rampart i.e. the *vapra*. The process of the formation of the rampart is a joint operation with that of the moats the *parikhas*, as termed in Sanskrit literature.

According to Kautilya[15] a fort should have 3 ditches with an intermediary distance of 1 *danda* or 6 feet from each other and 14, 12, and 10 *dandas* i.e., 84, 72 and 60 ft. in width, with a depth not less than by one quarter i.e. 21 ft. 18 ft. and 15 ft. or by one half of their width and square at bottom, and one-third wide as at their top, with sides built of stones or bricks filled with water from perennial sources and contain crocodiles and lotus plants.

The main idea behind moat is to make the approach of the enemy difficult. Kautilya therefore prescribes not less than 3 moats one behind the other. The moats are of two kinds viz., a dry moat and wet moat. The dry moat is also known as ditch, which is filled up with stocks of hay, wild thorns, and creepers, concealing underneath, poisonous weapons. The wet moat is filled up with deep pools of water upto the mouth and contain crocodiles and other poisonous creatures.

As far as Keesaragutta is concerned, the huge tanks at the foot of the hill on the west and east must have served as a moat for the protection of the fort.

Traces of moat on the other side of the fort are not clearly visible now. Neverthless it is quite probable that the natural formation of steep and slopy rock on all the other sides might have served as natural barriers for protection of the fortification wall.

Prakara : *Prakara* forms the most important part without which a fort cannot be truly called a fort. Kautilya[16] prescribes it to be created at a distance of 4 *dandas* i.e. 24 ft. from the inner most ditch, about 6 *dandas* height, 36 ft., and twice as much broad i.e. 72 ft. by heaping up and upwards and by making it square at the bottom and oval at the centre pressed by trampling of elephants and bulls. It should be of sufficient thickness and height, which vary according to the contours of the grounds.

The *prakara* wall is to be made strong by filling it up with the massive stones to make it look a grand gigantic structure.

The main material for building ramparts are mud, brick and stone. In ancient period we find largely the mud and brick fortifications. The strength of a fort is determined by the number of ramparts it possesses and their height and width.

Forts in ancient Andhra are mainly built of perishable materials like mud and brick as against stone which became the chief material in later times.

As has been stated earlier, the fortification wall at Keesaragutta had a base of stone work supporting a superstructure of burnt bricks, as evidenced from the ruins of the fortification. On the base rock surface, a masonary wall was built with brick and mud to a height of about one metre with a width of three and half metres and the brick work was bound into a solid fabric by means of stones so interpersed that the more brittle material rested upon the harder, while moist clay had been used for mortar.

Four courses of rubble structure are still visible on the southern side of the fort. The *prakara* from the base must have been originally 5 to 6 m.

From the fact that whenever the height of *prakara* is reached to 5 to 6 m. the walls are invariably finished off with a course of small stones. As there are no fallen blocks of stone lying near, we may assume that this was the original height of the *prakara.*

The perimeter of the fortification wall is about seven kilometres, which runs along the steep and slopy rocks at some places and on plain natural soil at some other over the hill.

Towers of Turrets : Another important element in the fortification is the raising of the towers on the parapets in all the four directions. These parapets were interpersed at regular intervals (100 *hastas* i.e. 150 ft. or 45 m.) with towers and they were provided with moveable stair-cases, and doors so constructed as to provide the comfortable ascent and descent. Panini and Kautilya call this *carika-devapatha.* Bastions or towers are mainly meant to reinforce the strength of the fort wall which run for long distances continuously, spaced at regular intervals of distance and at corners.

According to Kautilya, the wide road on the top of the parapet built along with the line of battlements (Indrakosas) was called *Devapatha.*[17] The height of the brick fort wall (*prakara*) above the mud-rampart (*vapra*) there is stated to be 36 ft. rising from the ground level and the battlements were built above it. The *Devapatha* extending along the city wall should be understood with reference to its great height resembling the celestial passage (*Devapatha*) in the heavens, justifying the comparison with the latter.[18]

One conspicuous point that attracts ones attention is that there are no evidences of the existence of bastions for this historical hill-fort at Keesaragutta. In the absence of any such material evidence it may be safely concluded that there was no need for the construction of bastions in those days. The importance of bastions was much less in early years of the Christian era, as the wars were generally fought on the plains in those days rather than attacking the fortified cities or towns as can be seen from the contemporary history of Andhra Desa in the post-Satavahana period.

The utility as well as the purpose of the bastions of a fortress increased in the later period, that is, just before and after the Early Chalukyans rose to power in the beginning of the 7th century AD.

Thus, it may be inferred that the Vishnukundins dispensed with the bastions probably keeping in view of the military needs of their times.

There is a semi-circular projection at a distance of about 160 m. east of northern gate. At this point the fortification wall takes a curve towards east. Thick layer of morrum and brick is noticed over the natural rock. The width of the fortification wall here is 4.60 m. Traces of superstructure are missing. On the south-east corner of the fortification, displaced stone boulders numbering about five are lying scattered near the basement formed by natural rock. The rectangular stone slabs might have been used as superstructure.

From this place four to five kms. distance is clearly visible in day light on account of its high altitude. The distance between the two boulders is nearly ten metres and width is about five metres. This is about 150 m. from the southern gate. There is every possibility to believe that the above two structures might have been used as watch towers.

Gateways : Gate-ways (*Dvarah*) form an important obstacle in the structure of the fort, next to the rampart. According to Kautilya, an entrance gate to the fort should be one-sixth as broad as the width of the street (*Kavata*).

Gateways were in the form of pyramidal towers of imposing aspect. They were called *Gopurams* literally the defensive structure of the town and thus fittingly adding to the fortification of the town. They formed a characteristic feature of the Indo-Aryan architecture. The Arthasastra of Kautilya mentions four principal gates on the four principal quarters and designates them as *Brahma, Aindra, Yama*, and *Sainapatya* according as they are laid on the North, East, South and West respectively.[19]

The gateways are to be provided with *pratoli*[20] a gateway sometimes provided with flight of steps, a small turret, the main road of town.

As stated earlier, the Keesaragutta fort was provided with four maingates on the east, west, south and north.

Huge dressed rectangular stone slabs were used in the construction of the gateways. Such boulders are found even today as a representatives of the glorious past.

Northern gate: Topographically, northern, side of the fortification wall appears to have been given importance and the main gate is located here. Nearly 15 to 20 stone slabs of different sizes are lying scattered near this gateway. One of the biggest slabs measure 4.35 m. in length 0.06 m. in width and 0.30 m., thickness. Another slab is the size of 3.30 m. × 0.60 m. × 0.25 m.

The width of the gateway is about 4 m. Topography of the hillock indicates that this gateway is the lowest point from the (ground) sea-level.

There are traces of curtain walls in semi-circular shape as a protection to the gate from the direct onslaught of the enemy. In all probability this must be the main gate of this fortification.

Eastern Gate: The eastern gateway is slopy. Stone pavement is visible but no stone slabs are traceable. The width of the gate is about 6 m. There is a big tank just by the side of this gate down below the fortification wall which might have served as a moat. The natural rock boulders and slopy sheets of rock served as side walls for the gateway. The gateway leads to the villages Parvathapuram, Rangapuram etc.

Southern Gate: The width of the gate is nearly 6 m. No stone boulders are visible. Probably natural rock boulders must have served as a gateway. The gate faces towards Bhogaram, Madhavaram, Kondapur, Ghatakeswaram etc. Innumerable natural rock boulders protect this gateway. A platform like brick sturcture is seen at the entrance of the gateway but no superstructure is existing.

Western Gate: The Western gate faces towards the village Keesara. This gate is about 7 m. in width. Stone slabs of the size of 2.70 m. × 0.70 m. × 0.35 m. are lying near the gate. Two big slabs probably used as door jambs are also found at this place. About 150 m. from this gate inside the fort there is a square brick shrine probably of Saivite shrine.

The northern gate is exactly at a distance of 1,265 m. from the western gate. The distance between northern and eastern gates is about 1,750 m. Eastern and southern gates are at a distance of 2,360 m. Western gate is situated at a distance of 1,250 m. from southern gate.

The Kautilya Arthasastra, one of the oldest treatises of politics and sociology, gives the names of the four principal gates of the Aryan's town or village.

The eastern gate, the starting point of the circumambulatory rite, was dedicated to *Brahma*, the creator represented by the rising sun. The southern gate, which symbolises the sun at noon was dedicated to Indra the vedic god who ruled the firmament during the day. The western gate was dedicated to the setting sun, or to Yama, the Lord of Death, and the northern gate to *Senapati* or Kartikeya the war-God. The nature symbolism of the Vedas was changed into philosiphic concept of the Upanishads. Vishnu-Surya took the place of Indra at the zenith, Lord Siva was substituted for Yama and Vishnu Narayana replaced Kartikeya.[21]

Inner fortification : Inner fortification wall is provided surrounding the entire palace complex, the traces of which are very much disturbed.

The starting point is taken from the water tank which is about 200 m. from the western gate of the main fortification wall. The secondary wall starting from the above point runs towards north and then towards east. The wall then runs towards north and then towards east. The wall then runs towards south and finally joins the eastern side of the watertank. The tank remains outside this secondary wall, and it virtually separates the palace complex and the tank.

The circumference of the wall is about 920 m. Brick, and stones are used for construction of this wall. The method of construction also appears to be similar to that of main fortification. Traces of only one gate on the western side near the tank are visible. One more gate might have existed on the eastern side and another gate connecting the palace complex to the tank.

Early years of the Christian era witnessed an increased tendency to construct hill forts. This was in consonance with the teachings of Kautilya and other writers on military affairs. The typical site preferred for a hill fortress was a precipitous cliff sloping to a river on one, two or even three sides and with steep slopes falling away on the other side. At the highest point was built a fort serving as a citadel.[22]

The account of Hiuen Tsang goes to show that towns, even of a small size, were enclosed by walls. The Chinese piligrim says "The towns and villages have inner gates, the walls are wide and high. The earth being soft and muddy, the walls of the town are mostly built of brick or tiles."[23]

Impact of warfare on construction of forts

A study of the military organisation of various kingdoms and the representation of arms and weapons in the sculptural carvings of various periods help us to understand the system of warfare.

An Amaravati rail pillar[24] shows vividly the art of warfare and military organisation of these times. Cities were well defended with high walls, ramparts and gates, walls and gateways were surmounted by *toranas* as at Sanchi.[25]

Warfare in ancient Andhra appears to have been based on the conventional form of "*Chaduranga bala*" i.e. four fold division of army into infantry, cavalry, elephants and chariots. During this period, infantry played a major role forming the front line of attack. Hence, the wide prevalance of field warfare, or land battles, fought at a chosen site or terrain, between the two warring factions, far away from their capital cities, the idea behind which was not to disturb or cause hinderance to the civilian population. The main weapons of warfare, as seen from the sculptural carvings at Amaravati and Nagarjunakonda, are stones, sticks, clubs, mace which are called as "crushing or stunning weapons".[26]

Archaeological evidences of fortifications in early Andhra Desa

The excavations carried out at Nagarjunakonda, revealed a citadel, with its grand fortification wall, ditches, gates and barracks, which threw light on the town planning and flourishing condition of the capital of Ikshvaku kings during the 3rd century AD[27]. Enclosing a trapesoidal area about 900 m. × 600 m. the citadal wall ran along the right bank of the Krishna on the west at an average distance of 105 m. from it, while on the south it overlay the summit of the 51 m. high Peddakundellagutta hill, it's maximum extant height on the plains being about 4.80 m. above the outside ground level. Trenches laid across the wall, both on the east and west, showed, that it had been built in two phases, the first or lower phase was presented by a rampart of morrum or mud above 24 m. wide at the base, resting on the natural soil, except on the western (river) side, where it overlay an earlier occupational deposit represented by a floor and a few hearths; the second phase was represented by a burnt brick wall 2.75 m. to 4.27 m. thick, generally built either directly on the existing rampart or on a secondary filling over it, but on naturally high grounds directly on the bare rock surface. The fortification wall was surmounted by a ditch on all the three sides, 3.65 m. in depth and varying 22.20 m. to 39.60 m. in width. Two main gate-ways, one each on the eastern and western sides, and a narrow postern gate, on the eastern and possibly serving as an emergency exit were exposed; close to the eastern gateway were barracks including stables and a nicely plastered masenary cistern. The western gateway, with a minimum width of 5.10 m. lay near the '*asvamedha*' site excavated.[28]

It is noteworthy that the shape of the fortification at Keesaragutta is almost similar to that of the brick fortification wall unearthed in Nagarjunakonda.

REFERENCES

1. Ramachandra Murthy, N.S.; 1979; Forts in Andhra Pradesh; Thesis-Karnataka University, Dharwar, p. 71
2. Data, G.T.; Art of Warfare in Ancient India, chapter IV, p. 29.
3. Sinha, B.P.; 1971; "Art of War in Ancient India" (Article from Studies in the Cultural History of India, Dharwar).
4. Sinha, S.D.; 1965; Ancient India Warfare with Special reference to the Vedic period; E.J. Brill Laiden, Netherlands, p.170.
5. *Arthasastra* of Kautilya; 1924; Translated by R. Shamsastry, Mysore, p. 309.
6. *Ibid*., p.50.
7. Buhler, G.; Laws of Manu, S.B.E. Series, XXV, Delhi, pp.228-229, Verse 76.
8. Shukla, D.N.; 1960; Hindu Science of Architecture, p.76
9. *Arthasastra* of Kautilya, *op.cit*., p. 56-57.
10. Prabhakar, V. Begde; 1978; Ancient and Medieval Town Planning in India, New Delhi, p.81.
11. Mahabharata; 1909-1919; N.S.P. Bombay, Shantiparva.
12. *Arthasastra* of Kautilya *op.cit*., Book II, chapter 3.
13. *Ibid*., p. 349-350.
14. *Ibid*., p. 54.
15. *Ibid*., p. 51.
16. *Ibid*., chapter III.
17. *Ibid*., p. 52.
18. Agarwala, V.S.; 1939; India known to Panini, Varanasi, p. 139.
19. *Arthasastra*; *op.cit*., Book No.II, chapter II.
20. Acharya, P.K., 1946; Encyclopaedia of Hindu Architecture, Bhopal, p. 321.
21. Prabhakar, V., Begde; 1978; *op.cit*., p.10-11
22. Beal, Samuel; 1888; Life of Hiuen Tsiang, London, 1, 73-74.
23. Chakravarti, P.G.; 1972; The Art of Warfare in Ancient India, New Delhi, p. 138.
24. Burgess, J.; Buddhist sculptures from Amaravati, ASSI Vol.I, plate XI, fig.1.
25. Gopalachari, K.; 1976; Early History of the Andhra Country, Madras, p. 109.
26. Krishna Murthy, K.; 1977; Cultural Study of Nagarjunakonda, Delhi, chapter IX, p. 191.
27. Indian Archaeology-A Review; 1957-58, New Delhi p. 5.
28. *Ibid*., p. 5-6.

Secular : Palace complex

The excavations at Keesaragutta have brought to light several brick structures which may be broadly classified as secular and religious. The religious structure have been dealt with in detail under "Brick temples". The remaining structures that have been exposed during the three field seasons of excavations may be grouped under secular.

There are six structures within a square enclosure wall measuring 54.30 m. each side. The total area inside the main enclosure wall is about 2948-50 Sq. m. The enclosure wall has one main entrance on the northern side and one on the eastern side.

Another structure is just outside the above enclosure wall at a distance of 3.5 m. from the northern main entrance; one more structure has been noticed in juxta-position and contiguous to the above structure outside the enclosure wall, which has not been exposed completely during the current field season.

For the purpose of detailed study the structures inside the enclosure wall are numbered as structures I to VI and the other which is outside the enclosure wall as structure VII.

Enclosure Wall

The wall around the square constructed with brick, mud and mortar has been exposed. The wall is 1.05 m. wide and runs 54.30 m. each side. Only to a height of about one m. has been exposed completely on the northern and eastern sides. The other two sides could be exposed partly only as the permanent structures like guest house have come up preventing further excavations in that direction. However, the alignment of the wall has been traced completely.

Northern main entrance : The total length of this entrance from the first step inside the enclosure wall to the first step outside the entrance is 8.75 m. and 5 m. from inside upto the wall and 3.75 m. outside the entrance. There is a raised platform of 2.90 m., in breadth connected with a flight of steps from inside and outside. Two steps are there at present from outside and two steps are missing. Stone slabs used for steps measure 2.20 m. × 0.55 m. in length, and width respectively. A railing was constructed with brick, mud and mortar on both the sides of the steps and stone slabs of the size 1.60 m. × 0.42 m. × 0.09 m. were placed over it on either side. The width of the entrance is 2.20 m.

A stone slab of 2.40 m. long and 0.50 m. wide placed horizontally in the centre of the raised platform contains two holes on either side probably for fixing pillars of the superstructure. Each hole is of the size of 8 cm. × 6 cm. which was drilled in the middle of the rectangular base cut to a depth of about 2 cm., extending 35 cm. × 25 cm. in length and breadth, probably for raising the door jambs on both the sides.

There are eight steps leading to the court yard from the main entrance. The flight of steps is provided with side railing 1.20 m. high from the ground level. After eight steps, one half *chandrasila* is placed as the first step the diametre of which is 95 cm. The stone slabs used as steps are almost of the same size as those used for the steps outside the entrance.

Eastern entrance : The entrance has been brought to light during the present excavations. The width of the entrance is 1.14 m. and its breadth is 0.58 cm. Flight of steps could not be exposed during the current field season.

It is quite likely that one more entrance existed on the western side also, leading to the water gate of the secondary fortification wall contiguous to the watertank.

The square plan of the enclosure wall is in accordance with the ancient Indian Silpa Sastras. According to 'Manasara' when a site is selected for constructing a building the ground is divided into different number of squares.[1] The square Vastu-Purushamandala symbolises the celestial world. It is rigid and cannot be moved, thus representing a perfect and absolute form.[2]

Structure I

This structure mainly consists of five cells and a rectangular hall with a porch of 4.10 m. long and 3.00 m. wide from outside followed by flight of steps. The first step from below is a stone slab 1.70 m. in length and 0.56 m. in breadth with a thickness of 10 cm. The second step is *Chandrasila* with a diametre of 1.15 m. There are five more steps raised on the basement constructed with brick mud and mortar. The steps are provided with railing on the sides but the stone slabs over the railing are missing.

The flooring of the porch is 0.75 m. high from the ground level. Nine courses of bricks are traceable. From inside the porch to the first step below the length is 4 m. Further steps leading into the porch are missing.

The porch is rectangular with a length of 1.90 m. and width of 2.10 m. The thickness of the wall is 1.10 m. Immediately after passing through the porch, we enter the big rectangular hall with 19.35 m. × 4 m. length and breadth respectively including outer walls. The inner measurements of the hall are 15.85 m. × 2.65 m. The height from the ground level to floor level of the hall is 2 m.

Contiguous to the hall there are five cells separated by a brick wall having a thickness of 1.20 m. The individual measurments showing the length and breadth of the five cells from west to east are as follows:

Ist cell	..2.65 m. × 2.40 m.
IInd cell	..2.53 m. × 2.30 m.
IIIrd cell	..2.60 m. × 2.25 m.
IVth cell	..2.60 m. × 2.30 m.
Vth cell	..2.60 m. × 2.40 m.

The cells are separated by the walls with a thickness of 0.85 m. The first and third cells are filled with sand while the other cells are filled with rubble and morrum.

The back wall with a thickness of 1.80 m. on the south runs from west to east.

Lime plastering of nearly 5 cm. thickness is visible on the outer wall of the hall just below the porch. Projections in the corners outside the hall are noticed. Outer and inner basements are provided with a projection of about 20 cm..

The structure no.I is quite opposite to the main northern entrance at a distance of 20.60 m. facing north.

Structure II

Structure II is similar to that of structure I in plan but there are only three cells here followed by a rectangular hall and a porch with a flight of steps. This structure is 5.5 m. away from the north east corner of the structure I and faces east.

The first step is a rectangular stone slab and the second one is a semi-circular stone. Above this there are two more steps leading to the porch. The first step is 1.70 m. in length and 0.50 m. in width and the second one is a *chandrasila* measuring 1.00 m. × 0.50 m. Traces of railing are missing. The distance from the first step to the last step including the missing steps is 2 m.

The porch is 5 m. in length and 3 m. in breadth from outside, and 2.5 m. × 2.00 m. inside. The hall is 9.50 m. in length and 2.20 m. in breadth excluding the outer walls. From outside, its length and breadth are 12.60 m. and 6.10 m.

The size of the three cells from north to south are given below.

	Length	*Breadth*
Ist cell	2.70 m.	2.10 m.
2nd cell	2.70 m.	1.10 m.
3rd cell	2.70 m.	2.10 m.

The three cells are backed by thick brick wall. The outer walls are of a thickness of 1.60 m. and the walls between the cells are 0.80 m. in thickness.

Fine lime plastering is noticed on the front side of the walls near the porch.

Structure III

Structure III is about 2.20 m. on the proper north to structure II, containing a single cell and a hall with an entrance provided with steps facing towards east. The first step is a rectangular stone slab of the size of 1.60 m. × 0.50 m, × 0.10 m. in length, breadth and thickness respectively. Second one is a semi-circular stone with a diametre of 1.10 m. The breadth of the entrance is 1.50 m.

The hall is 3.50 m. in length and 2.50 m. in breadth inside and 4.50 m. × 3.50 m. from out side i.e. including walls.

The inner length and breadth of the cell is 2.80 m. and 2.00 m. respectively, while the outer measurements of it being 5.50 m. × 5.50 m. Inside the cell, lime plastering is noticed on the flooring and also on the walls. The lime plastering is intact. There are three niches in the middle of the back wall of the cell. The measurements of the three niches are as follows:

	Length	*Width*
1.	30 cm.	20 cm.
2.	25 cm.	20 cm.
3.	28 cm.	20 cm.

A globular earthern pot[3] with a lid decorated with serpents, and other figurines was recovered in the north-west corner of the hall. A human skeleton in an inverted position was also found under the debris of a fallen wall just outside this structure III. This structure is in east-west orientation facing east.

Structure IV

Exactly opposite the structure III there is another structure nearly 23 m. away towards east. This structure IV, facing west, contains a hall and a cell. This is very much disturbed. The wall separating the hall and the cell is not traced.

The hall is 3.70 m. in length and 3.50 m. in breadth. The size of the cell is 3.20 m. × 2.60 m.

The outer walls are of a thickness of 1.20 m. Steps are missing. The whole structure is 10.50 m. in length and 6.40 m. in breadth.

Structure V

About one metre to the proper south of structure IV there is another structure with two rectangular halls on the back and the front separated by three cells in the middle contiguous to the front hall. The structure also faces west, and is just opposite to structure II. Steps are not traced. The entire structure is 16.50 m. in length and 13 m. in breadth.

The inner length of the front hall is 13 m. and it is 2 m. in breadth.

The central hall is divided into three cells with the following measurements.

	Length	*Breadth*
Ist cell	2.50 m.	2.50 m.
2nd cell	3.50 m.	2.50 m.
3rd cell	2.50 m.	2.50 m.

The length of the back hall is 10 m. and breadth is 3.20 m.

Beautiful stuccos, pot sherds, beads, coins, etc., were found associated with the structure V. One red-ware storage jar was recovered in the north-west corner of the front hall.

A fragment of panel of about 28 cm. long and 15 cm. wide and 7 cm. thick has been found outside this structure. The panel is plastered with lime and a green coating is applied over it with a thickness of 1.5 cm.

Structure VI

To the proper south of structure V at a distance of about 12.50 m. another structure has been exposed. A rectangular hall measuring 12 m. in length and 6.70 m. in breadth with the walls having a thickness of 1.10 m. have been noticed. The inner length and breadth of the hall is 10 m. and 4.60 m. respectively. Two courses of bricks only are visible all along the structure.

A wall contiguous to this structure running south-wards took a semi-circular curve and turned towards west. This wall constructed with rubble projects exactly at the south-east corner of the enclosure wall and runs towards west taking a semi-circular curve. As in the case of other structures at the site, the superstructure is completely destroyed. Only rubble is visible. In continuation of this rubble wall a few slabs planted vertically have been noticed almost in the middle way. The other part of the wall could not be exposed as the entire site is under heaps of debris. It is likely that this wall continued and joined the other corner viz., south-west corner of the main enclosure wall thus forming a complete semi-circular or half-moon shape. Probably, this must be a retaining wall for the main enclosure wall on the south. This reminds us to the apsidal (chapa-like) plan.

If the apsidal plan is analysed it is seen to be composed of a semi-circular and an oblong part. In other words it is a combination of elements of both circular and the square forms.

Trough

A trough made of stone slabs measuring 2 m. in length and 0.75 m. in width has been brought to light inside the brick enclosure wall, 5 m. from the main entrance on the north. Small heaps of lime mortar, lime mixed kankar are seen piled up in a row along the enclosure wall. The length of the tub on the top is 2.25 m. and 1.78 m. at the bottom, the width at the top and the bottom being 75 cm. and 25 cm. respectively. The depth of the tub is 43 cm. Thus, it is wider at the top and narrower at the bottom; the sides are slanting. It is quite likely that this trough was used for mixing lime for plastering of the various structures in the building complex mentioned above. The Silpa Ratna,[4] describes different kinds of lime plaster; mainly powdered. *Vajralepa*, according to the Silpa Ratna[5] is a high grade lime plaster with two percent resin in its composition and other binding and adhesive substances. Preparation of *vajralepa* is described in Brihat Samhita[6] and Vishnu Dharmottara.[7] The term *Vajralepa* denotes a special kind of plaster particularly described in the Silparatna, the Manasollasa[8] and the Isana Gurudeva Paddhati.[9]

The walls to which lime plaster (*suddha*) has been applied should then be coated with a paste of hide-glue mixed with white earth in three layers, and above it another final coat of the same paste mixed with powdered conch etc.[10] From the above literary evidences it appears that the tub was used for mixing the lime plaster glue, or *Vajralepa* for fine plastering of the walls, panels, stuccos, pillars etc., of the building complex. Number of stuccos, terracottas, fragment of plastered bricks probably used for the pillars of the superstructure for decorative purpose recovered in the course of excavations inside the enclosure wall strengthens the above view.

Some of the stuccos are beautifully painted in red, ochre, yellow and green, some of the bricks are lime plastered and painted in red, ochre, green and yellow. Fine lime plastering is noticed on the walls at the basement level. At some places plastering was done with mud and over this mud plastering lime plastering was applied. As has already been mentioned, a panel plastered with lime and green coating over that lime plastering is found near the structure No. V. The thickness of the plaster is about 1.5 cm. All the above facts go to prove that the plastering material was prepared within the building complex itself in a most scientific method with technical skill and aptitude.

Structures outside the enclosure wall

Structure No.VII : Structure VII is outside the enclosure wall at a distance of 3.5 m. from the main northern entrance of the enclosure wall towards north-east. The structure is facing east. The total length of it is 14 m. and the breadth is 13 m. It is also constructed with bricks upto basement. Huge stone slabs are placed over the brick wall. There are four rooms in four corners measuring 2 m. × 2 m. each. A flight of steps is provided to a length of 4.5 m. with a breadth of 2 m., constructed in bricks on the eastern side. The main entrance to this structure appears to be on the northern side since a flight of steps and a porch are noticed here. The plan of the structure appears like a "*chatuh-sala*" mentioned in the ancient Indian *Silpa-Sastras.*[11]

The frequent mention of *chatuh-sala* houses in Sanskrit literature makes it quite clear that they were quite characteristic of the buildings in ancient India.[12] *Chatuhsala* occupies all four sides of the house with a central open court. This class of *sala* house was most common in ancient India. According to the texts, houses of the Brahmins should be square like temples. If the houses of Brahmins are not square, they should nearly resemble a square i.e. the length may exceed by one-tenth only.

Another brick structure has been brought to light during the current field season, in juxtaposition to the existing modern road.

About 10 m. east of structure VII at a depth of 0.75 m from the ground level, a brick wall, 19 m. long running in north-south direction connected to a square porch at the northern end has been brought to light during the course of recent excavations. The breadth of the wall is the same as that of the main enclosure wall of the palace complex, viz., 1.05 m. After running for 19 m. towards south, the wall turned to the east at right angle, parallel to the main enclosure wall with an intervening space of 12 m. This wall could not be exposed completely as there is a modern road over the structure on the eastern side. Coming to the porch, it is 5.5 m. × 2 m. inside and 7.5 m. long outside. The total length of the porch from west to east is 8 m. Flight of steps to the west are noticed. A brick wall is traced to the north of the porch in alignment to the 19 m. wall on the south; here also the wall could be traced only upto about 2 m. as the wall is leading towards the modern road, which prevented further excavations.

Leaving a space of about 3 m. from the porch to the west another brick wall running towards west parallel to the structure VII with a square porch just facing the northern entrance of the structure VII has been traced. This porch is similar to the northern entrance of the palace complex. Only two courses of bricks are noticed in this wall. The wall is 14 m. long from the eastern side, of the porch. The complete alignment of the above two structures could not be exposed due to the construction of pucca roads on the east as well as on the north of the site where the archaeological excavations have been taken up.

It is quite likely that these two walls described above must be the enclosure walls, consisting of number of mansions inside, similar to the palace complex described in the preceding paras.

The alignment of these structures that have been brought to light during the course of the excavations are shown in the plan.

The structure I with five rooms prefaced by a rectangular hall, a square porch and flight of steps must be a multi-storeyed building. The flat roof made up of rectangular terracotta tiles and plastered with lime was laid over horizontal rafters supported by wooden pillars raised outside the walls. (The superstructure is completely destroyed). The massive style of architecture of the multi-storeyed secular buildings at Keesaragutta and decorative features may indicate that it may be the palace complex of Vishnukundin period, protected by a secondary fortification wall of rubble which encompasses an approximate area of 1 Km.[13]

The following literary evidences also support the above view, right from the selection of the site to the completion of the building.

Exponents of the *Silpa-Sastras* have laid great stress on the selection of a proper site for founding a new village or town. According to Manasara,[14] the site is to be examined and its fitness determined from its smell, colour, taste, shape, direction, sound and touch. The ground should be smooth and level and inclined towards the east. It should produce a hard sound. The odour of the site should be agreeable. It should have good quality soil. The site should produce water when dug to the depth of a man with his arms raised above his head. The temperature of the site should be moderate. The site which does not possess such qualities is not fit for habitation.

According to Mayamata,[15] the site should be fertile enough for all kinds of seeds. The earth of the site should either have a uniform colour or of all colours, white red, yellow and black. It should also have all the varieties of taste and should have a mixture of a small proportion of sand.

After the study of general site conditions such as geology, topography, drainage, vegetation, wild life and climate a detailed study of the ground and its soil conditions is to be carried out. Manasara[16] divides the soils into four kinds and lays down the order of priority with reference to seven traits such as colour, smell, taste, form, direction, sound and touch. The best soil is classified as "*Brahmin*" the other types being

'*Kshatriya*', *Vaisya*, and '*Sudra*'. It is important to note that the qualities of the ground and soil mentioned do not necessarily mean that they were inhabited exclusively by the respective *varnas*. In *Silpa-Sastras* the term '*Brahmin*' does not denote the caste but the quality. Thus, '*Brahmin*' means the best.[17]

The *Matsya Purana* describes a mystic method of determining the best building sites for the four classes.[18]

After the selection of the site, the next important step was to determine the cardinal directions by means of a gnomon[19] which is expounded in detail in the sixth chapter of Manasara. The square Vastupurushamanadala, as we noticed in the building complex at Keesaragutta, symbolises the celestial world. It is rigid and cannot be moved, thus representing a perfect and absolute form.

The site planning principles expounded by Kautilya and Sukracharya are not based on the principles of Vastupurushamandala but on sound common sense and logic. Kautilya[20] lays down that the demarcation of the ground inside the fort shall be made by opening three royal roads from west to east and three from south to north.

Kautilya[21] further describes the various cardinal directions towards which the quarters of various classes were to be situated. The king's quarters were situated in the centre of the city slightly towards north and occupied one-ninth of the total site inside the fort. The palace faced east or north.

Kautilya[22] further states that in the centre of the city and in every other quarter shrines of the guardian deities of the communities residing in them are to be built. At a distance of 100 *dhanus* (1 *dhanu*=6 ft. or 1.85 m. approximately) from the ditch or moat outside the fort in open country places of worship and pilgrimage, groves and buildings shall be constructed. Vatsayana recommended the building of a house else to a pond with an '*udayana*' garden outside.[23]

Ancient *Silpa-Sastras* divided buildings into four categories namely houses for the common people, palaces and gorgeous mansions for the princes and nobles, temples and lastly the public buildings such as public rest houses, etc. The architectural treatment of these four classes of buildings has been distinct in nature and definite in its contribution. Ancient Indian *Silpa-Sastras* lay comparatively less stress on the secular architecture. This does not mean that such housing is not given due importance. The older treatises like Manasara and Mayamata deal mainly with palace and temple architecture. Secular architecture acquired prominence during the early medieval period, but this was in conformity with the house architecture followed during ancient times.[24]

With slight variations all *Silpa-Sastras* agree that palace should be located in the centre of the town. Kautilya[25] states that the palace should occupy one-ninth of the total area inside the fortifications of the town and shall be located slightly towards north.

Manasara[26] divides palaces into nine categories with regard to their size and also according to the nine classes of the kings for whom they are meant. The palace complex generally comprised of various buildings which were essential because of manifold needs of the princely class. Manasara makes out a list of 42 palace establishments.

Manasara divides royal palace into two main categories. The first one is known as *Antah-sala* (interior palace with courts) and the other *Bahis-Sala* (exterior palaces and courts) the interior *salas* with their courts are obviously meant for the residences of the king and his family, while the outer *salas* are for the administrative establishments such as *sabha* halls and so on. Another important feature of ancient Indian palaces is the effective use of water reservoirs in various *salas*. The use of water bodies was provided for both ritualistic purposes as well as for pleasure. The various water bodies expounded in the *Silpa-Sastras* are *Kupa* (well) *Vapi* (stepped well), *Kunda* (deep pond), *Pushkarini* (shallow-pond), *Tadaga* (lake) and so on.[27]

According to the building-by-laws enforced in the ancient India, from the plinth to the ground level, a flight of steps shall be provided. A '*Vedika*' or a raised seat shall be provided on both the sides of the entrance door to the house. This rule is laid down by Brihat Samhita, Visvakarma Vidyaprakasa,[28] Visvakarmaprakasa[29] and Mayamata[30], which indicate that this rule was widely observed.

Now coming to the shape of the building complex, this resembles the "Maulika" mansion described in Manasara.[31] The storeyed mansions consist of rows of buildings varying in number of storeys upto twelve are artistically joined up. They are classified under six main groups called *dandakam, svastika, maulika, chatur-mukha, sarva-tobhadra*, and *vardhamana*. The '*maulika*' mansion is shaped like a winnowing basket and consists of three rows of buildings.

The contents of the chapter II in the Manasara describe in detail the measurements of length, breadth, and height of buildings of one to twelve storeyes, assigned to persons of different ranks. A palace of five to twelve storeys is stated to suit the emperor or the universal monarch, highest in rank among the nine classes of kings. Residence of one to three storeys are assigned to the heir-apparent and the chief feudatories, and so on.

In the light of the foregoing facts, it may be safely concluded that the structures I to IV inside the enclosure wall were the royal mansions consisting number of storeys. The open space in the centre of the buildings must be the court yard. The main entrance must have had a tower or *gopura* like superstructure with a square porch below it. Structure III and V appears to be single celled shrine where the guardian deities[32] were set up but unfortunately no such images have been brought to light in course of archaeological excavations except a decorated earthern pot,[33] and a human skeleton near the structure III.

Structure VII which is outside the main enclosure wall, identified as *Chatuhsala* according to *Silpa-Sastras* appear to have been occupied by the Brahmins-royal teachers or priests. Kautilya[34] says that the Brahmans shall reside to the north. The structure VII is exactly on the northern side of the main palace complex.

The six brick structures inside the main enclosure wall consisting of cells, with rectangular halls in front, and a spacious open court yard within the compound may be mistaken as monastaries of the Jains. The Jaina temple in the vicinity may give support to the above argument. A monastery has a big open court yard in the centre with monks cell arranged along the walls of the enclosure.[35]

In architecture both Buddhist and Jain structures are more closely connected with the Hindu ones. The Jain style was 'essentially Hindu', declares Fergusson, and was doubtless largely common to all Hindu sects, but in its evolution it became modified by Jain taste and requirements.[36] The religion of the Buddhists and that of the Jains were so similar to one another, both in their origin and their development of doctrines that either architecture must also at first have been nearly the same. A strong presumption that the architecture of the two sects was similar arises from the fact of their principal sculptures being so nearly identical that it is not always easy for the casual observer to distinguish what belongs to the one and what to the other.[37] There is, however, a marked difference of the Jain architecture of the South. The first peculiarity that strikes one as is the division, of the temples into two classes, Bastis (*Basadi, Vasati*, monastery or temple) and Bettas (? Vasahika, buildings, including monastery and temple). The former are temples, in the usual acceptance of the word, and always containing an image of one of the twenty four '*Tirthankaras*', which is the object worshipped there.

But the brick structures both, secular and religious brought to light during the excavations at Keesaragutta definitely belong to Brahmanical Architecture. Further there is no need for such a huge and massive fortification, secondary walls and masonry enclosure walls just for the sake of protecting of Jaina monastery. Moreover, not even a single image of *Tirthankaras* has been noticed associated with the structures inside or outside the enclosure wall.

The availability of Siva lingas in alignment, square brick shrines of Saivites with brick pedestals in the centre the massive style of architecture of the multi-storeyed secular buildings, the decorative features, and other concomitant evidences such as Vishnukundin coins, pottery, beads, terracottas, stucco, etc., go to prove beyond any reasonable doubt that the building complex under discussion was a palace complex belonging to early kings of the Vishnukundin dynasty.

REFERENCES

1. *Manasara* Ed. P.K.Acharya, 1932; Bhopal chapter VII.
2. Prabhakar V, Begde; 1978; Ancient and Mediaeval Town Planning in India, p. 29.
3. Vide IV 'Material Culture' (i) Pottery pp. 118-119.
4. *Silpa Ratna*; 1922; T.S.S., Trivendrum, XIV, p. 58-75.
5. *Ibid.*, XIV, p. 75.
6. *Brihat Samhita* of Varahamihira, with commentary of Utpala; 1895-1897; Vizianagaram series, LVII, p. 501.
7. *Vishnudharmothara*; 1912; S.V.Press, c.10-11.
8. *Manasollasa* of Bhatta Someswara; 1926; Govt. Oriental series, Mysore.
9. *Isana gurudeva Paddhati*; 1920-1924; T.S.S.Trivendrum IV, chapter XXXIII, p. 66-69.
10. Raghavan, V.; "Two Chapters on paintings in the Narada Silpa-Sastra", Journal of the Indian Society of Oriental Arts; Vol.III, p. 19 f.
11. *Manasara*; *op.cit.*, chapter xx.
12. Prabhakar, V.Begde, 1978; *op.cit.*, 106.
13. Krishnasastry, V.V.; 1979; "Keesara-capital of Vishnukundins" JAAP. Vol.I, p. 106.
14. *Manasara*; *op.cit.*, chapter III.
15. Prabhakar V. Begde; 1978; *op.cit.*, p. 26.
16. *Manasara*; *op.cit.*, chapter III.
17. Prabhakar V. Begde; 1978; *op.cit.*, p. 27.
18. *Matsya Purana*; 1970 A.S.S Poona, chapter 227.
19. *Manasara*; *op.cit.*, chapter VI.
20. *Arthasatra* of Kautilya; 1924.
21. *Ibid.*, p. 61.
22. *Ibid.*, p. 61.
23. Prabhakar, V. Begde; 1978; *op.cit.*, p. 38.
24. *Ibid.*, p. 105.
25. *Arthasastra*, *op.cit.*, chapter IV, p. 60.
26. *Manasara*; *op.cit.*, chapter XL.
27. Prabhakar, V. Begde; *op.cit.*, p. 109.
28. *Visvakarma Vidyaprakasa*; 1895; S.V.V., Bombay.
29. *Visvakarmaprakasa*; 1937; Ed. Matraprasad Panday, Banaras, Ch. SL.

30. *Mayamata* of Mayamuni; 1919; T.S.S. Trivendrum, chapter 29.
31. *Manasara*; *op.cit.*, chapter XXXV.
32. *Arthasastra*, op.cit; chapter IV, p. 62.
33. Vide IV 'Material Culture' (i) Pottery pp.112 ff.
34. *Arthasastra*; *op.cit.*, p. 61.
35. Ground plan of a monastery from "Nagarjunakonda" at p.29 Bulletin of the Madras Govt. Museum, Vol.VII, No. 4.
36. Fergusson, J.; 1910; History of the Indian Eastern Architecture II, London p. 5.
37. Acharya, P.K.; 1979; Hindu Architecture in India and Abroad, Bhopal, p. 76.

CHAPTER 3.2

Art

Architecture as a fine art must possess certain aesthetic features and must also indicate creative effort in the shaping of human actions towards the attainment of intellectual progress and elevation of life in its various aspects.

The Vishnukundin period witnessed allround progress in the field of fine arts.

Miniature temples

Adjacent to Yeleswaraswamy temple at Yeleswaram, *Devakulas* or votive shrines were found constructed in different orientation. Inside these shrines *Banalingas* were installed with or without *yonipithas.*

They might have been a part of the custom that developed here which enjoined the devotees to take vow to install a Siva linga and build a small shrine and leave it there after dedicating it to the Lord.

Five miniature votive shrines about more than 0.90 m. in height were found near the temple complex in Yeleswaram. These shrines have a low *adhisthana*, flat *kapota* by a semi-circular *Sikhara* incised with an inscription, the characters of which resemble to some of the inscriptions of the Vishnukundin period. It has a linga on vedi inside. Such votive shrines bearing the same architectural features except some of them represented with *kudu* arches on the *vimana* are also found in Mahanandi and Kadamalakalva. The other miniature shrines found at Yeleswaram have the same architectural features as described above, but they contain sculptures of Siva, as Ardhanariswara, Harihara, Umamaheswara and also a linga on vedi. There is a row of six miniature stone-cut shrines to the south of the *mandapa*, and two more rows of twelve shrines behind the Mahanandiswara temple, of which the following are important.

1. Shrine with a low *adhistana*, flat *kapota* and *vimana* of two steps with a *Nagara sikhara* above and a linga on vedi inside.
2. Shrine with flat *kapota*, *vimana* of four moulded steps,
3. Shrine with flat *kapota*, *vimana* of four moulded steps, an *amalaka sikhara* above and a linga on vedi inside.
4. Apsidal shrine on an *adhistana* with plain wall, moulded *kapota*, *griva* and apsidal *sikahara*. The front part of the *sikhara* contains *nasika* or gable with a smaller *nasika* inside it with a human figure.

There are four smaller shrines behind the Mahanandiswara temple. One of these has a *vimana* of four steps crowned by an *amalaka sikhara.* Another is also of same type and of the *vesara* order but has a *nasika* on the face of each of the three steps. The third is a stepped *vimana* of the Nagara order. The fourth has a *vimana* of seven steps crowned by an *amalaka sikhara.*

There are sixteen miniature stone-cut shrines within the compound of the Bhimalingeswara and the Ramalingeswara temples at Satyavolu. They all have lingas on vedi inside, of varying sizes.

Sculptures

The sculptures of Siva as Ardhanariswara, Harihara and Umamaheswara elegantly and exquisitely carved in deep niches of the miniature shrines found at Yeleswaram are described below.

Siva as Ardhanarisvara : Lord Siva is shown in half-male and half-female form in *Tribhanga* posture. In his right upper hand he is holding a *Trisula* and in his lower right hand which is raised carries probably a *Damaruka.* The Devi in her left upper hand carries some indistinct object probably *Nilotpala* or a mirror and her left hand is in akimbo, *patrakundala* worn by woman is shown in the left ear of lord Siva and right ear has a *Makarakundala*. This sculpture is adorned with *Graiveyaka, Katisutra, keyura* and bracelets. The *jata* is beautifully bundled up to form a *ushnisha* over his head bedecked with flower.

Harihara : Both the figures are shown in *Samabhanga* posture and their stance is indeed graceful. Both of them are represented with four hands. The right upper hand of Siva carried a *Trisula*, the outer counter of which is almost circular. The lower right hand which is raised carries *Damaruka,* upper left hand is in *aikmbo* and the lower left hand which is also raised carries an indistinct object. He is also adorned with *Udarabandha* round his waist, *keyura* and *kankana* on his arms. The third eye is present and his *jata* is arranged in the form of *Mukuta* bedecked with flowers. Vishnu carries a *Gada* in his right upper hand, conch in the raised lower right hand and the upper left hand in *katyavalambita* posture and the lower right carries the *chakra.* So far as the ornaments are concerned they are same as worn by Siva except that he is wearing a tapering *kirita.*

Umamaheswara : This panel depicts Siva with Parvati, Skanda and Ganesha. Siva and Parvati are sitting on a high pedestal in *Lalithasana* posture having Ganesha on the right of Siva and Skanda clinging to her breast. Ganesha has only a single pair of arms and has no crown over his head. Siva is represented with four hands and Parvati with two.

The right leg of Siva is hanging down and resting on the foot-rest while the left leg is bent and resting on the seat. Below in front is a couchant Nandi. His right upper hand is resting on the thigh and the lower hand which is raised carries, probably, *Damaruka*. The left upper hand passes round the back of Parvati and the lower left hand carries some object over his left shoulder. Here he is wearing *Yajnopavita* probably of *Mukuta*, *Udarabandha* of three bands round his attenuated waist, eleborate *Kundalas* beautify her ears. Particularly the pose of Parvati is very graceful, in a caressing attitude she has placed her right hand on the thigh of her Lord and holds Kartikeya in her left arms clinging to her breast like a devout mother. She is also wearing armlets and bracelets, *Mekhala* of two bands round her waist, a beautiful necklace and her braid is artistically adorned and decked with pearls.

Early Vishnu sculpture : A beautiful sculpture of Vishnu, whose head and feet were mutilated was found at Yeleswaram. The modelling of torso and body was chaste and beautiful. This appears to be an early form of Vishnu holding a *sakti* or staff in his right hand and a conch in the left. On stylistic grounds this may be assigned to 4th and 5th century AD.

An early sculpture of Narasimha : This sculptured panel was discovered over a hillock inside a square shrine which is now in dilapidated condition, at Kondamotu, located on the outskirts of Piduguralla village nearly 65 Km. from Guntur on the road to Macherla.

It is an oblong panel of limestone measuring 1.5 m. × 0.61 m. carved with six standing figures in bas-relief.

The figure on the extreme left is standing in *abhanga* posture, his right hand resting on the *Ikshuchapa* (sugar cane bow) and in his left hand he holds a *makaradhvaja*. The figure next to him stands in *Samabhanga* posture. His right hand is shown in *abhaya* pose. He carries a conch shell in his left hand which is in *katyavalambita* pose. The third is a very peculiar figure of a couchant lion with legs taut and tense and the face is devoid of teeth but in centre of the chest is prominently shown the Vaishnavite Lanchana '*Srivatsa*'. To this couchant lion at the level of the neck two hands are added, shown in uplifted position holding the attributes of Vishnu, *gada* and *chakra* in his right and left hands.

Flanking the left side of this icon is a standing image shown in *tribhanga* holding a flute and a bow in his right and left hands. His right hand is shown in *katyavalambita* pose. Next to this figure there is another shown in standing position holding a tyron or a wine goblet in his right hand and the left in akimbo. The last figure carries in his right hand a sword which resembles the incurved blade and a shield in his hand. There might be another figure by the side of the first figure mentioned above as it can be seen clearly that the demarcating plaster which is shown on the right side is conspicuous by its absence on the left side where the slab is broken. This has disturbed the symmetry of the entire composition but in its original state it appears that the sculpture had maintained perfect symmetry and balance by carving a group of three figures on either side of the central figure *Narasimha*.

The central figure has two arms bearing a *gada* and a *chakra* and tries to emphasize more the animal aspect i.e. the entire lion is shown in couchant form while its anthropomorphic form is suggested by its two hands which are added at the neck level.

Normal representation of *Narasimha* shows a human body or torso with a lion's head. Literature[1] refers only to seated and standing forms of *Narasimha* having a human body with lion's head. Considering the strange nature of the representation of this icon, it is quite possible to assume that in the early period i.e. early 4th century A.D. the anthropomorphic representation is an exception rather than a rule.

The first figure from left, which carries *Ikshu-chapa* (sugar cane bow) in his right hand and a *Makaradhavaja* in his left, appearently, looks like Manmatha, Pradyumna the eldest son of Krishna through Rukmini.

The next figure may be identified with two armed Vishnu, the right hand is in *abhaya* pose, the left one carries a conch shell.[2]

The third figure is of *Narasimha* in its *kevala* form.

Some difficulty arises in identifying the fourth figure. Vasudeva is not generally shown holding a bow or *dhanus* like Rama. The flute that he carried in his right hand helps us in identifying it as Krishna. But the image of Krishna should hold a *kridayasti* or a flute in his right hand and the left hand has to be raised to the level of the elbow and shoulder and the remaining features should be as in case of Rama.[3] Hence, this is an indication that Krishna can also be represented holding a *dhanus* or bow.

The fifth figure standing on the left hand side of Vasudeva who carries a wine goblet in his left hand might be Sankarshana as sometimes he is shown holding a drinking vessel emphasizing his inebriety.

The last figure next to Sankarashana who carries a sword in his right hand and a shield in his left might be Aniruddha, the grandson of Vasudeva who usually carries *khadga*[4] in his right hand and a *khetaka* or shield in his left.

The sixth figure is completely missing now might have been Samba, another son of Krishna by Jambavati.

It is clear by the perusal of the above description that Vasudeva, Sankarshana, Pradyumna and Aniruddha were worshipped as 'Panchaviras' in such early date in Andhra Desa.

The importance of this sculptured panel has to be assessed from its provenance and the period to which it belongs. Its discovery in the coastal Andhra is significant as the coastal Andhra in the beginning was fervantly devoted to the Buddhism, perhaps upto the fall of Ikshvakus. With the rise of the Pallavas Brihatphalayanas and Anandagotrin and Vishnukundins under whose aegis Buddhism received a set back and Hinduism with its sects like Saivism and Vaishnavism received encouragement, there must have been a school of reformists which aimed at the establishment of the glory of *Hindu Dharma* and the sculpture of early *Narasimha* may be manifestation of the spirit of the age when people conceived numerous forms for their pet gods and goddesses and Vishnu along with Siva was shown in all hybrid forms. We find the tendency in early sculptures to represent gods and goddesses in usual human forms.

The Vishnu of this panel who holds conch in one hand is shown in no way superior to the other members of *Panchavyuha* depicted in the panel. The other important thing which one can notice in this panel is that symbolism still continued and persisted as Lakshmi is not shown in human form but is suggested as in the early Buddhist sculpture by the symbol like *Srivatsa* on the chest of the image of *Narasimha*.

The importance of this sculptured slab can be guaged from the fact that no sculpture of Vishnu ascribable to such an early date was discovered in the Andhra area. This sculptured panel showing Vishnu in anthropomorphic form and also in animal form is perhaps the earliest extant. As such it is a rare and unique discovery.[5]

Stone plaque

A stone plaque, which is square in shape, each side measuring 12 cm. with a thickness of 1.5 cm. has been recovered from Keesaragutta excavations.

Mother goddess in sitting posture, legs bent and wide open, both hands raised holding a Siva linga in right hand and head of a lion in the left hand is depicted on the plaque, Nandi (bull) looking upwards towards Siva linga on the right side and a human figure sitting and facing towards mother goddess are also engraved. This human like figure appears to be of a worshipper or an attendant holding a fan or *Vinjamara* in one hand. Just above the central figure and in between the Siva linga and the lion's head there is a semi-circular and globular two tier structure resembling an inverted lotus. There are criss-cross lines on this lotus. Waist and genitals of the Mother Goddess are covered with a scarf which goes around the waist and the other end hanging down.

Some believe that she is popularly known as Yellamma or Renuka, the female counter part of Jamadagni and the mother of Parasurama.

Mother goddess appears under various names and forms giving raise to diverse myths. Indian traditions represent the great Mother Goddess (Adi Sakti) with a large number of names; but it has been suggested that they are not merely names of same goddess; but that they originally indicated different goddesses worshipped by different tribes in different parts of the country and that they were afterwards identified with the Mother Goddess. It is also believed that the aboriginal elements have largely contributed not only to the conception of Siva, but also to that of his wife. Siva's relation with hill tribes is indicated by his name Girisa, 'one who is Lord of the mountain'.[6] As regards the significance of the lion, it is almost constantly associated with the Goddess.[7] The Indian earth goddess is also called a lioness in a passage in the Yajurveda[8] and Satapatha Brahmana,[9] and later on the lion is a favourite animal of Parvathi just as the bull is of Siva.

The symbolism of the lotus flower is especially applied to the rising or setting sun, which is likened to a lotus flower floating on the cosmic waters-hence the poetic expression of the Vishnu's or Siva's lotus feet.

The name of lotus dome was given to it by Indian craftsmen who worshipped the rising sun as the mystic world-lotus.[10]

The cult of the Mother Goddess besides the linga worship has been depicted in this small plaque datable to circa 4th century AD.

Decorated Globular pot

The potters' craft was also fairly well developed in the Vishnukundin period and the globular pot with a lid richly decorated with serpents and terracotta figurines recovered from Keesaragutta is the best example for such craftsman-ship. The importance of the pot has been described in greater detail separately in the chapter on pottery.[11]

Terracottas and Stuccos

Keesaragutta : In the course of the excavations, beautifully modelled human and animal stucco figurines used for decorating the walls of the building were exhumed. Terracotta spools about 5 cm. in diametre have been recovered.

A spool is beautifully designed with incised rays emanating from a common centre. The other spool of black grey ware is incised with a lotus design inside a circle. The third one has punched star pattern around the periphery and in the middle are seven stars encircling a single star.

Beads made of terracotta are also met with. The shapes among terracotta beads are pear, spherical, *amalaka*, and tabloid. Terracotta plaques immensely decorated semi- circular in shape have been recovered.

A terracotta figure depicting a mother holding a child in her left hand has been found, the head of the figure is broken. The tradition of figuring Mother Goddess was a prominent feature in Indian art in historical times.[12] Most conspicuous iconographic features of these terracottas are the nudity, enoromous breasts and hips, position of arms to hold a child and the figures showing child suckling the breast of the Goddess. All these suggest that iconographically they are the representation of the fertility goddess.[13]

Stuccos

The collection of stuccos include (a) a stucco with a diametre of 12 cm. containing floral designs, (b) a stucco head of a lion-mouth and nose distinctly visible eyes and ears broken; (c) stucco of a bird probably a swan; head and beak only visible; (d) stucco of animal face with wide circular eyes probably a *yala* figure; (3) a beautifully moulded stucco of a tiger head with nose, mouth and two incisor teeth prominent.

Some of the stuccos are painted in red ochre, yellow, and green.

Bricks

Chistled or carved bricks semi-circular rectangular in shape, have also been found. Some bricks are plastered with lime and painted in red ochre, yellow and green.

Another type is a round and perforated brick with a hole in the centre.

Another interesting speciman is a rubber like square clay object probably (for rubbing the skin during bath) used as flesh rubbers during bath.

Yeleswaram

The excavations yielded a large number of terracottas comprising of male and female figurines, animals, birds, toy-carts, etc., which revealed the folk art of the remote past. Majority of the female terracotta figurines, represent female devinities with very elaborate coiffeure, dressed in a tunic or nude to the waist and with a dhoti or skirt. Despite the garment, special care is taken to reveal the mount of Venus in apparent nudity. They may be auspicious representation of the Mother Goddess Aditi, bestower of fertility and proto types of Mayadevi and Lakshmi.

Gollathagudi

The excavations at Gollathagudi temple complex also yielded a large number of terracotta figurines made in stucco which included human and mythical animals. Some types contain floral designs.

REFERENCES

1. *Silpa Ratna*; 1922; T.S.S.Trivandrum. *Vaikhanasagama*; of Marici; 1935; T.S.S.Trivendrum.
2. *Brihat Samhita* of Varahamihira; 1873 (H. Kern); G.57 V.35, JARS.
3. Gopinatha Rao, T.A.; 1921; Elements of Hindu Iconography Vol.I, pt.2; Appendix. C; p. 45-46.
4. *Ibid*., Appendix. C; p. 65.
5. Abdul Waheed Khan, Md.; 1964; An early Sculpture of *Narasimha*; APGAS No.16, Hyderabad.
6. Sircar, D.C.; 1971; Studies in the Religious Life of Ancient and Medieval India, Delhi, p. 103.
7. Hastings James; 1908; Encyclopedia of Religion and Ethics Vol.I to XII, Edinburgh.
8. *Yazurveda*; 1940; Moradabad. *Yazurveda*; 1899; Griffith, R.T.H. Benaras, V.12.
9. *Satapatha Brahmana*; 1882-1900; Achyuta Granthamala, Kasi, III, IV, 2.12.
10. Havell, E.B.; 1978; Indian Architecture through the Ages; New Delhi, p. 145.
11. Vide IV 'Material Culture' (i) Pottery, pp. 112 ff.
12. Balaram Srivatsava; 1978; Iconography of Sakti, Varanasi, p. 8.
13. Coomaraswamy, A.K.;1955; Mother Goddess in Marg VI, pp. 31 ff.

CHAPTER 3.3

Religion

It is rightly said that the age of the Vishnukundins is a transitional period in the religious history of the country.[1] Buddhism which was dominent during the time of the Satavahanas began to show signs of decay under the Ikshvakus, and it continued to loose ground steadily until it became practically extinct by the end of the Vishnukundin period.

Several Ikshvaku kings were staunch Saivas, and they erected several temples in their capital Vijayapuri dedicated to the God Siva and his attendant deities. The existence of several temples dedicated to Kartikeya, brought to light by the spade of the archaeologist at Nagarjunakonda shows that the worship of War God Kumaraswamy was also popular under the Ikshvakus.

Though the early kings of the Vishnukundin dynasty like Govindavarman I and Vikramendrabhattaraka I adored Buddha, built *stupas* and the *Viharas*, the subsequent rulers of the family were all staunch followers of Brahmanic Hindu dharma.

Govindavarman I, the founder of the Vishnukundin dynasty and his queen Paramabhattarika Mahadevi, were Buddhists in faith. He is said to have built in all provinces of *Dakshinapatha, Viharas* adorned with sculptures of various kinds by which he accquired *brahma-punya*. He accepted Buddhism after a study of *shad-abhijna prtiharya darsana*. Though he embraced Buddhism, he was tolerant; he built temples for the Hindu Gods. He believed that his wealth was for the enjoyment of the *bhikshus* etc., and gave away all his possessions in charity. Paramabhattarika Mahadevi his queen was also a devout follower of Buddha and she built a spacious *Vihara* at Sakrapura for the use of the *bhikshus*.

Madhavavarman II was a devoted follower of vedic Brahmanism. Madhvararman II and IV are credited with the performance of several vedic sacrifices. The performance of vedic sacrifices appears to have become popular, for most of the ruling kings of this age claim to have performed '*asvamedha*' and a number of other sacrifices. The worship of the gods of the puranic pantheon, specially Siva and his attendant deities, was very much in vogue.

The Vishnukundins described themselves as *parama-brahmanas* and granted to the brahmins *agraharas*, or land free from the payment of the taxes. *Agraharas* were granted to brahmins by the rulers for a definite purpose to enable them to devote themselves exclusively to the study and the teaching of the vedas, and perform sacrifices, which were believed to bring prosperity to the country and its people. The *agraharas* became centre of learning, and spread light and knowledge in the country. Both Indrabhattaraka and his son Vikramendra II actually styled themselves as "*Paramamaheswaras*".[2]

The following names of the deities figure in the Vishnukundin records:

I "*Sriparvathaswamin*" in
Tummalagudem set II, Line 2,
Pulombur-Line 1
Chikkulla-Line 1-2
Tundi-Line-1
Ipur-I-Line 6
Ipur II-Line 1
Ramathirtham-Line 1
II "*Somagirisvaranatha*"-Chikkulla plates-Line 23
"*Triymbaka*"
III "*Vinayaka*"-in Velpur inscription line-16.

i. '*Sriparvataswami*' was their family deity. Some writers identified *Sriparvataswami* with the God Mallikarjuna (Siva of the modern Srisailam).[3]

Another scholar viewed that it is doubtful whether *Sriparvathaswami* in the title *Sriparvatha-svami-pad-anudhyata* refers to the God Mallikarjuna of Srisailam in the Kurnool District, for in the first place, there is no evidence to show that there existed at Srisailam a shrine dedicated to Mallikarjuna or as to that matter any other deity at such an early date, and that as such *Sriparvataswami* to whose worship the Vishnukundins were devoted was to God Siva or what is more probable Kartikeya of Vijayapuri (Nagarjunakonda).[4]

It has already been mentioned that *Sriparvatasvami*, the family deity of the Vishnukundins might be the Ramalingeswaraswamy of Keesaragutta.[5]

ii. '*Somagagirisvaranatha*' that figures in Chikkulla plates indicated the worship of Siva with his consort Parvati. It may also denote Siva as the lord of the Moon (*Soma*) and Parvati.

Vikramendra Varman II issued this charter from his victorious camp at Lendulura which records the royal gift of the village 'Regonram' to the Three eyed God (*Triyambaka*) named Somagirisvaranatha (Siva).

iii. '*Vinayaka*' the elephant faced God was also worshipped according to Velpur inscription during the period of Vishnukundins.

In one of the Vijayawada cave temples[6] there is a figure of Ganapati in a niche. This deity has four hands and holds *modaka* in the lower right hand on which rests the top of the trunk. Another figure of Ganapati is seen in one of the niches in cave No.2. This deity is seated with his left leg folded and resting on the seat and the right bent at the knee and upraised. In one of the niches in the east wall of cave IV of Mogalrajapuram there is a figure of Ganapati with the head of real elephant.

The popularity of the worship of that deity in much earlier times is known.[7] The elephant headed God Vinayaka is a non-Aryan divinity adopted into the Brahmanical pantheon not much earlier than the 3rd or 4th century AD[8]. Ganapati is the lord of Ganas. He is popularly known as Ganesa. Ganapati is also named Brahmanaspati or Lord of Magnitude.[9] The elephant's head of Vinayaka was made the symbol of the inflated ego or the conscious "I", the first principle which emanated from the unmanifest Prajapati, for the simple reason that the elephant is of the most huge size amongst all creatures.[10]

Ganapati who is accepted by the Hindus as the son of Siva and Parvati was, as his name signified, placed in command of the *Ganas* by his father. He is also called Vinayaka from his being associated with the Vinayakas reckoned among the Gods, and who are said to observe all the actions of men and remove evils. Another name under which he is worshipped is *Vighneswara*, as Siva is supposed to have charged him with the task of hindering wicked people from performing sacrifices and other various acts and of rendering assistance of good men in their endeavours to perform such acts by removing difficulties when he is *Vighnahara*.

His worship appears to have been introduced just at the point when he became the God of the sect known as Ganapatyas[11] and gained popularity under the patronage of the Vishnukundins.

Nataraja from Vijayawada

Cave II, which is the largest and most beautiful of all the cave in Mogularajapuram is adorned with a fine figure of Siva as Nataraja with the portion below the waist broken. This deity is represented as dancing on the prostrate body of the *apasmarapurusha*. He has eight hands.

There is another sculptured figure of Siva with four hands dancing on the prostrate body of the *apasmarapurusa*.

In his character as Nataraja, Siva is shown dancing in *Tandava* dance. Siva is said to perform this dance in the evening in the presence of Parvati seated on a diamond throne in order to relieve the sufferings of the *devas*. The dance of Nataraja is believed to symbolise the action of cosmic energy in creating, preserving, and destroying the visible universe.[12]

Durga

The back wall of the cell of cave IV in Mogalrajapuram contains a shallow niche in which there is a half relief figure of Durga sculptured. This deity stands facing the right with her right foot resting on a small stool and the left stiff and resting on the ground. She has four hands, the upper right holding *trisula*, the lower right resting on the bent knee and the lower left in *katihasta*. The upper left hand is worn-out.

Durga is one who is "Beyond the reach".[13] She is one, who destroys difficulty and affliction and also removes the terror. She has been described as assuming many forms out of one besides the emanatory forms, which comes forth out of the Adisakti Mahalakshmi.[14] The theory of incarnations has influenced in the course of development of Sakti pantheon.

Saivism

In the two varied kinds of phenomena which nature presents, the early habitants saw the power of the Omnipotent, but that which appeared to them to be terrible and dispiriting and wrought destruction they named Rudra. They also believed that the same power of the Almighty, which brought about ruin and destruction, was turned into a benignant deity if appealed and appeared by prayer, and so they named it Siva-the auspicious.[15] In the Atharvaveda, Siva is called Pasu-pati, meaning Lord of animals, thus forming a link between the Vedic Siva and Siva worship of later times. His worship suffused with feelings of intense love advocated under the impulse of the teaching of *Bhakti*, which was then stimulating men's minds in carrying everything before it in matters of religion. Here he is the supreme lord to be worshipped with complete selfsurrender, his devotee undertaking the observance of the Pasupata vow consisting in giving up anger and greed, practising forgiveness and insisting upon the use of ashes signifying the transitoriness of all mundane things. In this may be discerned the germ of the Pasupata sect, which came into being in the early times, about 150 BC[16].

Just about the time, when the Pasupata sect was reorganised, a new school of thought in Siva worship became enshrined in books called the Agamas. The followers of the school were known as Maheswaras, worshipping Siva under the name of Maheswara, not differing much from the ancient Pasupata sect.

The earliest worshippers of Siva of whom mention is made in the Epics are the Pasupatas-followers of the Pasupata doctrine. Pasupata is formed from Pasupati-Lord of folks. Pati is the Lord, and man is the pasu, bound by the fetters of the world and requires to be released by the Lord. The doctrine was supposed to have been taught in the beginning of God Siva himself, namely, that Siva himself, was the source of the whole creation and that final union with him should be the desired aim of his worshippers. The Pasupatas worshipped Siva in the form of the linga, conceiving him as a deity of wild aspect as Bhairava, and they admitted even the goblins, ganas and others in their worship with him. They admitted all classes within their fold which accounts for a large following for the sect.

The doctrine of a new school of thought already in existence began to influence men's minds which subsequently became, enshrined in books called Agamas numbering about twenty-eight. The followers of these Agamas worshipped Siva mostly as Maheswara. The Agamas mark the appearance of Sakti ideas among the Saivites and contains rules regarding temple-building, image-making, and religious practices such as the wearing of the sect, mark the *Tripundara*, and the belief generated in the efficacy of the use of mystic rites and charms. These hold that Siva possesses or develops in himself a Sakti or power consisting of the rudiments of the individual soul and the material world, and from this Sakti, the world is developed. Man is by nature fettered by ignorance, and *kama*-the material cause of the world. Man can, therefore, only be liberated by the grace of the Lord, which is also a product of Siva's Sakti.

About the 4th century AD the doctrine of the Pasupata sect adumbrated in the Epics, made its appearance in the Vayupurana composed at that time, parts of which contain panegyrics and hymns in honour of the God under his names Maheswara and Nilakanta. From this time onwards, Saivism became the next dominent creed in the land, and counted all classes from princes and chief to ordinary individuals as its votaries, and the invocation addressed by the poets and men of letters of the times to God Siva at the beginning of their literary compositions.

This has greatly influenced the south Indian rulers of that period. Everywhere elaborate temples in honour of Siva were erected. Thus, the Pasupata sect, which has its beginning in the early epics, was reorganised about the 2nd century A.D. and had gained popularity among the ruling classes as well as masses.

Another doctrine called "Panchayatana" came into vogue in the early years of Christian era. They observe the worship of five Gods, namely the Sun, Ganesh, Siva, Vishnu, Devi, but give preference to Siva.

The Kapalikas, not sufficiently distinguished from the Kalamukha, appear to be an old sect, almost coeval with the Pasupata sect. They indulged in rites and ceremonies of a very revolting nature, and they worshipped Siva in his fierce aspect as Bhairava. The Kalamukhas, maintained that for the attainment of desires in this world and the next, the votaries of Siva in his Bhairava aspect, should eat his food in a skull, besmear the body with ashes of a dead body, eat the ashes, hold a club, keep a pot of wine and worship the God. From their habit of eating their food in skull and holding the club, they were easily and closely identified sometimes with the Pasupatas and sometimes with the Kapalikas.[17]

We have seen that some of the Vishnukundin kings were styled themselves as 'Paramamaheswaras' and that the family deity of the Vishnukundins was Sriparvataswamin. We have also seen that they worshipped Ganapati, Siva, Vishnu, Devi (Durga) as evidenced from the carvings of Vijayawada group of cave temples, with special preference to Siva, and that they built a number of temples throughout their kingdom, in honour of Siva which include innumerable miniature votive shrines found at Yeleswaram, etc., and row of lingas at Keesaragutta. Though there are no direct evidences to show that the Vishnukundins worshipped 'Sun God' it can be asserted with confidence that the worship of 'Sun' was also prevelant in that period. "*Chitra Rathaswami*" — the Sun God, was the tutelary deity of Salankayanas. There was a temple by that name at Vengı.

The foregoing evidence prove beyond any reasonable doubt that the Vishnukundin kings were the staunch followers of Pasupata sect-influenced by Agamas, and also patronised the doctrine of "Panchayatana".

Siva Lingas on Keesaragutta

There is a live temple by name Ramalingeswara temple on the top of the hill and just opposite this temple, more than 70 lingas arranged in 4 rows with an intervening space of 3.5 m. are found. These lingas were carved in black basalt with smoothly rounded top, octogonal shaft and square base installed into brick courses measuring 50 cm. × 25 cm. × 8 cm. Brahmasutras were incised over the lingas in a typical shape. In the earlier phase, no stone panavattas, were noticed. Besides the brick used for panavattas, a terracotta linga recovered during excavations with similar conical shaped Brahmasutras, is a clue to date the lingas and the bricks used for pedestals to the early historical period.

Almost every pond of water over the hill had a linga on one of its bank. Most of the lingas were provided with brick pedestals and introduction of stone *panavattas* in the later period are noticed.

Brick is the most ancient material for a sacred building. *Istikanyasa* (the installation of the bricks) is performed as a part of the main foundation rite of the temple. Later on with the introduction of stone as building material the *Istikanyasa* was substituted for *silanayasa* in both secular and religious buildings.

The *Samaranganasutradhara*[18] mentions about half a dozen substances of which the temples are made. On earth temples can be built, of any of these substances, stone, burnt brick, wood, cloth, bamboo and mud. "*Mahanirvana tantra*" says that it is 100 times more meritorious to give a brick temple than a thatched temple (i.e. wooden temples) and 10,000 times more meritorious to give a stone temple than a brick temple.

Manasaras' classification of lingas is the most scientific and it takes all the bases in its account. *Samaranganasutradhara* has devoted a separate chapter, a big one of more than three hundred lines to it (chapter 70).

Manusha lingas or man made lingas form the largest group of the Shtira-lingas and are made up of three parts known as *Brahmabhaga, Vishnubhaga* and *Rudrabhaga.* The first in the square lowest section, the second the octagonal middle one, while the third or the top most one is generally cylindrical. *Rudrabhaga* is known also by the name of *Pujabhaga*, for the offerings of water, flower and other objects are usually put on its top; the two other sections are inserted inside the pedestal (*pithika*) and the ground.

Rudrabhaga of all the Manusha lingas are carved certain lines called Brahmasutras and the tops of the lingas technically known as *Sirovartana* are fashioned in a number of forms. As regards the *Brahmasutras*, it is the tracing of certain lines in the lingas. These lines are also called *laksanadharana, manirekha parsvasutra* etc.[19]

Asthavara lingas or *Achalalingas* are broadly classified into four types viz., Svayambhuvas, Daivika, Ganapa and Arsa.[20]

1. *The Syayambhu* lingas are those that rose up and came into existence by themselvs and had existed from times immemorial.

2. *The Daivika* lingas are recognised by their characteristic shapes. The Daivika lingas do not possess the brahma or parsva sutras.

3. *The Ganapa* lingas are those that are believed to have been set up by *ganas*. They are of the shape of the fruits of cucumber, citron, wood apple, or palm.

4. *The Arsa* lingas are those that are set up and worshipped by asceties, they are spheroidal in shape, with the top portion less broad than the lower portion, in other words

they are like an unhusked coconut fruit. The Ganapa lingas and the Arsa lingas like the Daivika lingas are without *Brahmasutras*.

From the foregoing facts it can be deduced that the scattered and unsheltered lingas over Keesaragutta are Manusha or man made lingas carved by the artisans possessing full knowledge of *Silpa-Sastra.*

No *Deva-puja* is so old and so famous in India as that of Siva. Historically, it is as old as the Indus valley civilisation. Siva-puja from the point of view of iconographical interest is of two kinds, one is symbolic-the phallus as an emblem i.e. the linga *puja* and the other is anthropomorphic as of others.[21]

The great Siva devotee Bana, it is said, founded as many as fourteen crores of Siva-lingas which later became famous as *Banalingas*.[22]

Kurma Purana has an elaborate account of Linga-*puja*, its origin and development. The Vamana Purana has given the glorious descriptions of the famous ancient sites where the Siva-lingas were founded.[23]

Some times the worshipper himself was an image-maker. The temporary lingas made of clay, sand, rice curd, etc., used to be shaped then and there; hence such productions were a part of daily routine in Indian life.

Worship as an institution is as old as the civilisation of mankind itself and it was a life-companion throughout the ages. The objects of worship or the symbols of worship have been different in different periods of human civilisation. Many a mountain has been our object of worship from times immemorial. It is mountains from where we have derived the worship of Salagramas and *Banalingas*, later on, deemed representatives of Vishnu and Siva respectively. This symbolism in worship is the fundamental fact of being grateful to an object which some way or the other has been conducive to the well being of human life and its primary necessities.

The Gods are installed not only in *Tirthas*, on banks of rivers, lakes and the sea-shores, at the confluence of rivers and esturies, but also on hill-tops and mountains slopes etc.

The Vishnudharmottara[24] (Part III, chapter XC III-25-31) speaks of an installation of consecrated images (Arca), "Installations should be made in forts, in auspicious cities, at river sides, in forests, gardens at the side of ponds, on hill-tops, in beautiful valleys and particularly in caves".

According to Mayamata[25] stone is allowed to be used for temples by Brahmanas, Kshatriyas and hermits but one should not use it for Vaisyas and Sudras.

Stone when quarried and cut is an enduring and noble material, fit for gods, priests and the ruling classes.[26]

It is seen from the Vishnudharmottara and other texts that the science of selecting and testing the stone is most developed where the stone has to be chosen for "linga". Stone indeed is the aboriginal substance of the linga. Gold, the purest of all substances is not considered in this respect. It loses its value and is only given second consideration when a linga is to be made.[27]

The Linga Purana[28] (Chapter XLVII.5) speaks of a linga made of gold and jewels, or of silver or copper, as alternatives only for the linga made of stone, and which is the embodiment of Brahma, Vishnu, and Siva. Stone as menhir is specially connected with linga and also with the *Adharasila*.

Siva is preferred as Brahman or Truth in the Vedas and Upanishads and his form of linga is worshipped.

There is only one God. Although he is one, people, have various notions about Him.

Origin of Linga worship[29]

The earliest refrences to linga worship are to be found in the Rigveda, where the phallus is called "Sisnadeva", in the later or puranic period the references are more explicit.

"Markandeya Purana"[30] says that Rudra and Vishnu are the creators of the universe and they form the *Ardhanarisvara* aspect of the former deity. The allusion is to the Haryardha form of Siva, in which the female generative principle is identified with Vishnu. That the male and the female principles are inseparable and are ever found together in cosmic evolution is the real import of the *Ardhanariswara* or Haryardha forms of Siva, the same idea is also conveyed in a brief way by the symbols "the linga" and the "yoni"

The Linga Purana states that pradhana (nature) is called the linga and Paramesvara is called the lingin (the sustainer of the linga) and that the pedestal of the linga is Mahadevi (Uma) and the linga is the visible Maheswara. A more express allusion to the generative power of the linga and the yoni, the emblems of the Saiva cult, is found in the Vishnu-Purana, wherein we are told that Brahma asked Rudra, born of his anger, to divide himself; thereupon Rudra, divided himself into two, a male and a female portion.

We learn from the "Siddhanta Saravali" that the bringing about the union of the 'pitha'which is the symbol of Sakti and the linga, that of Siva, in accordance with the rules laid down in Saiva Sastras in called *pratishtha.*

According to T.A. Gopinatha Rao[31] the most ancient linga in Andhra Desa is the one at Gudimallam situated at a distance of about 20 Km. from Tirupati. The linga is known from ancient times by the name of Parasurameswara. The linga is composed of two parts, the nut and the shaft of the membrum virile, each of them shaped exactly like the original model, in a state of erection. Then the sculptor has modelled this linga in imitation of the human phallus.

There is very close resemblence of the figure of Siva on this Linga to that of a Yaksha in the Sanchi Stupa, figured on page 36 of Grunwedel's" Buddhist Art in India" (translated by Gibson and Burgess). The date of the sculpture has been presumed to be the 2nd century B.C. but some scholars have disputed the date.

The two great generative principles of the universe, Siva and Sakti, or Purusha and Prakriti, the father and mother of all creations, the energy and matter of the physical scientists is symbolised briefly in the form the linga and the yoni. For the past two thousand years, if not more, the Hindu males and females have been offering worship to this symbol of the Great Architect of the universe.

The worship of linga and the yoni is absolutely and thoroughly free from any kind of immorality or idecency.

This shows the significance and the place of linga worship in the day to day life of the people as well as the rulers of early Andhra Desa particularly the Vishnukundins.

Vaishnavism

We have seen that the Vishnukundin kings were staunch followers of vedic religion. In Tummalagudem copper plate II the names of Vaishnava deity like Vishnu,[32] Govinda[33] are mentioned. Moreover the names of the Vishnukundin kings are of Vaishnava gods, viz., Govindavarman, Madhavavarma, and the first part of their dynastic name 'Vishnukundin' refers to the Vaishnava god.

The royal emblem of the rulers was lion which is also a symbol of *Narasimha*, a man lion avatara of Lord Vishnu.[34] The Vishnukundin coins contain a lion inside a circle on the obverse. The head of a lion is depicted on the stone-plaque[35] of Mother Goddess found at Keesaragutta.

The Undavalli cave temples contain a huge figure of Vishnu Anantasayi. The pillars of the *mandapa* are adorned with sculptures viz., Gajendramoksa, lions, Vishnu, Varaha with Prithvi, Narasimha, Vamana and Bali, Trivikrama etc. The open portico before the *mandapa* contains on its eastern edge the figures of two lions. On the back wall of the *mandapa* are the figures of the devotees and fine figure of Vishnu seated on Sesha.

The *nasika* on the east in cave No.II at Mogalrajapuram contains three heads, representing Brahma, the central and western *nasikas* contain two heads each representing Siva and Vishnu with their consorts. There is a representation of *Gajendra moksha* on the first pillar in the front row to the east. To the right is Vishnu flying on Garuda, with two hands resting on the head of the elephant and the other upraised. There is also sculpture showing Putana suckling Krishna.

There are two niches to the west of Cave IV of which one is empty and the other contains the standing figure of Vishnu, with four arms. The Central chaitya window of the Mogalrajapuram cave contains the figure of Lakshmi-Narayana.[36] We have already seen in the previous chapter that the early sculpture of Vishnu found at Yeleswaram and early-Narasimha sculpture of Kondamotu belong to Vishnukundin period.[37] The man-lion incarnation of Vishnu became popular in the early centuries of the Christian era. The fact that the '*Avatara*' is often mentioned in early records of Simha instead of *Narasimha* may suggest that the deity was once conceived by some as having the form of a lion (not a combined form of man and lion).[38]

But about the 4th century AD Vaishnavism and worship of Vishnu seems to have taken certain set forms due to the increasing influence of the bhakti cult.

One of the caves of Mogulrajapuram was dedicated to the Hindu Trinity i.e. Brahma, Vishnu and Siva.

These evidences indicate that the worship of Vishnu was popular during the Vishnukundin period.

Saktism

A mention has been made in the previous chapter[39] about the stone plaque of Mother Goddess found at Keesaragutta. This plaque of Mother-Goddess gives us to understand the religious beliefs of the people during the Vishnukundin period.

Cult of Mother Goddess

Man's link with his mother is patent. Mother, who bears the child, nurses and rears it up, leaves a deep impress on its mind. It is but natural for the child to magnify her glory and power and to think of her as the representative of creative and sustaining forces of nature. Perhaps since the childhood of mankind similar psychological process prompted man to deify mother. To a child, mother appears in different moods and forms. She loves and chastises the child as the occasion would demand. The attributes of the human mother are naturally ascribed to the Divine Mother and the Goddess too is conceived of in multifarious forms and moods.

The worship of Mother Goddess is one of the earliest characteristics of human behaviour. The Mother Goddess holds high antiquity; it seems that she is the earliest manifestation of the divine principle to be represented in a visual form in bone, ivory, stone and bas relief with the maternal organs grossly exaggerated with pendulous breasts, broad hips, round buttocks and excessive corpulency suggestive of pregnancy.[40] Thus, her iconographic forms were fixed and individualised and she got the status of an ultimate Goddess or Universal Mother, responsible for giving life, vitality and prosperity. Some scholars,[41] believe that the Indian nude goddess was a Goddess of Fertility and popular as a household goddess among the non-Aryan communities but later she became absorbed in the Brahmanical and Buddhsit pantheons as Sakti and ultimately became identical with the Great Mother, the supreme Devi of the Tantras.

The worship of Mother Goddess received Brahmanical sanction by interpreting them as manifestations of Sakti personified in the aspect of the consort. At a level Sakti was interpreted as the eternal reproductive principle (*prakriti*) united with the eternal male principle (*purusa*) in the generation of Gods and the universe.[42]

The nudity aspect of the Mother Goddess was an Universal feature of the Mother Goddess cult. This aspect is specially noticeable in the forms of Sabari, Parnasabari, Nagna-sabari, Aparna etc.[43]

It seems that the fusion of pre-historic Mother Goddess tradition with the vedic goddess tradition relating to *Vak* and Sarasvati is greatly responsible for the prominence of Sakti cult in the post-Vedic times. The identification of Rudra and Agni, the two Vedic Gods, inaugurated the process of fusion of Sakti and Siva (Rudra) cults. The seven fierce godesses such as Kali, Karala, Bhima, Chandi, Chamunda, etc.[44] identified with the seven tongues of Agni, became associated with Siva as the result of this fusion. All these Goddesses represented the destructive, terrible, fierce and wrathful aspects of the energetic female (*Sakti*). The peaceful and benevolent aspect of the goddess was promoted through the identification of Vedic *Vak* and Sarasvati with the Mother Goddess.[45]

The exclusive worship of the female principle, as distinct from the Divinity seems to have had its germ in the idea that when the one personal God wills to put forth energy for the purpose of creation, he is held to possess double nature partly male and partly female. The idea of the union of desire with God is exemplified by the concept of Heaven and Earth joining together and creating the Universe. We find this duality more clearly explained in the Brahmanas and Upanishads, for we find mention of the condition of the one being unhappy without a second. He divided himself into two. Thus we have here a distinct personality given to the power of God, which was named as Sakti.[46]

Another set of notions of some antiquity, which contributed to form the notion of Sakti were derived from the teaching of the Sankhya system, which taught the separate existence of two principles, Purusha and Prakriti, both coeval and co-existing independent principles, the play of which was deemed to be necessary for creation to take place.[47]

Saktism in the bare acceptation of the term is worship offered to the supreme deity exclusively as a Female principle.

Jainism

On the top of the hill at Keesaragutta, there is a Jaina temple with a brick, square *Garbhagriha*, later adjoined with a *Mukhamandapa* of granite pillars and roof slabs.

An early temple of Mahaveera with a sanctum, *antarala* and *Mukhamandapa*, and the foundations of two more temples were cleared of debris at Gollathagudi, which revealed the complete plan of the sanctum with its lime plastered brick walls and the *Mukhamandapa*. The excavations also yielded large number of Jaina sculptures. The excavations of Gollathagudi shed much light on the building activities of ancient Jains who preferred brick as their constructional medium to stone even while the contemporary Hindu temples were constructed purely in stone round about the region.

An inscription[48] of the Eastern Chalukyan king dated saka 684 indicate that there was a Jaina establishment at Vijayawada even before the Eastern Chalukyas entered the region i.e., during the time of Vishnukundins.[49]

Jainism effected reforms by refusing to accept the divine authority of the Vedas, in presenting a common opposition to certain unreasonable practices of the Brahmins, in preaching that salvation was possible to all irrespective of caste and creed and in introducing the use of the vernacular in the addresses to the people in preference to the classical Sanskrit, which few could understand. Jainism is considered to be a reform movement against the unreasonable practices and teachings of the Brahmins, but it accepted the view then held on the theory of transmigration of the soul of man, that he is fettered to its mundane life by the laws of *karma* and that release from rebirth is obtained by man by means of the acquisition of right knowledge. For the attainment of this knowledge, it advocated the 'Sanyasa marga' on which much stress was already laid by the Upanishads, laying much emphasis on "asceticism consisting in subduing senses, withdrawing from wordly things, from communion with people, begging for alms, living in forests, observing cleanliness, internal and external, abstinence from injury to living beings, and sincerity, purity, freedom from envy, kindness and patience.[50]

There is no wonder, a section of the people, though not all, became the followers of Jainism during the period of the Vishnukundins who were known for their religious tolerance.

Buddhism

As has already been stated there are ample evidences to show that Buddhism flourished along with other religions during the Vishnukundin period. Hiuen Tsang who visited the Andhra Desa after the disappearance of the Vishnukundins mentioned the existence of about twenty Buddhist monasteries.[51]

Govindavarman, the donor of the Tummalagudem grant I, is stated to be the builder of *Viharas*, assembly halls and was the possesser of wealth enjoyed by the *bhikshus*. He made a gift of the village Penakapara for a monastery built by his chief queen Parama Mahadevi.

The word "*Mahabodhichittena*" and "*Bhagavato Dasa Balabalinah chaturvvairsaredyashtadas-avenika Buddhadharma Samalankruta*"................ mentioned in the line 12, 13-15 of the grant refers to Buddhism. *Bodhi-chitti-otpada* is the mental disposition of one whose chief aim is enlightenment. *Dasa-balas* or the ten-fold forces of a Tathagatha, like *Sthana-asthana-Jnana-balam* indicate the force of knowing possibilities and impossibilities.[52]

The expression *uttpadita-mahabodhichitta* is based on the doctrine of Bodhisatva which is the keynote of the Mahayana teachings.[53] The inscription seems to suggest that the monks should have firm faith in the Buddha and in his teachings and should study the scriptures and practise meditation. [54]

In Tummalagudem plate II, it is said that Govindavarman embraced Buddhism after studying the doctrines propounded by the Buddha. Vikramendrabhattarakavarman made a gift of the village of Irenderu to the *chaturdasa-arya-vara-bhikshu sangha* residing in the mahavihara built by Parama-bhattarika; Vikramendravarman was a *parama-saugata* (devoted Buddhist). It is also stated in the above inscription that Paramabhattarika married Govindaraja who built in every vishaya in the *Dakshinapatha* wonderful stupas and viharas adorned with several kinds of sculptural work by which he acquired *brahma-punya*. Govindavarman I accepted Buddhism after a study of *shad-abhijna pratiharya darsana*. Paramabhattarika Mahadevi, his queen, was a devout follower of the Buddha.

Under the Vishnukundins Buddhism continued to lose ground steadily until it became practically extinct by the end of the Vishnukundin rule.

REFERENCES

1. Venkataramanayya, N.; 1975; The Vishnukundins, Madras, p. 45.
2. Epigraphia Indica XII; 1914; p.133 ff., Ramathirtham Plates of Indravarman, Line. 6. Epigraphia Indica XXXVI; 1965; p. 7 ff., Tundi Plates of Vikramendra Varman II, line-18. Epigraphia Indica IV; 1896-97; p. 193 ff., Chikkulla Plates of Vikramendra Varman II, Line. 18.
3. Sankaranarayanan, S.; 1977; The Vishnukundins and their times, Delhi, p. 141.
4. Venkataramanayya, N.; 1975; The Vishnukundins, Madras, p. 27.
5. Vide chapter 3, i. pp. 36 ff.
6. Vide chapter 3, pp. 36-38, Cave No.1, at Vijayawada.
7. *Yagnavalkya Smriti*; 1936; N.S.P. Bombay, chapter I, verses, p.271-294.
8. Hopkin, E.W.; 1915; Epic Mythology, pp. 206-207.
9. Agarwala, V.S.; 1966; Siva Mahadeva, Varanasi, p. 53.
10. *Ibid.*, p. 54.
11. Pai, D.A.; 1928; Monograph on the Religious Sects in India Among the Hindus; Bombay p. 86.
12. *Ibid.*, p. 60.
13. Balaram Srivatsa; 1978; Iconography of Sakti, Varanasi, p. 27.
14. *Ibid.*, p. 27.
15. Pai, D.A.; 1928; *op.cit.*, p.12.
16. *Ibid.*, p. 13.
17. *Ibid.*, p. 64.
18. Shukla, D.N.; 1960, Vastu Sastra, Vol.I, para V, chapter VII, p. 459-460.
19. Shukla, D.N.; 1958; Vastu Sastra, Vol.II, Hindu Cannons of Iconography and Paintings, p. 244-245.
20. Gopinatha Rao, T.A.; 1921; Elements of Hindu Iconography, Vol.II Part I, p.78-86.
21. Shukla, D.N.; 1958; *op.cit.*, p. 54.
22. *Ibid.*, p. 35.
23. *Ibid.*, p. 35.
24. *Vishnudharmottara*; 1962; S.V.P., Bombay, Part III, chapter XC.III, 25.31.
25. Mayamata oriental manuscript Library Catalogue Vol.XXVII, Madras.
26. Krama Risch Stella; 1946; The Hindu Temples Vol.Calcutta, p. 113,
27. *Ibid.*, p. 153.
28. Linga Purana; 1885; Calcutta, CL.XLVII.5.
29. Gopinatha Rao, T.A.; 1921; *op.cit.*, p. 58-62.
30. *Markandeya Purana*; 1862; ASB. Calcutta.
31. Gopinatha Rao, T.A.; *op.cit.*, p. 68-71.
32. Tummalagudem Copper Plates II of Vikramendra Varman II, EA. Vol. II, p. 15 ff. Line 3.
33. *Ibid.*, line 28.
34. Majumdar, R.C.; 1954; The Classical Age, Ed.H.C.I.P., Bombay, p. 415.
35. Vide II Art; Stone Plaque; pp. 92-94.
36. Sankaranarayanan, S.; 1977; The Vishnukundins and their Times, Delhi, p. 142.
37. Vide II Art; pp. 88 ff.

38. Sircar, D.C.; 1971; Studies in the Religious Life of Ancient and Medieval India, Delhi, p. 268 foot note.
39. Vide II Art; Stone Plaque, pp. 93-94ff.
40. James, E.O.; The Cult of Mother Goddess, pp. 11-13.
41. Coomaraswamy, A.K.; 1955; Mother Goddess, Marg VI, pp. 31 ff.
42. James, E.O.; The Cult of Mother Goddess, pp. 101-102.
43. Banerjee, J.N.; 1941; Development of Hindu Iconography, Calcutta, p. 49.
44. Majumdar, R.C.; 1954; The Classical Age, H.C.I.P., Bombay, p. 444.
45. Balaram Srivatsava; 1978; *op.cit.*, p. 13.
46. Pai, D.A.; 1928; *op.cit.*, p. 15.
47. *Ibid.*, p. 15-16.
48. Desai, P.B.; 1957, Jainism in South India and Some Jaina Epigraphs, Sholapur, p. 19.
    — 1916-17, ARE, p. 116.
49. Sankaranarayanan, S.; 1977; The Vishnukundins and their Times, p. 150.
50. Pai, D.A.; 1928; *op.cit.*, p. 23.
51. Neelakanta Sastri, K.A. 1939; Foreign Notes of South India, Madras, pp. 98,100.
52. *Dharma Sangraha* of Nagarjuna; 1885; Oxford, p. 16, Sect., LXXVI.
53. Sankaranarayanan, S.; 1977; The Vishnkundins and their Times, p. 142.
54. *Ibid.*, p. 143.

CHAPTER 3.4

Material Culture

Pottery

The art of pottery making is interspersed with the social life of the man so much, as a result of which every age witnessed the silent and steady evolution of the pottery with its distinction. The archaeologists of today have recognised the importance of pottery in constructing the archaeological sequence of a site and have rightly termed it as 'Alphabet of Archaeology".[1]

The pottery evidence from Keesaragutta is very significant. The excavations yielded pottery associated with the structures in the palace complex consisting of red-ware, dull red-ware, and black grey-ware. Some fragments of blotchy red ware also have been recovered. The entire pottery is wheel-made. The paste, as a rule, is medium, sometimes coarser, tempered with sand which often contains larger particles of grit. Usually no surface wash is met with and, wherever available, it approximates to the colour of the paste. A pleasing effect is produced on some of the vessels by mixing powdered mica in the paste or dusting it on the pots before firing, vases are usually more absorbent. The firing is good, but instances of deformed pots due to unequal or bad firing are also noticed.

The fabric ranges from coarse to medium; some sherds of fine fabric have also been recovered.

The red-ware, both slipped and unslipped, is generally wheel-turned and has many shapes. These include vases, bowls, dishes and miniature pots, storage jars, etc.

The vases, mostly unslipped, are with flared rims, convex bottoms and outer surfaces corrugated; conical bowls and lid-cum-bowls are with featureless rims, and some are with flaring body. Nandi type of globular miniature pots with featureless rim and with conical base, spouted miniature pots with a sharp out-curved rim, recurring type of pots with concave neck, and sharp everted flat rim, are also found. Storage jars are with a prominent straight sided neck and with grooved rims devoid of any surface treatment. Lids are cupola shaped with carinated bottom and with a knob at the crest. Some lids are circular hat shaped and some are bell shaped with bottom like knob and carinated base.

Decorations are also met with. They comprise applied, incised and stamped patterns. The incised designs, usually confined to the external surface of the pots, consists of ropy bands, chevrons, floral and creeper patterns. The designs are mostly geometric and linear, consisting of parallel bands on the shoulder.

All the pots are grouped according to their utility for the better understanding of the culture trait of the people. The pottery can be further classified into utilitarian and ritualistic.

Storage jars

Jars are available in red-ware, and coarse dull red-ware. Among the red-ware storage jars, the first type has a prominent straight sided neck with grooved rims, fine fabric devoid of any surface treatment. This was probably used as "*Ghata*" to carry and also to store water. The second type is of a coarse dull red-ware with incised triangular motif below the ridged neck portion, incisions probably stamped, inside the motifs are linear incisions stamped at regular intervals.

The third type is a huge storage pot with a narrow out-turned and constricted rim, top portion of the rim is grooved below which are obliquely incised patterns.There are three reliefs just below the rim. First relief contains thin lined groovings below which are crescent shaped nail impressions a few inches below it is another relief curvilinear triangles with similar technique. The red slip is visible outside and partly inside.

The fourth type has a thick out-curved rim. The edge of the rim is incised with oblique ropy pattern (bands). There are also grooved linear parallel bands all along the neck portion. Below this are incised inverted triangle with linear incisions within them. These triangles are arranged in a panel like form.

The fifth type has two bands of rope designs with oblique incisions.

The sixth type is of blotchy red-ware and has a flared rim and the rim top contains circular motifs of rossettes rim tappering. Below the ridged neck portion are incised chevron shaped designs and nail head section.

The seventh type is a red-ware pot with a petal shaped design.

The eighth type has a flaring rim with applied protruding circlets over the rim surface. This is illfired.

The ninth type is without curved rim. Its neck portion is decorated within two reliefs with nail incisions in linear patterns.

The tenth type has constricted flat rim of coarse grained fabric. There is a grooved line all along the outer edge of the rim. No surface treatment is given.

These jars were probably used for storing grains and other food stuffs for daily consumption as well as to keep sufficient stocks in reserve for use during the times of war or any such emergency as is evident from the place these fragments were found.

Ornamental jars

These are the jars available in red-ware; fabric ranging from coarse to medium. The first type has an outcurved rim. The designs are divided into two compartments separated by a ridge just below the outer rim and there are incised wavy designs extended all along. Just below the ridge there are applied and stamped uniform motifs. They must have been used for keeping valuables and rare articles by the members of the royal family who lived in palaces as the type of jars are profusely and attractively designed.

The second type is of a red polished ware. It has designs incised with chevrons, floral and creeper patterns.

The third type is a coarse red-ware pot with a floral design probably stamped.

The fourth type has relief showing incised chevron shaped motifs with dotted line. Outside surface is given slipped treatment.

The above three jars appear to be of aesthetic type and predominantly used for beauty sake by the women-folk of the royal families.

Vessels

Vessels are available in red-ware, dull-ware and pinkish red-ware. The fabric varies from fine to medium. Some are red-slipped.

The first type is a carinated *handi* with a curved rim with soot marks at the bottom portion. No surface treatment was given.

The second type is similar to the first type but smaller in size with a flared rim. There is incised decoration just above the carination in the form of wavy triangular patterns.

The third type is a small *handi*. Soot marks are present all along the base. The red-slip is visible outside. Section is in the shape of inverted 'S'.

These appear mainly, to be cooking pots. The first type may have been used for storage of cooked food, as the rim is broad; the second type for storing sweetmeats or delicious food stuff and the third type for storing cooked food or heating it.

Conical bowls

Three types of conical bowls have been found and they are also available in red-ware and pinkish red-ware. The first type has a featureless rim with flat base. The second type is similar to the first type but slightly irregular in shape. Its fabric also is finer. The third type has a flaring body with a flat bottom.

These bowls were probably used for holding gruel or semi-liquid substances.

Miniature pots

Handi type globular miniature pots are available in dull red-ware only. The pots have small featureless rim and conical base devoid of any surface treatment. Another pot has a round base with a faint surface treatment in the form of grooved bands. The shape and the size of these pots indicate that they were used for holding liquids etc., for ritualistic purposes.

Spouted miniature pots

A spouted miniature pot with a sharp outcurved rim, globular in shape has been found. It's fabric is coarse and the surface treatment is very faint. This type of pots could have been used to pour milk or ghee for ablutionary purposes.

Small jars

Small jars are available in black and red-ware with fine fabric and also in red-ware. The first has a deep and flat body with wide bottom slightly carinated in the middle. The rim is everted. Grooves are present on the top and at the neck portion of the rim. It is slightly polished and burnished. Another type is a concave necked *handi* type of pot with sharp everted flat rim-nail shaped in section. Bands on the concave portion of the neck are present. The fabric is coarse. It is a slightly self-slipped red-ware which is ill-burnt.

These jars appear to have been used for domestic as well as ritualistic purpose to store grain or liquid or any hot preparations.

Vases

Vases have been found in red-ware only; one type has flared rims and hollow bottom. Outer surface is carrugated. The bottom is convex and there is a provision for a stand which is apparently missing. This deep vase could have been used as pitcher, liquid container, or for incense burning.

Lid-cum-bowl

Only two specimens of this type are found. They are available in coarse red-ware and dull red-ware. The first has featureless rim with carination at the neck portion. No. surface treatment is given The diametre of the lid-cum-bowl is 15 cm.

The second one is a small hollow lid of fine fabric devoid of any surface treatment.

Bowls appear as common variety of the period and probably were used as dining sets.

Beaker

One pinkish grey ware beaker type of pot of medium fabric has been found in the temple complex. It has everted sharp rim and flat base, slightly bulging in the middle. There are grooves at the shoulder region. The height of the beaker is 11 cm. These type of beakers were used to pour ablutions for the ritualistic purposes or for drinking purpose.

Dish on stand

Stand bases are available in coarse fabric. The first type has a very flat topped concave stand base. Inside is hollow. No surface treatment is seen.

The second type is also similar in fabric with no surface treatment. The top is flat with a perforation.

These stand bases must have been used for holding big pots, images, etc.

Lids

The lids are available in red-ware only. The first type is a cupola shaped hollow lid with carinated bottom. There is a knob at the crest.

The second type is a circular hat shaped lid with button shaped knob. It has a hollow bottom with notched edge.

The third one is a bell shaped lid with a worn out button like knob and carinated base; body slightly wobbling. These types of lids could have been used as finials.

The fourth type is similar to that of the other types but with a better treatment in fabric and finishing. Carination at the bottom is pronounced. The lid has a nipple shaped knob (Washed red-ware). This must have been used as a cover on a small pot.

Sprinklers

Three types of sprinklers have been recovered during the excavations.

The first type is a bottle-necked sprinkler with a flanged rim top, and a conical knobbed opening with a perforation at the top running through the neck. Of consistently fine fabric, it is treated externally with a bright-red slip. This is similar to samain ware. This type is fairly widespread and occurs at Arikamedu,[2] Brahmagiri,[3] Chandravalli,[4] Yeleswaram,[5] Hastinapura,[6] Kausambi,[7] etc.

The second type has a flanged rim top without any knob, body tapering, fine fabric with red slip probably intrusive ware.

The third type is similar to type two but with wide rim top, washed red-ware of medium fabric.

The first type of sprinkler must have used for attaching it to "*poornaghata*" or any such auspicious pot either for aesthetic or for religious purposes. The other two types appear to be of purely decorative pieces.

Spouts

The spouts are available in two types all in red-ware. (1) simple and tubular and the other (2) truncated type.

The first one is a polished red-ware with a fine fabric. It has wide bulbous body resembling the trunk of a sphnix. This is a unique spout unlike other ordinary spouts both in technique and finishing. Similar spouts were also found in Yeleswaram.[8]

The second type has a projecting conical hind part, and perforations at the proximal end with a wide cup-shaped opening at the distal end. Probably mould made; fabric well levigated, highly red polished.

It is quite probable that the above two types might be imported one.

The third one is a spout of inferior fabric and illfired with a wide tubular channel. There are decorations of white dotted patterns of doubtful import.

The fourth type has tapering body and smaller than the other types of medium fabric.

The fifth one is also a small spout with a lipped distal end and a wide trunk. The occurrence of the spouted vessels is noticed at Luristan,[9] Nal,[10] Jahanjhmer,[11] Brahmagiri,[12] Nagarjunakonda,[13] Tekkalkota,[14] and Piklihal.[15]

These spouts might have served for regulating the flow of liquids. Spouts are luted on vessels, basins and bowls. All these spouts are hand made and have been luted with the vessels. After the spout has been luted, a hole has been punched at the joint in order to pour liquid from the vessels.

R.C.Prasad Singh[16] mentions the usage of spouted vessel for religious functions. A Sanskrit text "Kriya kanda Varidni" written in Bengali script refers to Vardhani, vessel with spout. The vessel is used in the *chatus sastipada vastu Yajna.* According to the text, vardhani is tied around the neck of the pitcher used as kalasa. Another reference from the same text suggests that water should be poured into specially dug ditch in order to check the auspiciousness of the land under construction. Tying of vardhani around the neck of the pitcher and pouring of water through them suggest religious function. The word 'pranali' standing for spouted vessel, occurs in the *Srauta-Sutra* and through these pranalis *soma* used to be offered to the gods in the Vedic sacrifices.

Vessels must have been used by the royal families of the Vishnukundin dynasty for some such religious functions following the vedic traditions.

Decorated Pottery

R.C.Agarwal[17] rightly observed that the early centuries of the Christian era in India are marked by the appearance of embossed or decorated pottery in sufficient quantity.

An interesting specimen of a dull red-ware globular pot with a lid profusely decorated with snakes and human like figures, has been recovered outside the *Garbhagriha* of the temple structure at the north-west corner of the *antarala* during the recent excavations at Keesaragutta. This is very significant since this type of pot has not been found in any other excavations so far carried out by the Department of Archaeology and Museums, Andhra Pradesh.

It is a globular vase with flat out curved rim and narrow neck. The circumference of the vase is about 80 cm. and its height including lid is 37 cm. Five terracotta human like figurines encircled by serpents are placed on the belly of the pot at equal distance in a sitting posture resting their hands on the knees. The lid is also decorated with a figurine surrounded by a snake; the hood of the snake is broken. The size of each figurine is 8 cm. The head of one of the figurines is broken. The belly of the pot is decorated with seven serpents in their full length, beautifully moulded, exhibiting artistic skill. All the figurines appear to be of females with demonical features.

Its purpose and usage is shrouded in mystery. Nevertheless, it is not very difficult to unravel the mystery from the available literary evidence.

The snake is accepted by many scholars as being intimately connected with fertility cult since times immemorial.[18] Vogel says that in the whole of western and southern India, the cobra is worshipped upto the present day by women, who are desirous of off spring.[19] According to Hendrik Kern[20] the Nagas are essentially water spirits and they are to be regarded as personified forces of nature; in the first instance the snake like coiling rain-clouds emitting flashes of lightining the serpents of the sky-which are transported to the lakes and pools on earth and finally are "confounded" with real poisonous snakes. Kern's view emphasizes at any rate a very important aspect of Naga worship, viz., the close relationship between the Nagas and the elements which in a hot country like India is of such vital significance for human and animal existence. We often find a snake encircling a linga on the yoni-patta or otherwise lying in it at the narrower end of the yoni-patta. The cult of Earth Goddess is associated with snake symbols.

J. Mackenzie says "that in Gauripuja, women of all Hindu classes and creeds" adore the serpent, as it is supposed to remove their barrenness.[21]

The Goddess is to be invoked. According to some Tantric text as Gauri, Gandhari, Matangi, etc., in connection with snake bites when some paste of the leaves of certain medical herbs mixed with the juice of Kumari plant is to be smeared, in the *Uda-Kumbha vidhana* ceremony. The serpent is always the Agathodaemon, the bringer of health and good fortune.[22]

The practice of adoration of the serpent is very primitive in India and it has some Vedic association also. In *Grihyasutras* '*Sarpabali*' is one of the many house-hold rites and its performance as annual rite-prolonged for no less a period than the four months of the rains is reminiscent of the popular naga-worship in many parts of India.[23]

Naga cult in Buddhism during Satavahana period is also noteworthy. Serpents are represented as entwining stupas. Both at Amaravati and Nagarjunakonda, the Buddha is represented as seated on Nagas with their hoods just above his head. The snake cult was widely prevalent in these parts of Andhra Desa.

The exact usage of this pot is not known but it proves beyond any reasonable doubt that the pot maker or his masters who wanted him to make such a pot were inspired by the Naga-cult.

Yeleswaram

Yeleswaram pottery is not only striking and significant but also very much veriegated, drawing parallels from many important early historical sites excavated in India. The entire collection of pottery appears to be of wheel made with the fabric ranging from fine to coarse. Red-ware pottery is mostly slipped. During the early part of this period say upto 4th century AD dull red ware of Ikshvaku period continued by the grey ware emerged and predominated this pottery. Red polished-ware and black and red-ware were conspicuous by their absence after the termination of Ikshvaku period.[24]

The following are some of the specimens of pottery that were recovered from layer IV assigned to the Vishnukundin period:

1. A small vase of red-ware with a rounded body having a thicked rim externally grooved. It had deep grooves in the neck and on the shoulder.
2. A big red-ware water-pot with a globular body and grooved flat undercut rim. At the neck also it was decorated with horizontal grooves.
3. A red-ware pot with a hole for a spout.
4. A carinated lid of dull red-ware with a closing and slightly everted rim having a sharp flange in the waist. It had deep grooves in the neck. Two types have featureless

rims whereas one type was devoid of grooves. Similar types were recorded at Arikamedu, Brahmagiri and Maski.

5. A grey-ware spouted vessel with a rounded body having sagger base.

6. A grey-ware vessel with an externally thickened rim.

7. A dull red-ware lid with closing featureless rim, flanged waist and a solid knob. It contained a hoard of 49 Vishnukundin coins. Similar types were recovered in later periods as well, treated with lime or yellow colour.

8. A grey-ware lid with a hollow stand (must be finial).

9. A small grey-ware bowl with grooves.

10. A grey-ware miniature lid cum bowl with flanged rim.

11. A red-ware conical bowl with a flat base irregular shape.

12. A dull red-ware lower part of dish on a stands with curved edge at the bottom coarse fabric.

13. A dull red-ware fragment of dish on stand with soot marks in the disc coarse fabric.

14. A polished red-ware fragment of carinated *handi* with an out turned rectangular rim having sharp carination in the waist polished red-ware.

A fragment of a red-ware storage jar is met with in the recent excavations at Keesaragutta. There is applique design probably of an animal leg. The fabric is coarse and may be classified under decorated pottery.

Nelakondapalli

Fragments of red polished ware and red slipped ware of coarse to fine fabric have been met with during the excavations at Nelakondapalli. First type of storage jar has a usual rim, the lower portion of the rim is decorated with ropy design. Second type has a plain flat out-turned rim, below the rim is decorated with horizontal grooves. Third type has a splayed rim with horizontal grooves on the body. The first type must have been used as a jar for storing grains etc., and the other two types for storing water.

Fourth type is a large storage jar with oval shaped body probably with a rounded base with out-turned rim, horizontal grooves on the edges of the rim and below the rim of the jar. The neck portion of the jar contains ropy design.

Another type is a thick fragment of a vessel with flat out-turned rim and a loop design on the rim. The fabric is coarse and it is red slipped. Similar pottery is found at Keesaragutta, Yeleswaram etc.

Iron objects

Nails, knives, arrow heads, sickles are some of the iron objects that have been recovered from the excavations at Keesaragutta.

A flat iron piece with rivet measuring about 11 cm. length and 3 cm. breadth has been found. This piece might have been used as hinges for the door.

An iron spear head or a similar weapon has also been met with. It is 12.5 cm. in length including 1 cm. long pointed part at the tail end, and 1 cm. width in the middle.

Another iron object 5.5 cm. long, slightly bulging in the middle and pointed at both ends has been met with.

Beads

For an archaeologist, beads are valuable because they serve as a valuable source of information in tracing the influence of one culture on the other particularly in ancient times.

A number of beads have been recovered from the excavations at Keesaragutta. The beads are made of terracotta and precious stone. The shapes of terracotta-beads are pear, spherical, amalaka, and tabloid. But for a cylindrical amethyst bead, beads of precious stone are rare.

Similarly, a good variety of beads of terracotta and semi-precious stones have been brought to light at Yeleswaram. Terracotta was most popularly used in manufacturing beads. A variety of shapes such as barrel shaped, globular, discoid and faceted were noticed and all of them had as usual transversed holes. The favourite type appeared to be long barrel cylinder.

Bangles

A few bangle pieces have also been found at Keesaragutta. Some of the bangles made of shell are beautifully incised with concentric grooves and others are plain.

Stone objects

The stone objects found at Keesaragutta include a polished linga about 8.5 cm. long with a diametre of 3 cm. The top is round and the base is flat so as to insert into a pedestal.

Another object found associated with the linga is a conical bowl with perforation at the tip and the two perforations at the rim. It was probably suspended in the inverted position for letting down drops of water over the linga.

A head of a miniature female sculpture was found with bulbous eyes, her hair tied with a wavy fillot in the middle are made into a top knot. The sculpture was made of black basalt. There is also a small stone boat about 13 cm. long possibly used for grinding spices or ingredients of *tilak* etc. A part of the boat is broken and missing.

A stone-plaque of Mother Goddess is described separatly (Part II c.Art).

The large number of Siva-lingas carved out of stone beautifully and artistically go to show that "Keesaragutta" was a manufacturing centre of Siva lingas for exporting them to various places in the country during the Vishnukundin period. The Siva lingas on Keesaragutta and their significance has, however, been dealt in detail elsewhere.

Idols etc.

About ten idols which are detailed below were discovered at Nelakondapalli in the course of digging for *pati* earth:

1.	a. Buddha (standing legs and hands broken)	52.5 cm. × 25 cm.
	b. Head	20 cm. × 18 cm.
2.	a. Buddha (standing legs and hands broken)	80 cm. × 37 cm.
	b. Head	28.5 cm. × 22.5 cm.
3.	a. Buddha (standing hand broken)	
	b. Head	18 cm. × 15 cm.
4.	a. Buddha (standing)	65 cm. × 25 cm.
	b. Head	25 cm. × 24 cm.
5.	Buddha (standing)	82.5 cm. × 37 cm.
	Head	25 cm. × 24 cm.
6.	Buddha (standing)	50 cm. × 22.5 cm.
	Head	25 cm. × 24 cm.
7.	Buddha (standing)	80 cm. × 41 cm.
	Head	24 cm. × 25 cm.
8.	Buddha (standing complete shape except broken hands)	70 cm. × 22.5 cm.

9. Buddha (standing without legs) 88 cm. × 35 cm.
10. Broken pieces of Padma pedestals 9 nos.

All the idols are decorated with *Tilak* mark on the forehead and on stylistic grounds are datable to 3rd century AD.

The pit where the idols were discovered was extended and tub like brick structures, three in alignment separated by a drain, were brought to light. Number of broken fragments essential for moulding the broken idols, and a very interesting brick structure relating to the manufacture and preservation of the marble Buddhist idols were traced out. The trough measuring 4.45 m. × 1.96 m. × .80 m. appears to have been intended for preserving the idols under lime plaster and that they were given high polish later.

On the basis of the availability of lime-stone and marble deposits in the vicinity, number of brick tubs and fragments of Buddhist idols traced during the course of archaeological operations at Nelakondapalli, it may be concluded, that it was a manufacturing centre of Buddhist idols of different sizes and that the idols were exported to various other places in the country.

Coinage

A collection of 868 Vishnukundin coins preserved in the A.P. State Museum at Hyderabad have been examined by M. Rama Rao and he has described some of them in the catalogue.[25] All the coins are of copper and round in shape. These coins were obtained from Tangutur in Bhongir taluk of Nalgonda district and from Telkunta in the Sultanabad taluk of Karimnagar district. These coins contain a lion inside a circle on the obverse and a vase or *kalasa* flanked by a lamp stand on either side inside a rayed circle on the reverse. Eliot[26] described two coins of the above type. M. Rama Rao has divided the coins into twelve varieties based on the symbols on the obverse of the coins.

1. Well decorated lion facing left with the double *ya* symbol and crescent above and with the left fore-paw raised.
2. Animal as above with mouth open.
3. Animal as above sparsely decorated.
4. Animal as in no.2 with symbols before the mouth.
5. Animal facing left with mouth open, tail curled above, left forepaw raised and double *ya* symbol above.
6. Animal facing left with mouth open, tail uplifted and left forepaw raised.

7. Animal as above with crescent above and double *ya* symbol before the mouth.

8. Animal facing left with open mouth, tail uplifted, left fore-paw raised and double *ya* symbol before the mouth.

9. Animal as above with a symbol before the legs.

10. Big bold animal facing left with mouth open, double *ya* symbol before the mouth, tail uplifted, left forepaw raised and symbols before the legs.

11. Animal as above with crescent above.

12. Animal as above with symbols before and between the legs. On the reverse a vase or vase like symbol in one pellet with two straight horizontal lines and a pellet above etc., are noticed. The most curious feature of the symbol on the reverse side is that starting as a vase or *kalasa* on two slender legs with two lines and a pellet above and with a lamp stand on either side, all inside a rayed circle, it culminates in a well formed *sankha* passing through several intermediate forms.

These type of coins were attributed to Pallavas,[27] which was proved to be untenable and wrong.[28] The Vishnukundins issued a variety of coins. The round double die struck copper coins are generally found in coastal Andhra, Telangana, Vidarbha and Maharashtra. Two coins have been published with the following description:

"A well decorated lion facing right with gaping mouth, curled up tail, left fore-paw raised are found on the obverse, the sacred *kalasa* on a stand flanked by lamp stands on either side are seen on the reverse of the coins. The lion with all its vigour portrayed on the obverse invariably found on the coins, leads one to think that they have made it a dynastic crest, the lion symbolising the power. The reverse of the coins has a spiritual content. The flaming lights whose rays spread all over the world, meaning the diffussion of knowledge. The sacred *kalasa* standing on a pedestal in the centre contains the water of life, purity and fertility which is a symbol of prosperity of Vishnukundin rule. But they bear no legend on them.[29]

It is further reported that two unique coins with legends bearing the names of Indravarma and his son Vikramendravarma whose inscriptions were found near Tummalagudem, a place 32 Km. away from Bhongir, were collected in the neighbourhood of Bhongir. The tiny coin of Indravarma measuring 7 cm. dia. is stated to contain all the features of the commonly found coins described above, and that the letters of the legend are artistic and commendable of the engravers art on such a mini coin. It is further described that the other coin of Vikramendravarma contained the legend in Brahmi script (?). The size of the coin is given as 1.5 cm.[30]

There is no dispute in accepting that the above two coins are of Vishnukundins but the legend part of it is doubtful, in view of the fact that not even a single coin containing clear legend out of thousands of Vishnukundin coins discovered so far, has been met with. Further, there is no reason to believe why the weak Indravarma and Vikramendravarma alone should issue coins in their name while the powerful monarchs like Madhavavarman, Indrabhattarakavarman did not do so.

A coin within a circle with pellets around, lion and tail downward to right on the obverse, and "within broad circle of radiating lines was "on a stand between two tripod lamp stands or standards" was found in Prakash excavations,[31] on the banks of river Tapati. This coin is attributed to the Vishnukundins.[32]

An exceptionally large number of Vishnukundin coins has been reported from several ancient sites in Maharashtra. At first glance they give an appearance of being copper coins and look rather heavy in proportion to their size. But a recent matallurgical analysis has revealed a peculiarity of their composition in as much as they comprise an iron core with the coating of a thin sheet of copper on the surface.[33] Kautilya's Arthasastra says that copper coins made up of four parts of an alloy shall be a mashaka, half a mashaka, kakani, and half a kakani. This alloy shall be made up of four parts of silver, eleven parts of copper, and part of tikshana or any other metal.[34]

A solitary coin was recovered in the course of archaeological excavations at Brahmapuri. It bears a lion to the right on one side and jar flanked by a trident on either side within the rayed circle on the other.[35] A couple of coins recovered in the excavations at Nevasa in the Ahmadnagar district of Maharashtra, bear a lion standing facing right , in its front, a vertical linear staff with a thick dot capping it, all in a circle on the obverse, and a vase on a stand between two posts on each side, the entire motif in a circle with radiating lines on the reverse.[36] Following Elliot, Vincent A. Smith and other earlier numismatists, these coins were assigned by the excavators to the Pallavas. But these coins are now commonly accepted to have been issued by the Vishnukundins.[37]

The new varieties were unearthed at Paunar in the Wardha district, their obverse has the figure of a well decorated lion to the right with gaping mouth, curled up tail and left forepaw raised within a circle inside a dotted border or in a rayed circle, while the reverse show either the axle of a wheel and a cresent with a dot placed on it in each of the four corners or a conch-shell decorated with some fillet-like objects within a radiated circle.[38] Another Vishnukundin coin of the common type with lion on the obverse and a vase-on-stand flanked by the figures of a *trisula* on either side, on the reverse, was reported from a place near Nagpur.[39]

The biggest hoard of over three hundred Vishnukundin coins was discovered at Paunar in the Wardha district. They bear a lion on the obverse and an axle in relief, or a conch- shell or a vase-on-stand, all in a circle with radiating strokes, on the reverse.[40]

In the recent years a hoard of Vishnukundin coins have been reported from Ramathirtham of Vizianagaram district in Andhra Pradesh. A coin has been recovered in course of archaeological excavations at Nelakondapalli of Khammam district. A hoard of 273 Vishnukundin coins have been recovered near the Sri Ramalingeswaraswamy temple at Keesaragutta while digging a trench for extension works of the temple. All these coins are of copper and round in shape. The coins bear a squatting lion with a spiralled tail and raised forepaw on the obverse, a *poornaghata* flanked by two lampstands all enclosed in rayed circle on the reverse. None of these coins bear any legend.

It is not known as to why the Vishnukundins did not like to issue their coins with legend though they were learned kings and were praised with long epithets in their inscriptions. In the absence of any archaeological or epigraphical evidence it may not be proper to come to any conclusion why the Vishnukundins dispensed with the minting of coins with the legends unlike their predecessors and contemporary dynasties like Satavahanas, Pallavas, etc. But it may not be unreasonable to think that the Vishnukundins were confident that the conspicuous and significant symbol adopted in their coinage viz., the lion on the obverse and a *kalasa* flanked by two lamp stands, all enclosed in a rayed circle on the reverse, itself would stand for their dynastic appellation so far as their coinage was concerned.

REFERENCES

1. Krishnamurthi, K.; July, 1965; Some Technical Aspects of the Indian Pottery; the Orissa Historical Research Journal, Vol.XIII, No.2, p. 29.
2. Wheeler, R.E.M., etal.; 1946; Ancient India Vol.2.
3. Wheeler, R.E.M., etal.; 1947-48, Brahmagiri and Chandravalli excavations; Ancient India Vol.4, pp. 203 ff.
4. *Ibid.*, p. 203 ff.
5. Abdul Waheed Khan, Md.; 1963; A monograph on Yeleswaram Excavations, Plate XI, fig. XI- 1 and 3.
6. Ancient India No.10 and 11, p. 64, 65 Type XV.
7. *Ibid.*, p. 65.
8. Abdul Waheed Khan, Md.; 1963; *op.cit.*, plate XIV-B.
9. Wheeler, R.E.M. etal,; Ancient India Vol.4, pp. 203 ff.
10. Marshal, John, Sir; 1931/1973; Mohenjo-daro and Indus Valley Civilisation, Vol.I, Delhi, pl.XC II, fig. 31 and 34.

11. Indian Archaeology,; 1957-58; p. 18, pl.XXIV.
12. Ancient India Vol.4, p. 202.
13. Sankalia, H.D.; 1974; Pre-history and Proto-history of India, and Pakistan, Poona, p. 256 fig.121.
14. Nagaraja Rao, M.A. and Malhotra, K.C., 1965; Stone Age Hut Dwellers of Tekkalkota, Poona, p. 36.
15. Allchin, F.R.; 1960; Piklihal Excavations, APGAS No.1 p. 31.
16. Prasad Singh, R.C.; 1969; "Spouted Vessels in India", in potteries in Ancient India, Patna, p. 121-122.
17. Agarwal, R.C.; 1969; Potteries in Ancient India, Patna, p. 161.
18. Dikshit, S.K.; The Mother Goddess, Poona, p. 36.
19. Vogel, J. Ph.; 1926, Indian Serpent Lore, London, p. 19
20. *Ibid.*, p. 3-4.
21. Mackenzie, J.; 1875; Indian Antiquary, p. 5
22. Fergusson, J.; 1968; Tree and Serpent Worship, London, p. 3.
23. Shukla, D.N. 1958; Vastu Sastra, Vol.II p. 348.
24. Abdul Waheed Khan, Md.; 1963; op.cit. p. 14.
25. Rama Rao, M.; 1963; The Vishnukundin Coins in the A.P. Govt. Museum, APGAS No.10, p. 33-41.
26. Elliot, W.; 1886; Coins of South India, pl.11 Nos.49&50.
27. *Ibid.*, pl.11.
28. Rama Rao, M.; 1963; *op.cit.*, p.35.
29. Acharya, K.V.; 1977; "Vishnukundins and their coins", Andhra Pradesh, Vol.XXI, No.9, Hyd. p. 14-15.
30. *Ibid.*, p. 15.
31. Thaper, B.K.; 1967, Prakash Excavations, AI., Vols.20 and 21 p. 118.
32. Krishna Sastry, V.V.; 1979; "Keesara-the capital of Vishnukundins"; JAAP, Vol.I, No.1, p. 99.
33. Ajay Mitra Shastri,; 1973; Vishnukundins in Maharashtra p. 96.
34. *Arthasatra* of Kautilya; 1915; Translated by R. Shamasastry, chapter XII, p. 98.
35. Ajay Mitra Shastri; 1972; Coinage of Satavahanas and Coins from Excavations, Nagpur, p. 130.
36. Sankalia, H.D., Deo, S.B., Ansari, Z.D.; 1960; from History to Pre-History at Nevasa (1954-56), Poona, p. 199.
37. Ajay Mitra Shastri; 1973; *op.cit.*, p. 98.
38. *Ibid.*, p. 99.
39. JNSI Vol.XXXIII;1971, Delhi Part I, pp. 126 ff.
40. Deo, S.B.; Dhavalikar, M.K.; 1968; Paunar Excavations, Nagpur, page 14 , plates XVII and XVIII.

CHAPTER 3.5

Social and Economic conditions

The Vishnukundin polity conformed to the rule laid down in the Sastras; its keynote was the sovereign. Monarchy was hereditary. "Except in times of danger, sovereignty fell to the lot of the oldest (son) is always respected. Sovereignty may (sometimes) be the property of the clan, for the corporation of clans is invincible in its nature and being free from the calamities of anarchy, can have a permanent existence on earth" says Kautilya.[1] The king was the commander in war and led his armies personally to the battle field. Indrabhattaraka is said to be the victor in innumerable *chaturdanta* battles.[2] The kings of the dynasty were engaged almost constantly in wars, both defensive and offensive. As the guardian of the social and religious order, the kings' "fearless hand' was to be wet by the water powered out to impart fearlessness". He was to prevent "the contamination of the four castes". The true father of his people, he should sympathise with "the weal and woes of his citizens" and "never employ taxes except in confirmity with justice". He was to be the "furtherer of the homesteads of the low as well as of the twice-born". He should properly "devise time and place for the triple object of human activity". A king educated in these precepts among a moralising people would have been more than human if he had escaped the obsession of this conception of his duties.[3]

Social conditions

The four fold division of society-the caste system-prevailed in the Andhra Desa during the Vishnukundin period. We hear of Govindavarman's charities and gifts to numerous brahmins. He protected the *varnas* and *asramas* and patronised the brahmins. Their love for brahmins may have been due to the fact that they were themselves Brahma-kshatras. The Brahmins of the south in the early centuries of the Christian era had converted members of the ruling class into kshatriyas, including them to perform *yagnas* and conferring on them the enormous task of protecting dharma.[4] The advent of the land grants in the south, first made fashionable by the Chalukyas, Pallavas and Kadambas, witnessed a new age when the monarch began to lean more heavily on the Brahman settlers for the maintenance of law and order. Those monarchs also contributed, inadvertantly, to the liquidation of royal power through the alienation of basic functions like those of the enforcement of law and the collection of revenue. The story of land grant system as revealed in epigraphs will supply us an important aspect of social history connected with the role of Brahmin settlements in feudal formations all over India.[5] *Agraharas* were granted to brahmins by kings to enable them to devote themselves exclusively to the study and the teaching of the Vedas and perform sacrifices, which were believed to bring prosperity to the country and its people. The *agraharas* became centres of learning and spread light of learning in the country.

With their long historical prefaces and elaborate instructions for maintenance, the epigraphs supply many hints about political organisation and economic arrangements. Inscriptions of post-Mauryan period are connected by and large, with Brahmanical or Jain-Buddhist settlements or political commercial centres and reflect their elitist culture. Therefore, the direct information which they supply is limited to royal and ecclesiastical sectors of life. Vast areas of social activity lying outside them are naturally precluded from appearing in our epigraphic records except in terms of indirect and casual reference.

Women occupied a prominent position in society. The idea of women being the chattel of her lord with no rights and privileges which make life worth living, was quite alien to the Vishnukundin period. Paramabhattarika Mahadevi, daughter of Prithvimula, and the Chief Queen of Govindavarman was a worthy spouse of her husband. She built a spacious *Vihara* at Sakrapura for the use of the *bikshus* of Chaturdasarya-varasangha and persuaded her husband to grant the village Penukaparu for the repairs and white-washing of the monastery and for providing the comforts such as food, drink, couch, lamps, incense perfume and medicine for the resident monks.[6]

A miniature stone sculpture of a lady with[7] head and bulbous eyes, hair tied away with fillet in the middle and made into a topknot found at Keesaragutta, indicates the hair dress of the woman folk during that period. Men and women wore ornaments. Ear spools of various sizes made of terracotta found at Keesaragutta and Yeleswaram at the early historical levels show that the women were fond of ear ornaments. Strings of beads were also worn by them. The beads found at Keesaragutta are made of terracotta and precious stone. The shapes among the terracotta beads are pear, spherical, amalaka and tabloid. Similar variety of beads of terracotta and semi-precious stones were brought to light at Yeleswaram also.

Names

Almost all the names of the Vishnukundin rulers end with the suffix "Varma" viz., Govindavarma, Madhavavarma, Vikramendravarma, Indrabhattarakavarma. Like the Pallava king and the Brihatphalayana king Jayavarman, and Salakayanas, the

Vishnukundins have their names ending in 'Varma' and do not bear a metronymic.[8] 'Bhattaraka' is a title applied to priests.[9] Fleet has pointed out that in the Gupta and Vallabhi records 'Bhattaraka' and 'Paramabhattaraka' are titles applied to paramount sovereigns.[10]

K. Gopalachari observes that the expression 'Bhattaraka', a title applied to kings is evident from the fact that in Pallava grants it is applied to Maharajas.[11]

The copper plate grants of this dynasty show some names of brahmins- Agnisarma, Indrasarma, Sivasarma, Damasarma, Rudrasarma, etc., and a few names ending with suffix "Swami" e.g., Bolaswami, Kesavaswami. So the common name endings are Sarma, Varma, Swami, etc. Some names are borne by ladies and men e.g., Paramabhattarika Mahadevi, Prithvimula. The practice of naming the grandsons after their grandfathers was very common. As has been mentioned elsewhere, names of places are found in the inscriptions of the Vishnukundins and other contemporary dynasties of the Andhra Desa in the post-Satavahana and pre-Chalukyan period.

Trade

If the state of trade can be judged by the coinage i.e. by the variety and number of coins used or issued, it would appear that trade and industry flourished during the period of Vishnukundins. The vast trade of the period is also indicated by the charities of the rulers of this period. Govindavarman-I was munificent bestower of gifts of villages, fields, gold, elephant, horses, cows, bulls, couches, seats, vehicles, drinks, foods, vessels, houses, dresses, ornaments, virgins, and male and female slaves. The large number of Vishnukundin coins[12] from Ramathirtham, Yeleswaram, Bhongir taluk, and some places in Maharashtra such as Paunar in Wardha district, also attest to a busy trade in these parts of the kingdom.

Industries and commerce

Workers connected with buildings, polishers, iron workers, potters, artisans, writers (*lekhakas*), goldsmiths, stone-polishers, stone-masons, and carpenters appear to have been in the service of the kings. Most of these craftsmen were well to do and their artistic taste was noteworthy. The cave temples of Vijayawada, the secular and religious building complex at Keesaragutta and other places brought to light in the course of archaeological excavations, the copper plate grants and rings with circular seals, coins, etc., of these monarchs, the stone plaque of Mother Goddess, and the decorated globular earthen pot from Keesaragutta which are the best examples of their craftsmanship and artistic taste.

In the Vishnukundin kingdom, as in India at all times, agriculture was the main industry. Their inscriptions record gifts of villages to monastic institutions and *agraharas* to brahmins.

The land grants of the Vishnukundins do not show the division of administrative system. Incidentally, the inscriptions of the Salankayanas whom the Vishnukundins subjugated and occupied Vengi Desa, throw some light. The kingdom of Salankayanas was divided into Vishayas. The territory around the capital was not included in the Kudraharavishaya. Ahara, Rattha and Vishaya denote the same territorial division. Below the Vishaya was Grama and below that Pallika or Pallika Grama (a hamlet). No division between Vishaya and Grama is mentioned. Under the Eastern Chalukyas 'Desa' denoted a kingdom of which 'Vishaya' were divisions[13] therefore it may be safely concluded that the Vishnukundin dominion was also divided into number of Vishayas each consisting of number of villages, administered either directly by the kings or through the feudatories. Indrabhattarakavarma was stated to be the master of the entire Chakravarti-Kshetra[14] probably meaning the emperor's territory or domain.

The Vishnukundin monarchs must have evidently followed the Arthasastra of Kautilya in the administration of their kingdom though their copper plate grants are silent, in this regard. According to Kautilya,[15] the king shall employ as ministers such as are born of high family and possessed of wisdom, purity of purpose, bravery and loyal feelings in as much as ministerial appointments shall purely depend on qualifications. Having divided the spheres of their powers and having definitely taken into consideration the place the time where and when they have to work, such persons shall be employed as ministerial officers (*amatyas*). Villages consisting each of not less than a hundred families and of not more than five hundred families of agricultural people of 'Sudra' caste, with boundaries extending as far as a 'Krosa' (2250 yards) or two, and capable of protecting each other shall be formed. Those who perform sacrifices, spiritual guides, priests, and those learned in the Vedas shall be granted Brahmadeya lands yielding sufficient produce and exempted from taxes and fines. Lands prepared for cultivation shall be given to tax-payers only for life, unprepared lands shall not be taken away from those who are preparing them for cultivation. If cultivators pay their taxes easily, they may be favourably supplied with grains, cattle and money. The king shall bestow on cultivators only such favour and remission as will tend to swell the treasury, and shall avoid such as will deplete it.

A king with depleted treasury will eat into the very vitality of both citizens and country people. The king shall not only keep in good repair timber and elephant forests, buildings, and mines created in the past but also set up new ones.[16]

A wise king can make even the poor and miserable elements of his sovereignty happy and prosperous.[17]

The Vishnukundin kings were constantly engaged in wars and as such the duties concerning administration must have been carried by the ministerial officers (*amatyas*) assisted by other officials like headmen of the village, etc., mentioned as 'Vishayamahattara' in Pulomburu plates of the Eastern Chalukyan king Jayasimha Vallabha,[18] or "Grama Vriddha" mentioned in Godavari plates (set II) of Prithvimula.[19]

The Vishnukundin administration was keen in collecting different taxes. "The Vishnukundin charters usually exempt the gift villages from the payment of the 'Kara' alone and other exemptions are met with only in the Tummalagudem plates.[20] The word 'Kara; occurs in the Ramathirtham plates of Indravarma and Pulomburu plates of Madhavavarma IV, which denotes tax in general to be collected from the cultivators of land and people of other professions.[21]

Substantial part of the exchequer appears to have been spent for construction of temples, monastries, assembly halls, irrigation tanks, wells, and for keeping old ones in good repair. Their military administration also must have received a good part of the royal treasury. Madhavavarman II appears to have been a powerful war-lord, who had at his command an enormous army, consisting 8000 elephants, 10 crores of horses, and countless foot soldiers.[22]

The military strength is no doubt grossly exaggerated. Nevertheless, he must have had a large army in his service, to vanquish the kings of other dynasties and appropriate their royalty and bring under his sway vast territories. Kautilya[23] says that a large number of effete persons is better in as much as they can be employed to do other kinds of works in the camp to serve the soldiers fighting in battle fields, and to terrify the enemy by its number.

Vikramendrabhattaraka-II is said to be the victor in innumerable chaturdanta battles.[24] Hastikosa, and Virakosa, mentioned in Pulomburu plates of Madhavavarman IV, Vallabha figuring in Tummalagudem grant I, indicate the designations of the military officials. Hastikosa, Virakosa, and Vallabha may be the designations of the officers respectively, in charge of the elephant, infantry and cavalery forces of the king.[25] 'Skandhavara' at Kudavada,[26] and Velpur,[27] which figures in the Vishnukundin inscriptions indicate army headquarters or military encampments during war times. The skandhavara is a military encampment inhabited by the common people along with soldiers. In olden times the king used to be followed by a part of his civilian population too in order to ensure security. This encampment was generally situated near the prospective battle field.[28]

The expenditure must have been equally more on performing several Vedic sacrifices such as *Agnishtoma, Vajapeya, Bahusuvarna, Paundarika, Asvamedha, Kratusahasra, Sarvamedha, Rajasuya, Purushamedha,* etc., by the Vishnukundin monarchs like Madhavavarman II and also for maintaining *Ghatikas*.[29] The monarchs must have collected money for all the above mentioned activities by demanding from the subjects or by seeking subscriptions (*Bhikshata*, beg benevolences) from citizens and country people alike under false pretences of carrying this or that kind of business. Persons taken in concert shall publicly pay handsome donations and with this example, the king may demand of others among his subjects as laid down by Kautilya.[30]

People enjoyed "right to religion" during the period of Vishnukundins; all the important religions, viz., Buddhism, Jainism, Saivism, Vaishnavism, and other cults such as cult of Mother Goddess etc., flourished on account of religious tolerance of the kings. The performance of Vedic sacrifices appear to have become popular, for most of the ruling kings of this age claim to have performed the *asvamedha* and a number of other sacrifices. The very fact that they have taken credit for performing them shows that sacrifices and the Vedic religion of which they form an adjunct was very popular at the time. Besides the hieratic cult of sacrifices, the worship of the gods of the puranic pantheon, specially Siva and his attendant deities, was very much in vogue.

REFERENCES

1. *Arthasastra* of Kautilya, 1915; Translated by R. Shama Sastry, Book I, chapter XVII, page 40.
2. Kielhorn, F.; 1896-97; Chikkulla plates of Vikramendravarman, EI.; IV, S.G.P. Calcutta, p. 193 ff. Lines 12-13.
3. Gopalachari, K.; 1976; Early History of the Andhra Country, Madras, p. 79.
4. Narayanan, M.G.S.; 1975; The Vedic Puranics Sastraic Elements in Tamil Sangam Soceity and Culture Proceedings of the Indian History Congress, XXXVIth Session, (Aligarh), pp. 76-91 ff.
5. Narayanan, M.G.S.; 1978; Indian History Congress XXXIXth Session, Hyderabad p. 8.
6. Sastry, B.N.; 1974; Tummalagudem Copper plates of Vikramendra Varman II, EA. Vol. II, p. 15 ff. Lines 18-29.
7. Vide IV 'Material Culture', Stone Objects; pp. 121-122 ff.
8. Gopalachari, K.; 1976; *op.cit.*, p. 163. foot note.
9. Fleet, J.F.; 1888 (Edited) C.I.I. Vol.III, Nos.28 & 46.
10. Fleet, J.F.; 1905-1906; Epigraphia Indica Vol.VIII, Bombay, p. 17 and 41.
11. Gopalachari, K.; 1976; *op.cit.*, p. 173, note.
12. Vide IV 'Material Culture-Coinage' pp. 123-126 ff.
13. Indian Antiquary, Vol.VIII; 1879; Bombay, p. 76, Vol.XIII; 1884 pp. 213 ff.
14. Kielhorn, F.; 1930, Chikkulla plates, Line 11, EI.IV, pp. 193 ff.

15. *Arthasastra* of Kautilya *op.cit.*, Book I, chapter VIII, p. 15.
16. *Ibid.*, Book II, chapter I, pp. 52-54.
17. *Ibid.*, p. 321.
18. Pulomburu plates of Eastern Chalukyan King Jayasimha Vallabha, 1927-28, Epigraphia Indica XIX, Bombay, p. 256, JAHRS IV, 1930, pp. 74 ff.
19. Ramesan, N.; 1962; Copper Plate inscriptions of A.P. Govt. Museum, Vol. I APGAS No.6, pp. 241.
20. Sankaranarayanan, S.; 1977; The Vishnukundins and their Times, Delhi, p. 133.
21. *Ibid.*, p. 133.
22. Venkataramanayya, N. 1975: The Vishnukundins, Madras, p. 31.
23. *Arthasastra* of Kautilya, *op.cit.*, Book VII, chapter XII.
24. Epigraphia Indica XIV, p. 12.
25. Sankaranarayanan, S.; 1977; *op.cit.*, pp. 131-132.
26. Hultzsch, E.; 1923-24; Ipur plates I of Madhavavarman II, EI, XVII, Bombay, p. 334, Line-4.
27. Sankaranarayanan, S.; 1967-78, Velpuru Inscription of Madhavavarman II, E.I., XXXVII, pp. 125 ff.
28. Prabhakar, V. Begde; 1978; Ancient and Medieval Town Planning in India, New Delhi, pp. 53-54.
29. *Arthasastra* of Kautilya, *op.cit.*, pp. 301-303.
30. *Ibid.*, pp. 301-303.

Bibliography

Abdul Waheed Khan, Md. 1963: A monograph of Yeleswaram excavation, *APGAS*, No.14, Hyderabad.

Abdul Waheed Khan, Md. 1963-64: Yeleswaram excavations, *JAHRS*, Vol.XXIX, pp.7 ff.

Abdul Waheed Khan, Md. 1964: An early sculpture of Narasimha, *APGAS*, No.16, Hyderabad.

Acharya, K.V. 1977: Vishnukundins and their Coins, *Journal of Andhra Pradesh*, Vol.XXI, Hyderabad.

Acharya P.K. (ed.) 1932: *Manasara*, J.K. Publishing House, Bhopal.

Acharya P.K. 1946: *Encyclopaedia of Hindu Architecture*, J.K. Publishing House, Bhopal.

Acharya P.K. 1979: *Hindu Architecture in India and Abroad*, J.K. Publishing House, Bhopal.

Agarwal, V.S. 1939: *India known to Panini*, Veda Academy, Varanasi.

Agarwal, V.S. 1966: *Sivamahadeva*, Veda Academy, Varanasi.

Ajay Mitra Shastri (ed.) 1972: *Coinage of the Satavahanas and Coin from excavations*, Nagapur.

Ajay Mitra Shastrı 1973: *Vishnukundins in Maharashtra*, Vishveswaranand Institute of Sanskrit and Indological Studies, Punjab University, Hoshiarpur.

Allchin, F.R. 1960: Pikhlihal excavations, *APGAS*, No.1, Hyderabad.

Allchin, F.R. 1916-17: *Annual Report of Indian Epigraphy*.

Allchin, F.R. 1939-40 to 1942-43: *Annual Report of Indian Epigraphy*.

Banerjee, J.N. 1941: *Development of Hindu Iconography*, University of Calcutta, Calcutta.

Balaram, Srivastava 1978: *Iconography of Sakti*, Chaukhambha Orientalia, Varanasi.

Beal Samuel 1888: *Life of Hiuen Tsiang by the Shamans*, Hwuili and Yen-Tsung, London.

Bhaskaracharya 1929: *Siddhanta Siromani*, Kasi Sanskrit Series, Benaras.

Bhatta Someswara 1926: *Manasollasa*, Govt. Oriental Series, Mysore.

Burgess, J. 1887: *Buddist stupas of Amaravati and Jaggayyapeta*, Archaeological Survey of Southern India, London.

Burgess, J.: *Buddhist sculpture from Amaravathi*, Archaeological Survey of Southern India, London.

Buhaler, G.: *Laws of Manu*, SBE Series XXV.

Buhaler, G.: *Bulletin of the Madras Govt. Museum*, Vol.VII.

Buhaler, G. 1931: *Census of India*, Report page 406.

Chakravarthi, P.G. 1972: *The Art of War in Ancient India*, Oriental Publisher, New Delhi.

Coomaraswamy, A.K. 1937: *History of Indian and Indonesian Art*, London.

Coomaraswamy, A.K. 1955: Mother Goddess, *Marg*, Vol.VI, pp.31 ff.

Cousen, H. 1926: *The Chalukyan Architecture of the Kanarese Districts*.

Data, G.T.: *Art of warfare of ancient India.*
Deo, S.B. and Dhavalekar 1968: *Pauner excavations*, Nagpur.
Desai, P.B. 1957: *Jainism in south India and some Jaina epigraphs*, Sholapur.
1885: *Dharma Sangraha of Nagarjuna*, Oxford.
Dikshit, S.K. *The Mother Goddess*, Poona International Book Service, Poona.
Dikshit, S.K. 1961: *District Census Hand Book*, Hyderabad District, Hyderabad.
Dikshit, S.K. 1968: *District Census Hand Book*, Hyderabad District, Hyderabad.
Dikshit, S.K. 1961: *District Census Hand Book*, Nalgonda District, Hyderabad.
Dikshit, S.K. 1961: *District Census Hand Book*, Khammam District, Hyderabad.
Dikshit, S.K. 1961: *District Census Hand Book*, East Godavari District, Hyderabad.
Dikshit, S.K. 1961: *District Census Hand Book*, Krishna District, Hyderabad.
Dikshit, S.K. 1961: *District Census Hand Book*, Mahaboobnagar District, Hyderabad.
Dikshit, S.K. 1961: *District Census Hand Book*, Kurnool District, Hyderabad.
Dubreuil, G.J. 1917: *The Pallavas*, Pondicherry.
Dubreuil, G.J. 1879: Eastern Chalukyan Grants, *Indian Antiquary*, Vol.VIII, p.76.

Elliot, Walter 1886: *Coins of the Southern India.*
Elliot, Walter 1974: *Epigraphia Andhrica*, Vol.IV, *APGAS*, No.11, Hyderabad.

Fergusson, James 1968: *Tree and Serpent Worship*, London.
Fergusson, James 1910: *History of Indian and Eastern Architecture I*, London.
Fleet, J.F. (ed.) 1888: *Corpus Inscriptionum Indicarum*, Vol.III, Calcutta.

Ghosh, A. (ed.) 1957-58: *Indian Archaeology, A Review*, New Delhi.
Gopalachari, K. 1976: *Early History of Andhra Country*, University of Madras, Madras.
Gopinandha Rao, T.A. 1921: *Elements of Hindu Iconography*, Indological Book House, Varanasi/Delhi.
Griffith, R.T.H. 1899: *Yazurveda*, Benaras.

Hastings James 1908: *Encyclopaedia of Religion and Ethics*, Vol.I to XII, Edinburgh.
Havell, E.B. 1978: *Indian Architecture through the Ages*, Asian Publication Service, New Delhi.
Hemachandra Ray Chaudhuri 1927: *Political History of the Ancient India*, University of Calcutta, Calcutta.
Hopkins, E.W. 1915: *The epic mythology.*
Hultzsch, E. 1923-24: Ipur plates of Govindavarma's Son Madhavavarman, *EI.*, Vol.XVII, pp.334 ff., Govt. of India Central Publication Branch, Bombay.
Hultzsch, E. 1923-24: Ipur plates of Madhavavarman II, *EI.*, Vol.XVII, pp.337 ff., Govt. of India Central Publication Branch, Bombay.
Hultzsch, E. 1923-24: Ramathirtham plates of Indravavarman, *EI.*, Vol.XII, pp.133 ff., Manager of Publication, Delhi.
Hultzsch, E. 1957-58: *Indian Archaeology, A Review*, New Delhi.

James, E.O. *The cult of Mother Goddess.*
James, E.O. 1920-24: *Isanagurudevapaddhati*, Trivendrum Sanskrit Series, Trivendrum.

Keilhorn, F. 1896-1897: Chikkulla plates of Vikramendra Varma II, *EI.*, Vol.IV, pp.193 ff., SGP Calcutta.
Kramrisch, Stella 1946: *The Hindu Temples*, University of Calcutta, Calcutta.
Krishnamurthy, K. 1965: Some technical aspects of Indian pottery, *OHRSJ*, Vol.XIII, No.2, pp.29-42 ff.
Krishnamurthy, K. 1977: *Cultural Study of Nagarjunakonda*, Concept Publishing Company, Delhi.
Krishna Sastry, V.V. 1979: Keesara—the capital of Vishnukundins, *Journal of Archaeology in Andhra Pradesh*, Vol.II, pp.97-103 ff., Hyderabad.
Krishna Sastry, V.V. 1885: *Linga Purana*, Calcutta.

Longhurst, A.H. 1915-1916: *Annual Report of the Archaeological Survey of India*, New Delhi.
Longhurst, A.H. 1924: Pallava architecture, *Memoirs of ASI*, No.17, pp.22-30, New Delhi.
Longhurst, A.H. 1938: The Buddhist Antiquities from Nagarjunakonda, Madras Presidency, *Memoirs of ASI*, No.54, New Delhi.

Mackenzia, J. 1875: *Indian Antiquary*, p.5, Bombay.
Mackenzia, J. 1934: *Manasara—Sanskrit text with critical notes.*
Mackenzia, J. 1909-1919: *Mahabharata*, Nirnaya Sagar Press, Bombay.
Mallayya, N.V. 1930: Studies in Sanskrit Texts on Temple Architecture, *JAU*, Vol.IX, p.172.
Marshall, Sir John, 1931, 1973: *Mohenjo-daro and Indus Civilisation*, (Reprint) Indological Book House, Delhi.
Mayamuni 1919: *Mayamata*, TSS, Trivendrum.
Mayamuni 1919: *Mayamata* (Catalogue), Vol.XXVII, No.13078, Oriental Manuscript Library, Madras.
Mayamuni 1862: *Markandeya Purana*, ASB, Calcutta.
Mayamuni 1907: *Matsya Purana*, ASS, Poona.
Mc Crindle, J.W. 1884: Translation of Ptolomys' Geography, *IA*, Vol.XIII, p.353, Education Society Press, Bombay.
Majumdar, R.C. (ed.) 1954: The Classical Age, *HCIP*, Bharatiya Vidya Bhavan, Bombay.
Majumdar, R.C. and Pushalkar A.D. 1962: The Classical Age, *HCIP*, Bombay.

Nagaraja Rao, M.A. and Malhotra, K.C. 1965: *The stone age hut dwellers of Takkalakota*, p.36, Poona.
Narayana, M.G.S. 1975: The Vedic Puranic Sastric element in Tamila Sangam Society and Culture, *Proceedings of the Indian History Congress XXXVIth Session*, Aligarh.
Neelakanta Sastry, K.A. 1939: Foreign notices of South India, *University Historical Series*, No.14, Madras.

Pai, D.A. 1928: *Monograph on the religious sects in India among the Hindus*, The Times Press, Bombay.
Percy Brown 1959: *Indian Architecture (Buddhsit and Hindu periods)*, 4th edition, Bombay.
Prabhakar, V. Begde 1978: *Ancient Indian and medieval town planning in India*, Sagar Publications, New Delhi.
Prasad Singh (ed.) 1969: Spouted Vessels in India, *Potteries in Ancient India*, Patna.
Prasad Singh 1930: Pulomburu plates sets I & II, *JAGRS*, Vol.IV, pp.74 ff., *JAHRS*, Vol.V, p.183 note.
Prasad Singh 1927-28: Pulomburu plates of Jayasimha Vallabha, *EI.*, Vol.XIX, p.256 ff.

Raghavan, V. 1927-28: Two chapters on paintings in the Narada Silpa Sastra, *JISOA*, Vol.III, pp.15-32.

Ramachandramurti, N.S. 1979: *Forts in Andhra Pradesh*, unpublished thesis, Karnataka University, Dharwar.

Rama Rao, M. (ed.) 1943: *Jounal of Andhra History and Culture*, Vol.I, Guntur.

Rama Rao, M. 1963: Vishnukundin coins in Andhra Pradesh Govt. Museum, *Archaeological Series*, No.10, Hyderabad.

Rama Rao, M. 1964: Early Chalukyan temples in Andhra Pradesh, *APGAS*, No.19, Hyderabad.

Rama Rao, M. 1970: Select Andhra temples, *APGAS*, No.30, Hyderabad.

Ramesan, N. 1962: Copper plate inscriptions in Govt. Museum, part 1, *APGAS*, No.6, Hyderabad.

Ramachandran, T.N.: *Sculptures from Goli*, Madras.

Sankaranarayanan, S. 1967-68: The Vishnukundin charters from Tummalagudem, *Epigraphia Andhrica*, Vol.II, Hyderabad.

Sankaranarayanan, S. 1977: *The Vishnukundins and their times*, Agama Prakashan, Delhi.

Sankalia, H.D. and Deo S.B. 1960: From History to pre-History, *Nevasa* (1954-56), Poona.

Sankalia H.D. 1974: *The pre-History and proto-History in India and Pakistan*, Deccan College, Poona.

Sastry, B.N. 1974: Thummalagudem plates (set II) of Vikramendravarman II, *Epigraphia Andhrica*, Vol.II, pp.15 ff.

Sastry, B.N. 1976: *Andhrula Samghika Charitra*, Hyderabad.

Sastry, B.N. 1942: *Satapata Brahmana*, Sri Venkateswara Press, Bombay.

Sastry, B.N. 1882-1900: *Satapata Brahmana*, Atchyuta Granthalaya, Kashi.

Sastry, R. Shama (tr.) 1915-24: *The Kautilya Arthasastra*, Mysore.

Shukla, D.N. 1958: Hindu cannons of Iconography and Paintings, *Vastu Sastra*, Vol.II, Vastuvangmaya Prakashanashala, Lucknow.

Shukla, D.N. 1960: *Vastu Sastra*, Vol.I, Vastuvangmaya Prakashanashala, Lucknow.

Shukla, D.N. 1960: *Hindu science of Architecture*, Lucknow.

Sinha, B.P. (ed.) 1969: *Potteries in ancient India*, Patna.

Sinha, B.P. 1971: Arts of warfare in ancient India, *Studies in Cultural History of India*, Dharwar.

Sinha, S.D. 1965: *Ancient Indian warfare with special reference period*, E.J. Brill, Leiden.

Sircar, D.C. 1965: Tundi plates of Vikramendravarman II, *EI.*, Vol.XXXVI, pp.7 ff.

Sircar, D.C. 1971: *Studies in religious life of ancient and medieval India*, Motilal Banarasidas, Delhi.

Sivarama Murthi, C. 1957: *Early eastern Chalukya sculptures*, Madras Govt. Bulletin, Madras.

Sivarama Murthi, C. 1959: Andhravastu Kalaparinamamu, *Telugu Vignana Sarvaswam*, Vol.III, Madras.

Sivarama Murthi, C. 1976: *Amaravathi sculptures in the Madras Museum*, Govt. of Tamilnadu, Madras.

Somasekhara Sarma, M. 1959: *Telugu Vignana Sarvaswamu*, Vol.III.

Soundera Rajan, K.V. 1965: Architecture of the early Hindu temples of Andhra Pradesh, *APGAS*, No.21, Hyderabad.

Soundera Rajan, K.V. 1978: *The Art of south India Tamilnadu and Kerala*, Sundeep Prakashan, Delhi.

Srinivasan, K.R. 1964: *Cave temples of the Pallavas*, ASI, New Delhi.

Srinivasan, P.R. 1959: *Bulletin of the Madras Govt. Museum*, Vol. III.

Srinivasan, P.R. 1922: *Silpa Ratna*, TSS, Trivendrum.

Subrahamanyam, R. (*et al*) 1974: Nagarjunakonda, 1954-60, Vol.I, *Memoirs of ASI*, No.75, New Delhi.
Suktankar, V.S. 1917-18: Myakadoni inscription of Sripulomavi-II, *EI.*, Vol.XIV, pp.151 ff.

Thapar, B.K. 1967: *Prakash Excavations.*
Thapar, B.K. 1935: *Vaikhanasaagam of Marici*, TSS, Trivendrum.

Varahmihira 1895: *Brihat-Samhita*, English translation by Prof. Kern, Benaras.
Varahmihira 1915: *Brihat-Samhita*, English translation by V. Subramanyam Sastry, Benaras.
Venkataramanayya, N. 1936-37: Karnata, *JAHRS*, Vol.X, pp.89, 99 ff.
Venkataramanayya, N. 1975: The Vishnukundins, reprinted from *Journal of the Madras University*, Vol.XLVII, No.2.
Venkataramanayya, N. 1912: *Vishnu Dharmottara*, SVP, Bombay.
Venkataramanayya, N. 1971: Vishnukundin coins in Maharashtra, *JNSI*, Vol.XXXIII, pp.126 ff, Varanasi.
Venkataramanayya, N. 1921: *Vishnupurana*, Sri Venkateswara Press, Bombay.
Venkataramanayya, N. 1895: *Visvakarma Vidya Prakasa*, SVP, Bombay.
Venkataramanayya, N. 1937: *Viswakarma Prakasa*, Mata Prasad Pandey, Benaras.
Venkataramanayya, N. 1952: *Viswakarma Prakasa*, Sri Venkateswara Press, Bombay.
Vogel, J. Ph. 1926: *Indian serpent lore*, Arthur Probsthain, London.

Wheeler, R.E.M. and Ghosh, A. 1946: *Arikamedu Ancient India*, Vol.II, pp.101 ff.
Wheeler, R.E.M. 1947-48: Brahmagiri and Chandravalli, *Ancient India*, Vol.IV.
Wheeler, R.E.M. 1936: *Yagnavalkya Smriti*, NSP, Bombay.

Yazdani, G. (ed.) 1960: *Early History of Deccan*, Vols.I-II, (collected works) published under the authority of Govt. of Andhra Pradesh, Oxford University Press, London.
Yazdani, G. (ed.) 1940: *Yazurveda*, Moradabad.

INDEX

Figures and Plates

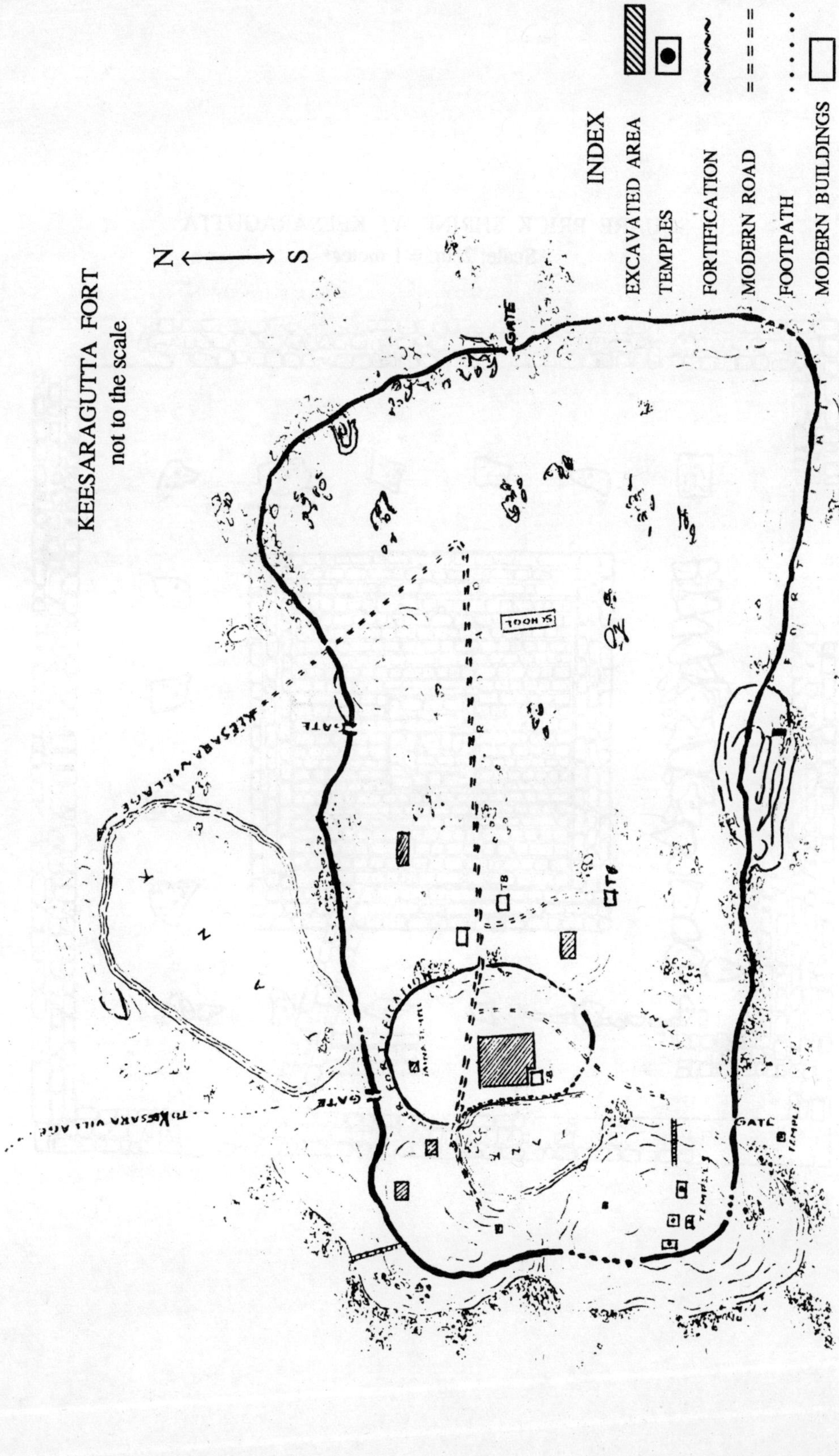
KEESARAGUTTA FORT
not to the scale
N
S
INDEX
EXCAVATED AREA
TEMPLES
FORTIFICATION
MODERN ROAD
FOOTPATH
MODERN BUILDINGS
GATE
SCHOOL
TEMPLE
TEMPLES

SQUARE BRICK SHRINE AT KEESARAGUTTA
Scale: 2cm. = 1 meter

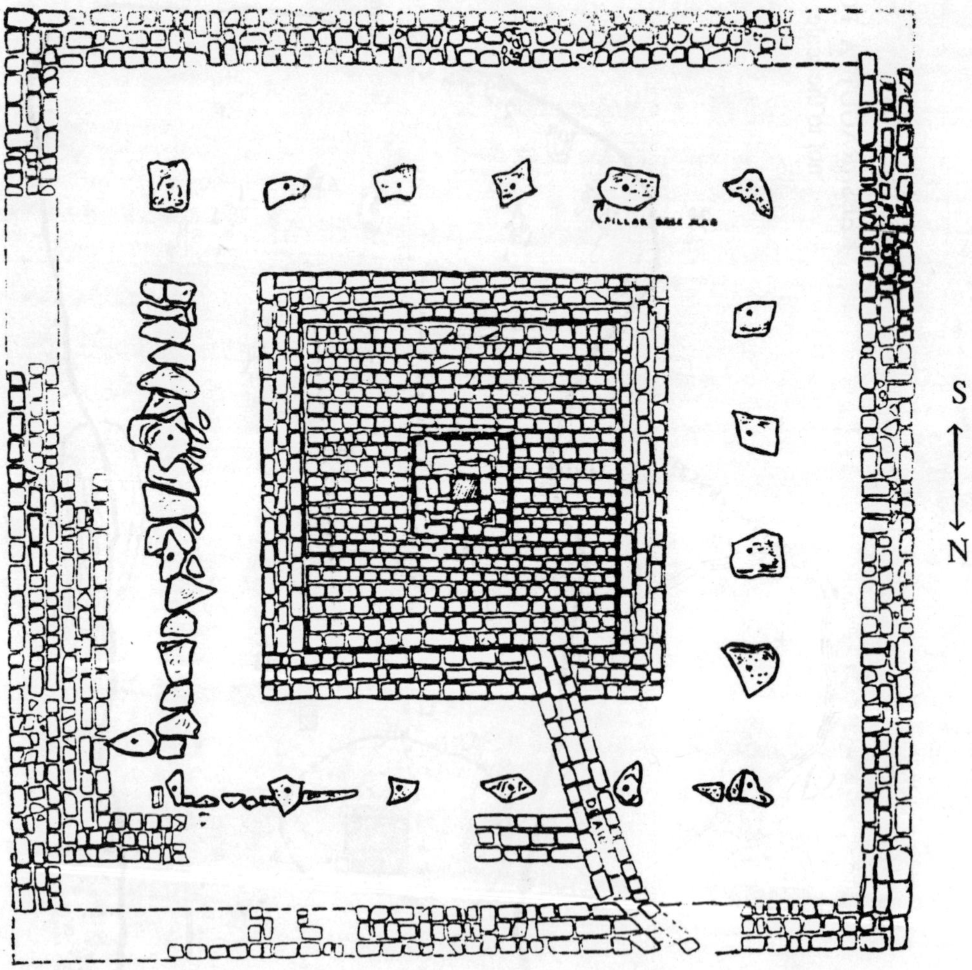

PLAN OF JAINA TEMPLE AT KEESARAGUTTA
Scale: 2cm. = 1 meter

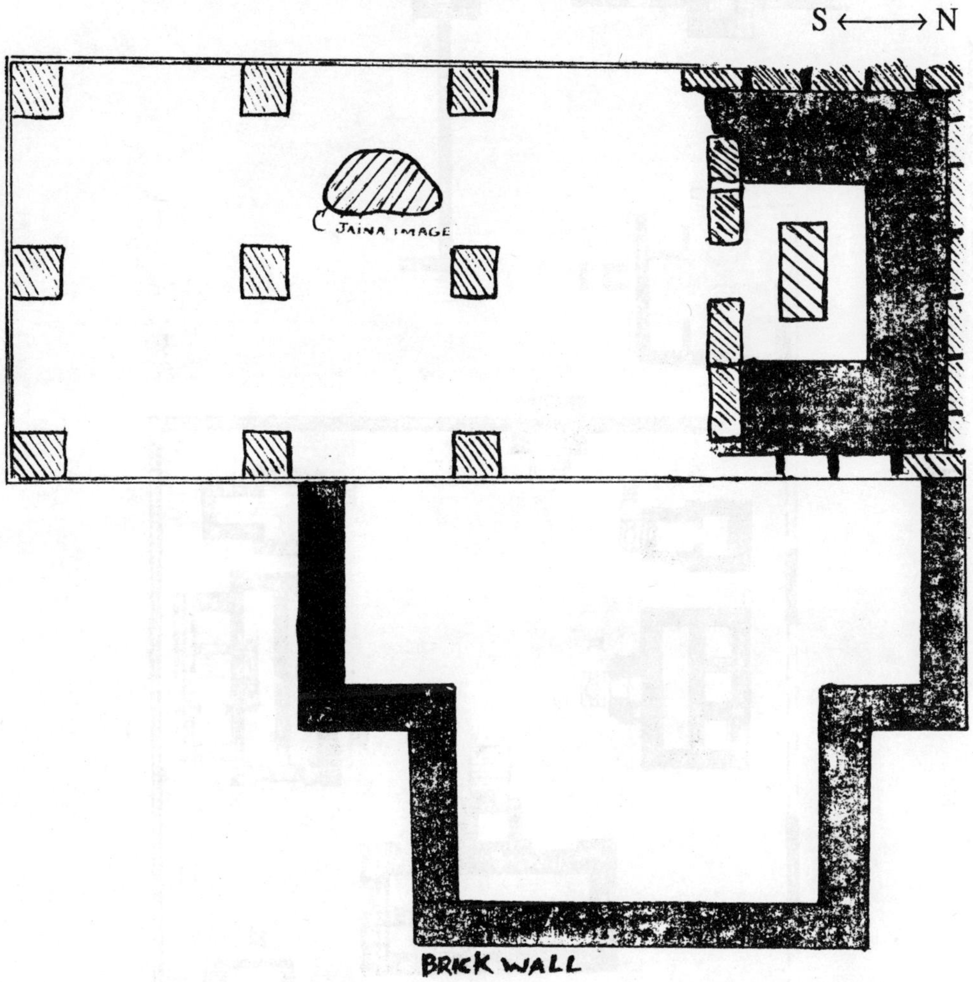

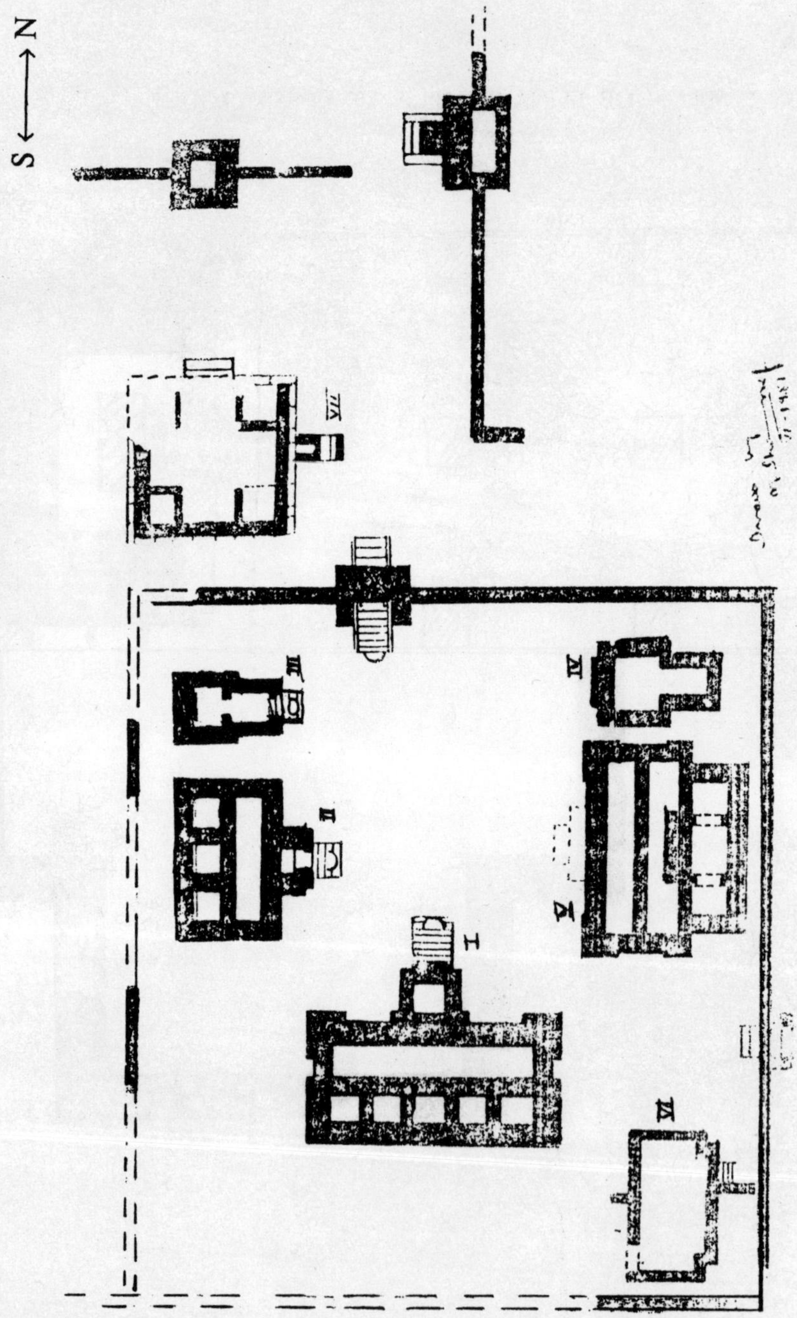

KEESARAGUTTA EXCAVATIONS—GROUND PLAN OF PALACE COMPLEX
Scale: 1/4 cm. = 1 meter

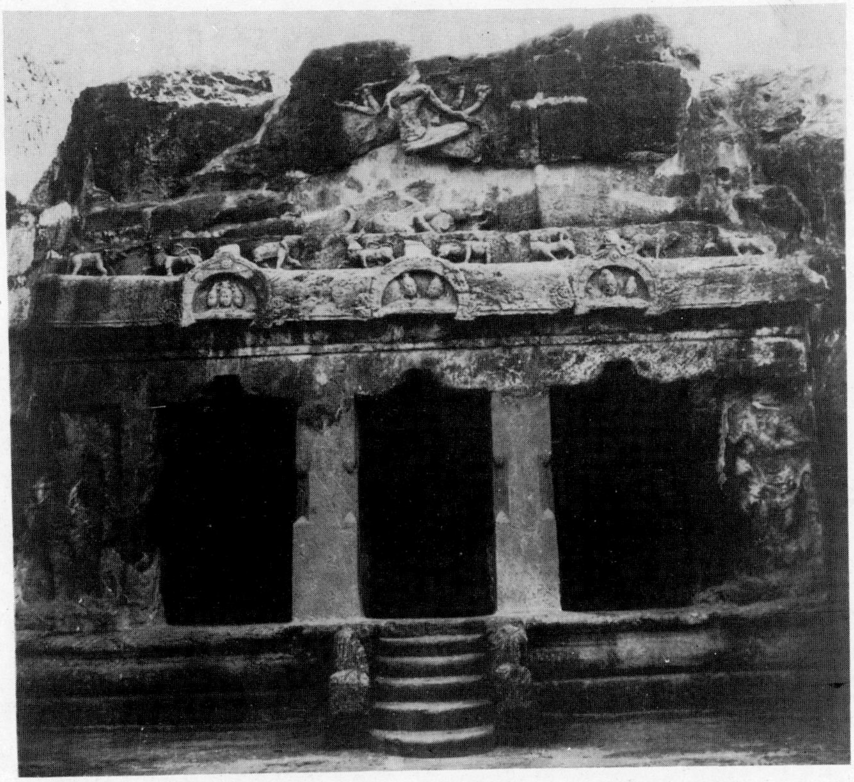

1. Vijayawada: General view of Cave-4 at Mogalrajapuram.

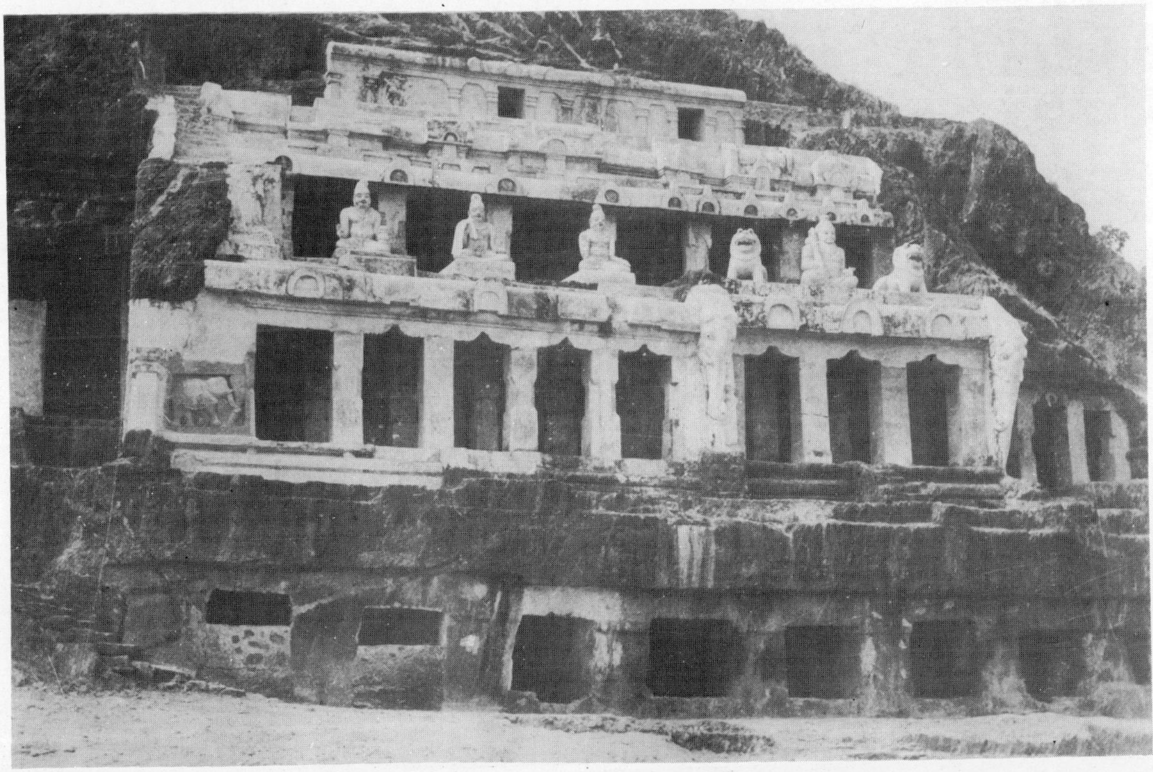

2. Vijayawada: General view of the Cave at Undavalli.

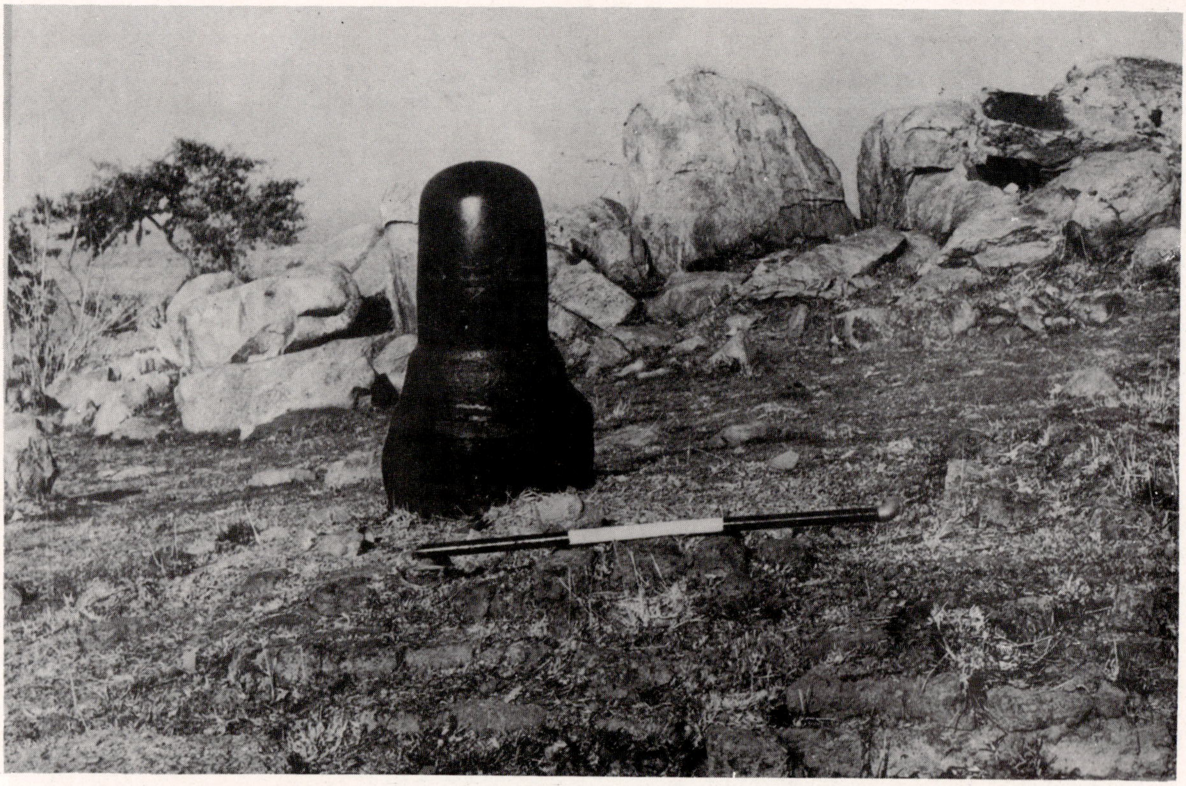

3. Keesaragutta: Sivalinga on Brick Yoni.

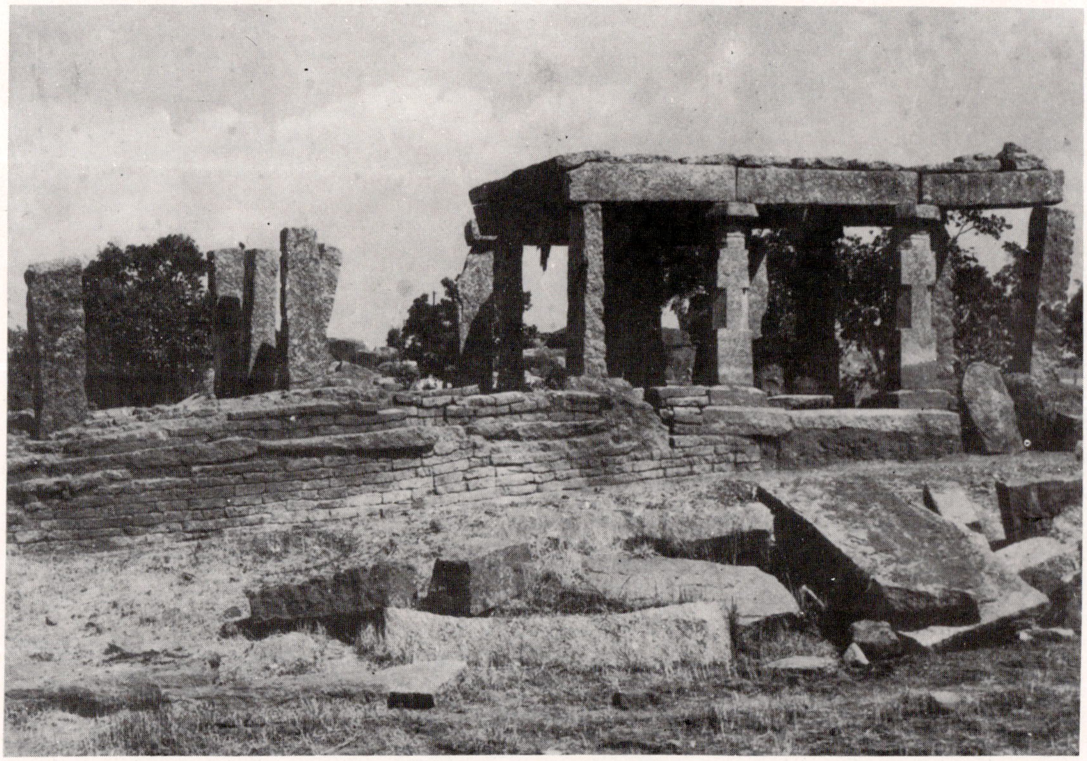

4. Keesaragutta: Jaina temple.

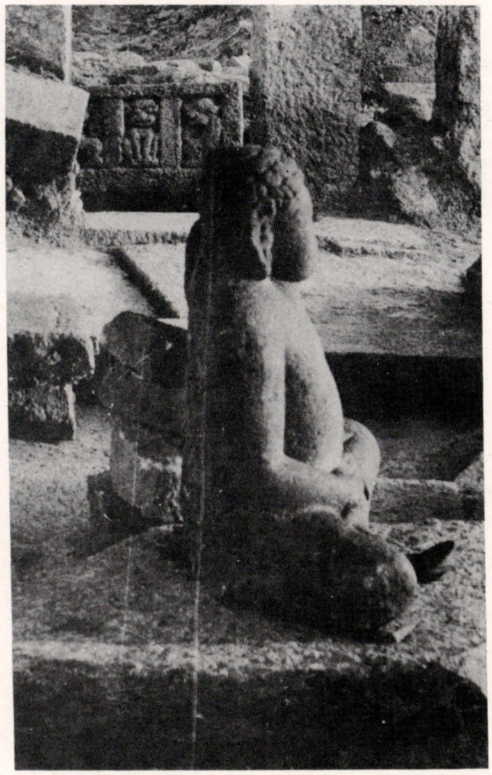

5. Keesaragutta: Image of JINA.

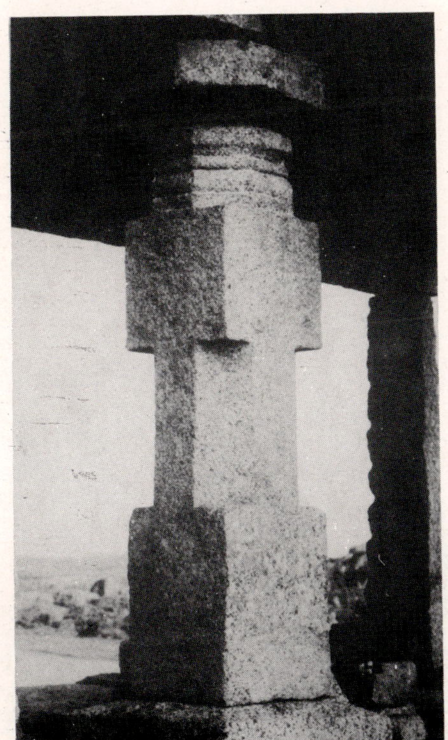

6. Keesaragutta: Pillar type—in the Jaina temple.

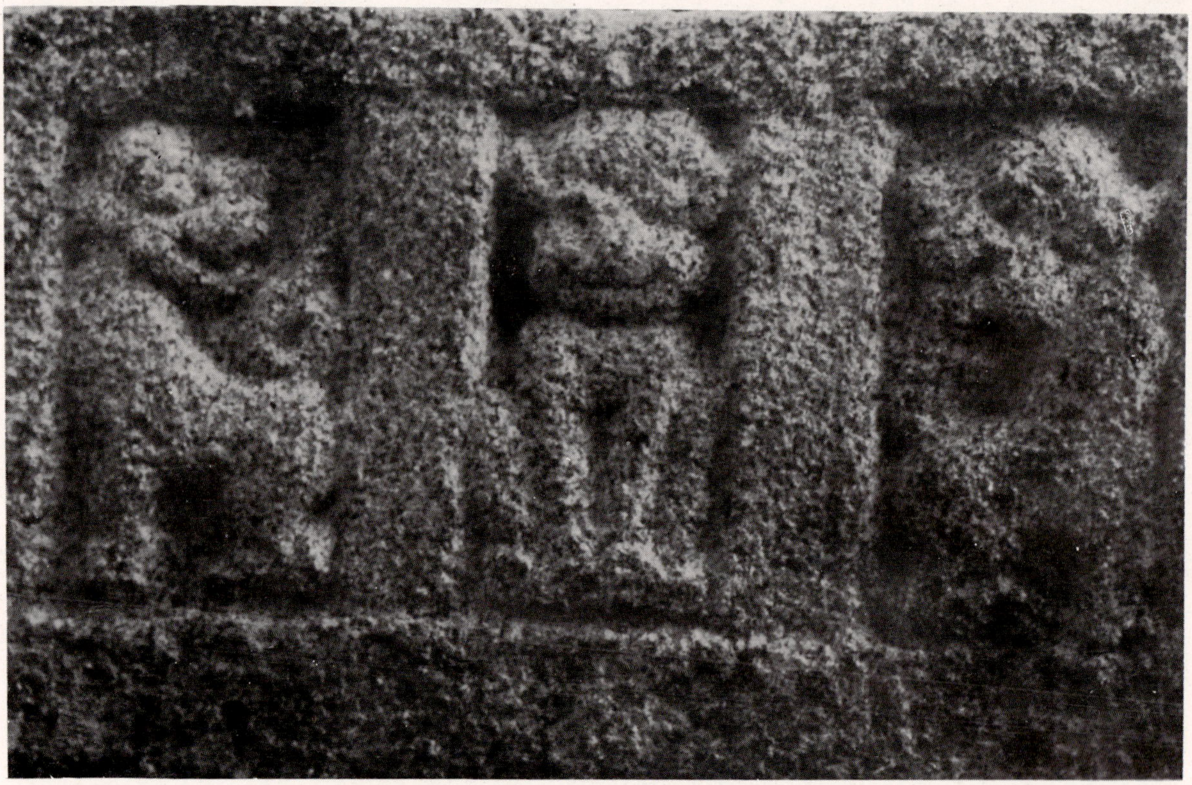

7. Keesaragutta: Panel showing lions.

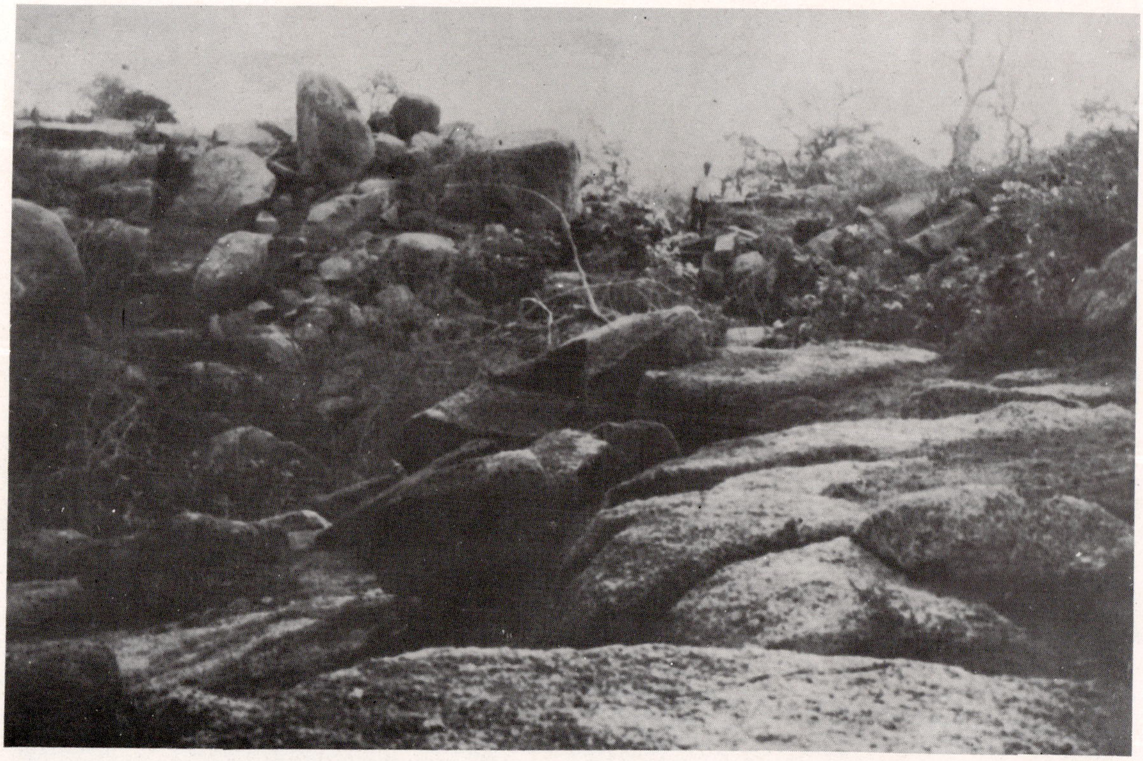

8. Keesaragutta: Fortification—showing the gate on the west.

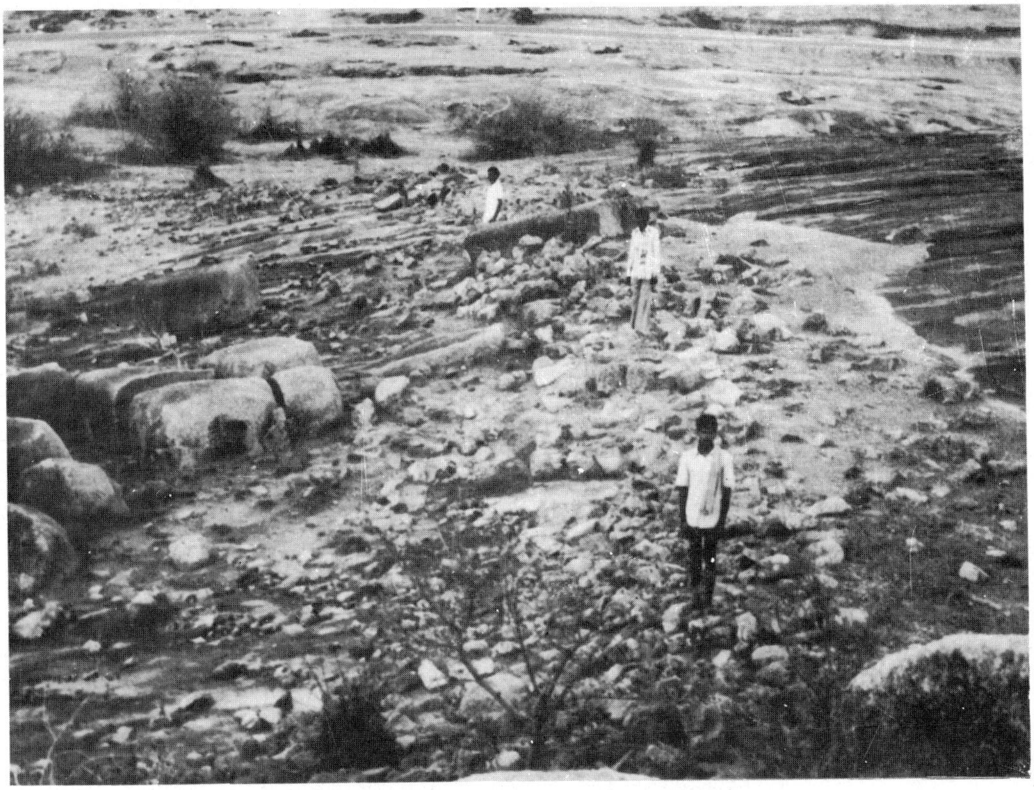

9. Bastion(?) of Keesaragutta Fort—north-east..

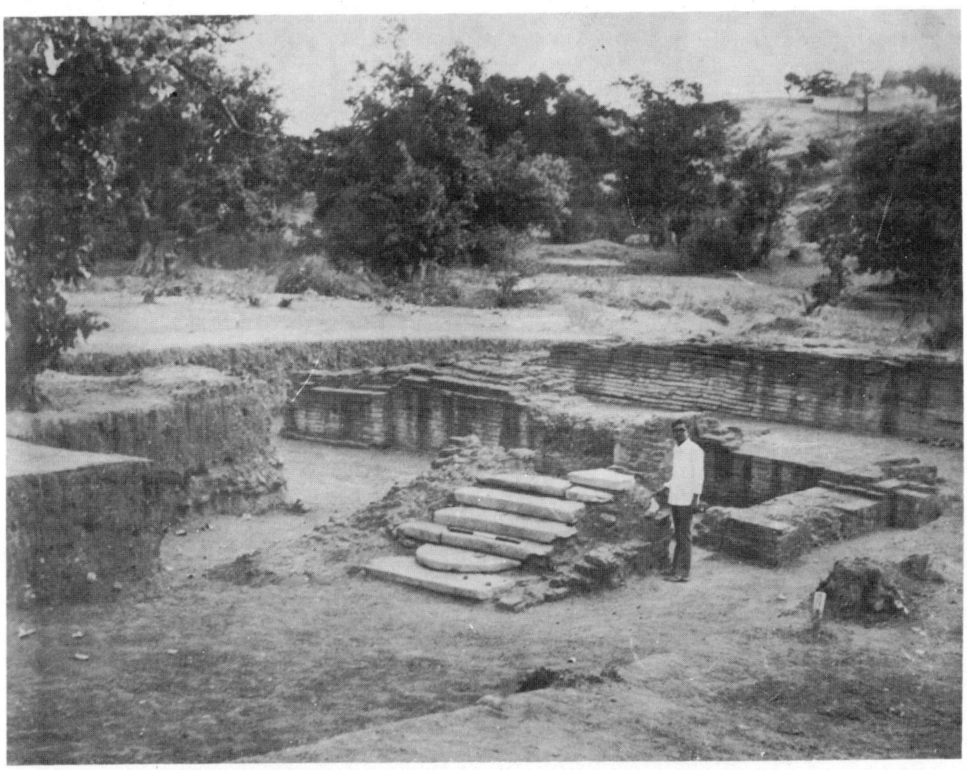

10. Keesaragutta: General view of the Palace complex.

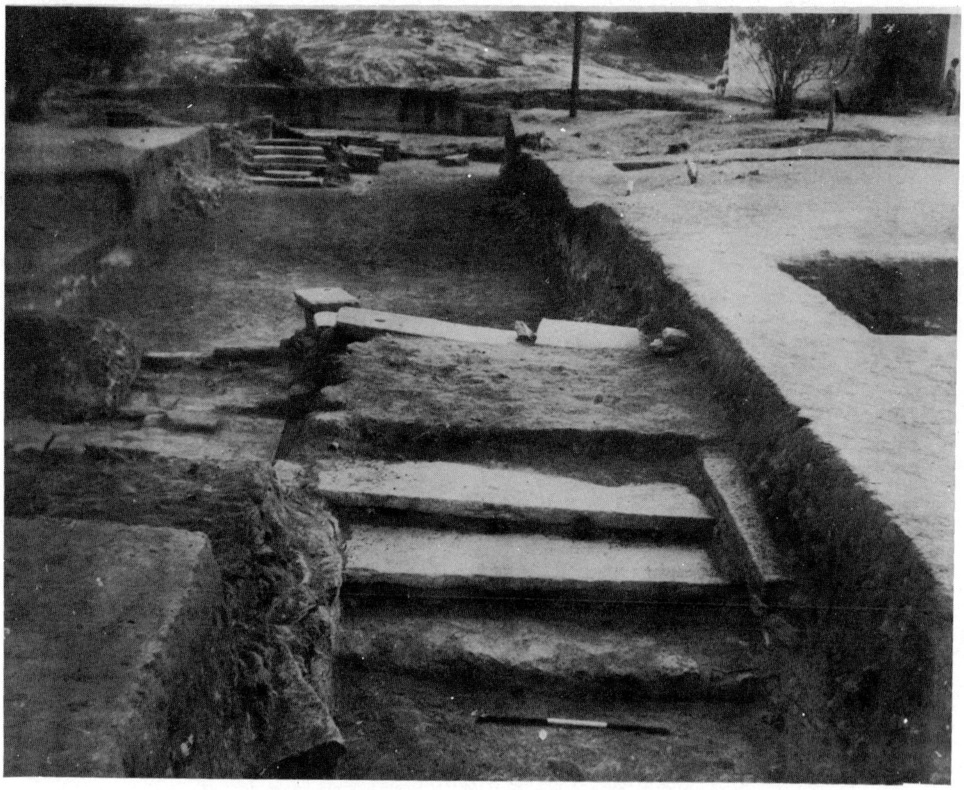

11. Keesaragutta: Palace complex.

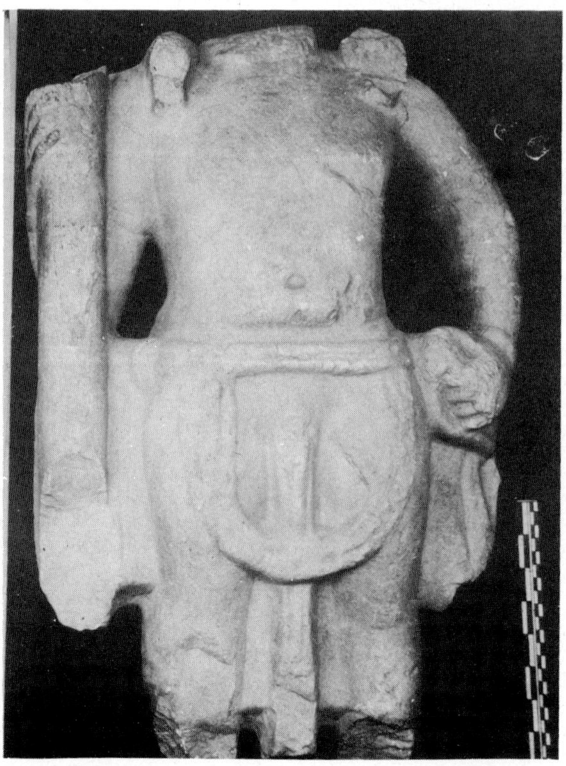

12. Early Vishnu sculpture from Yeleswaram.

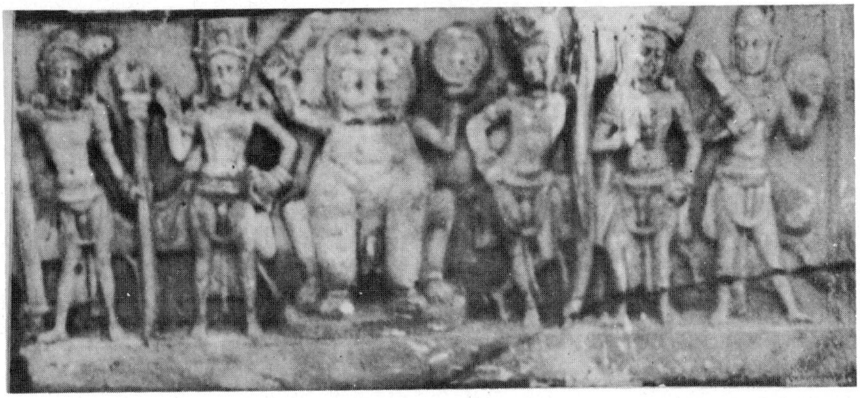

13. Early Narasimha sculpture.

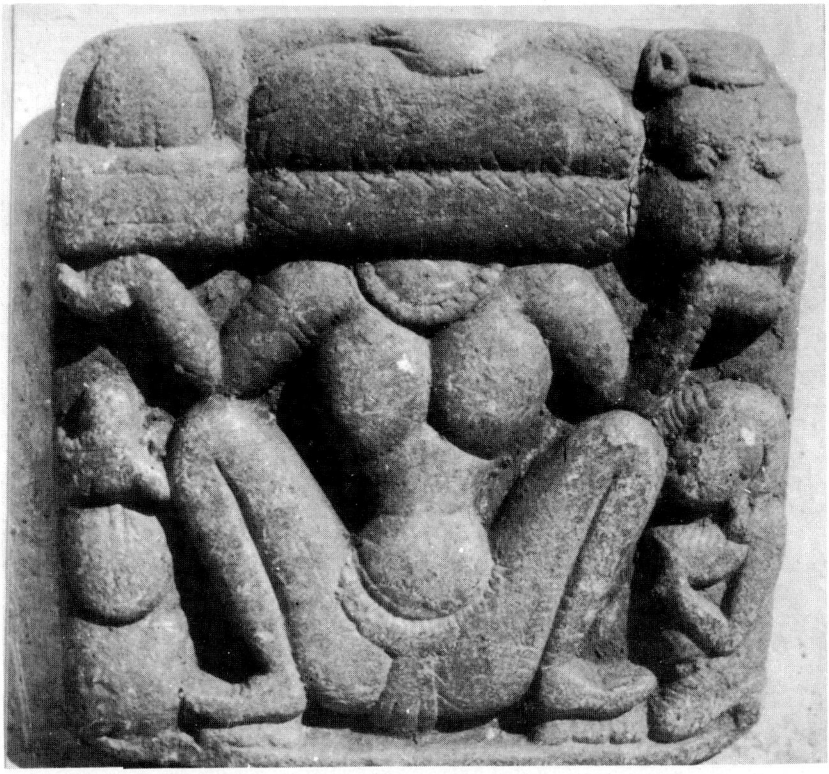

14. Keesaragutta: Mother Goddess—stone plaque.

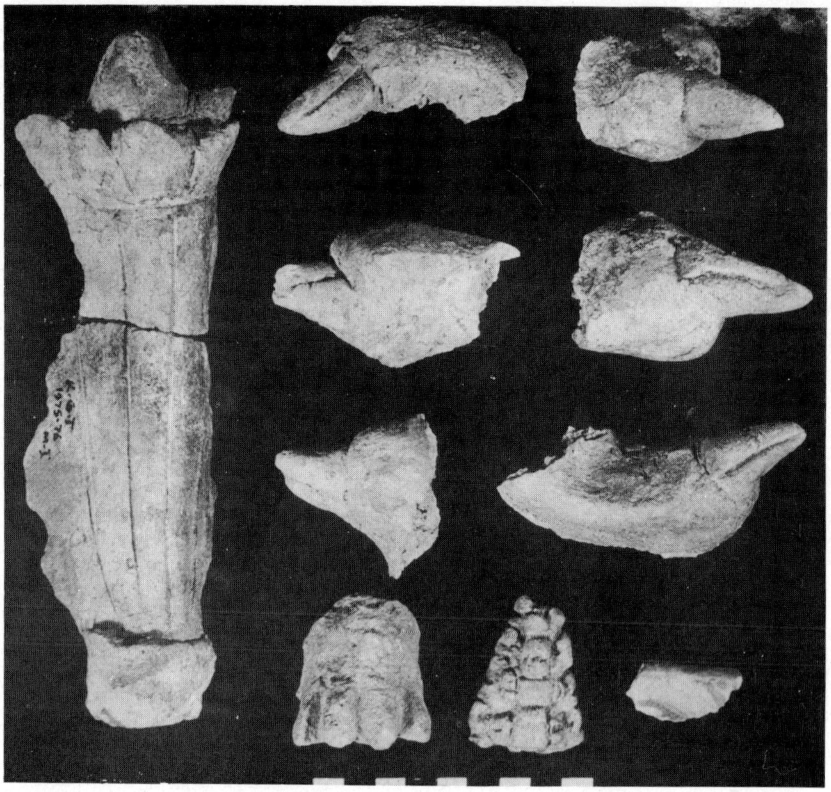

15. Keesaragutta: Stucco figurines.

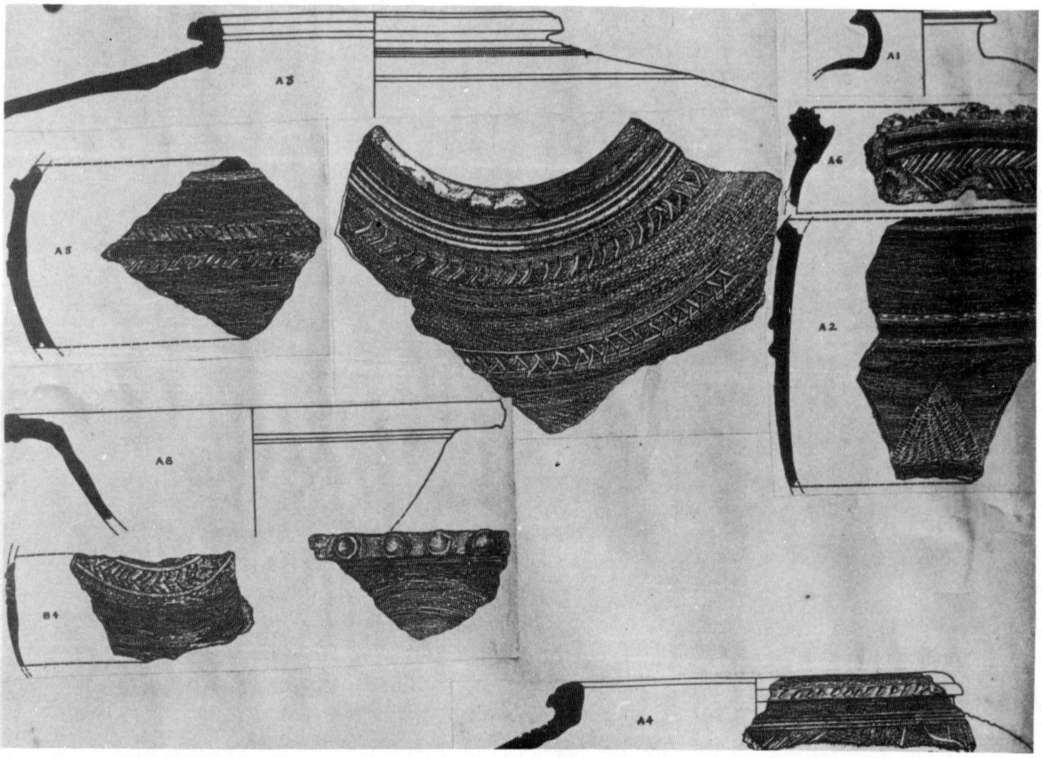

16. Keesaragutta: Pottery types.

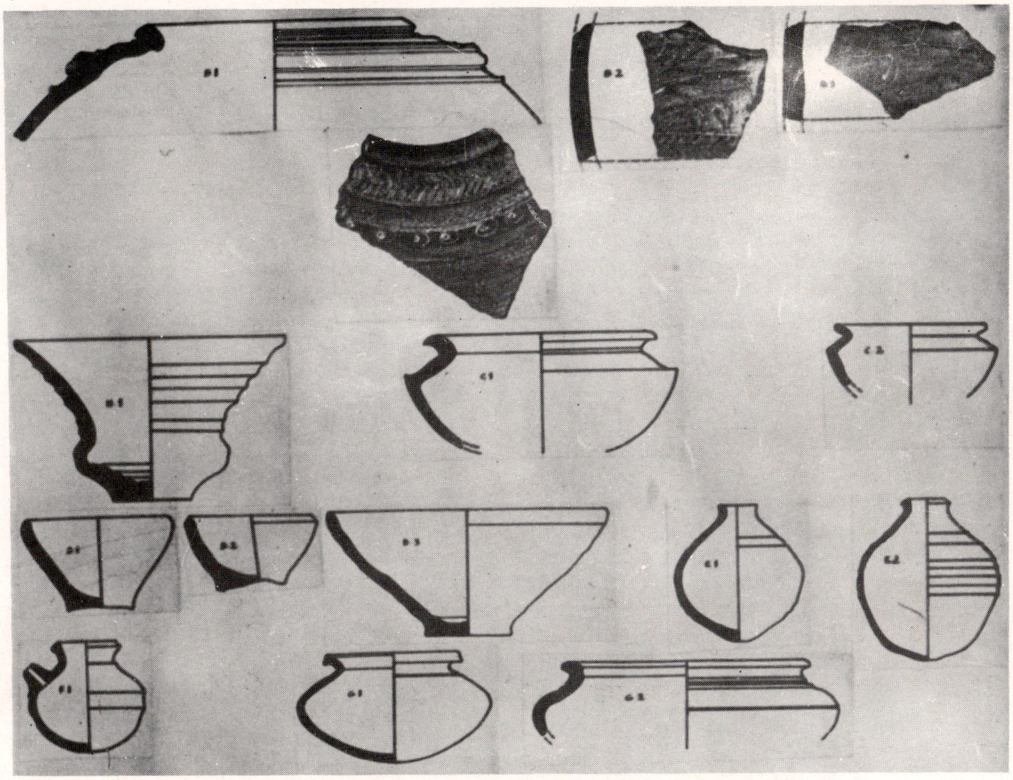

Keesaragutta: Pottery types.

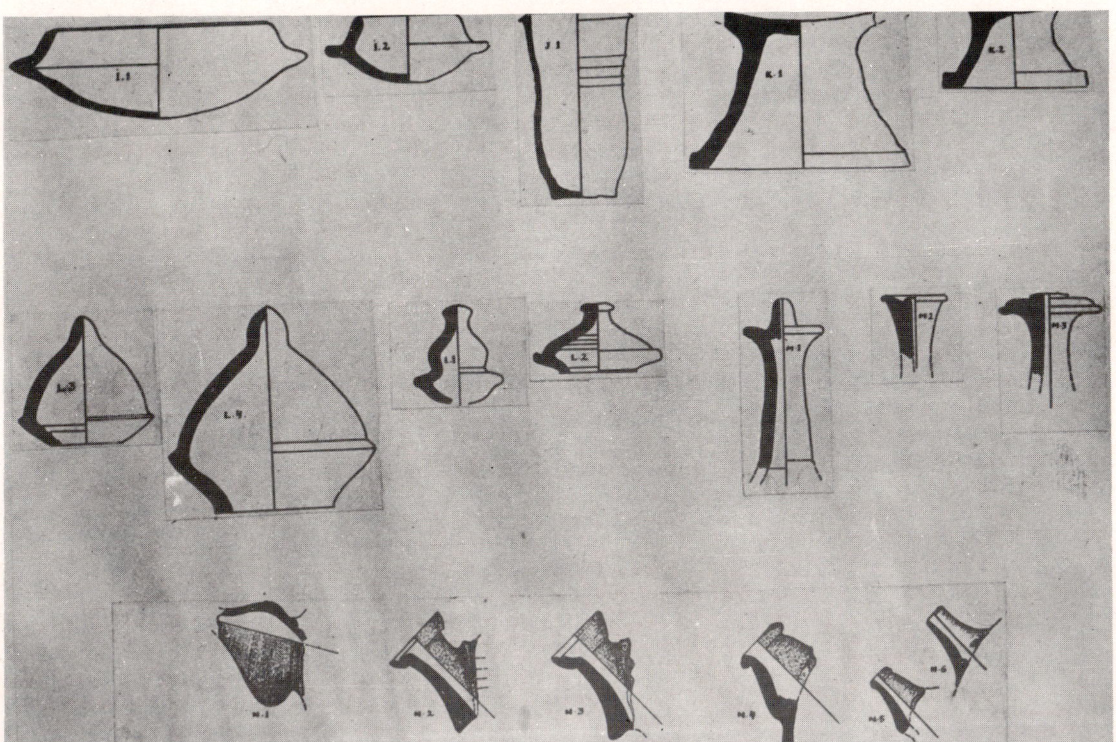

Keesaragutta: Pottery types.

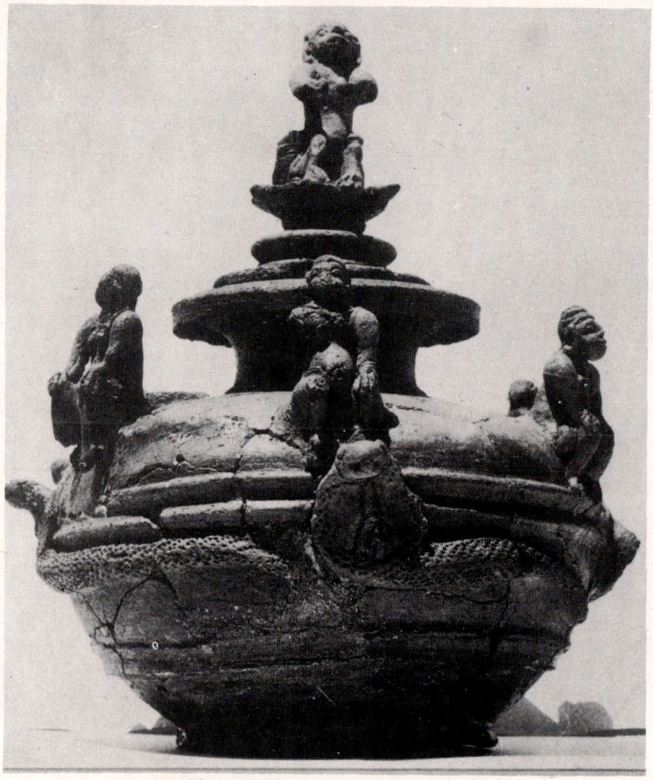

17. Keesaragutta: Decorated pot.

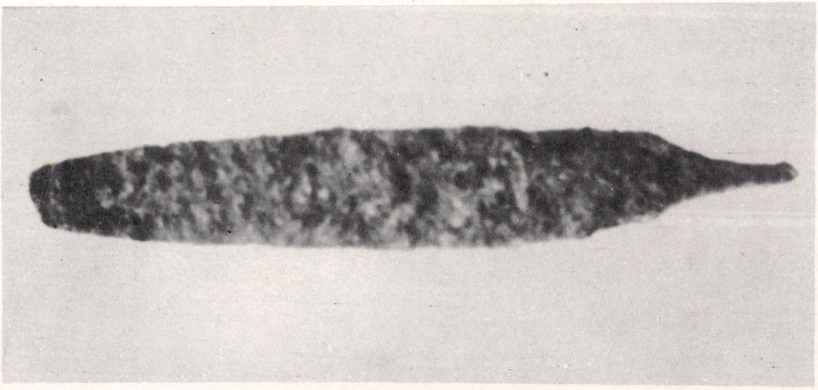

18. Keesaragutta: Iron tool.

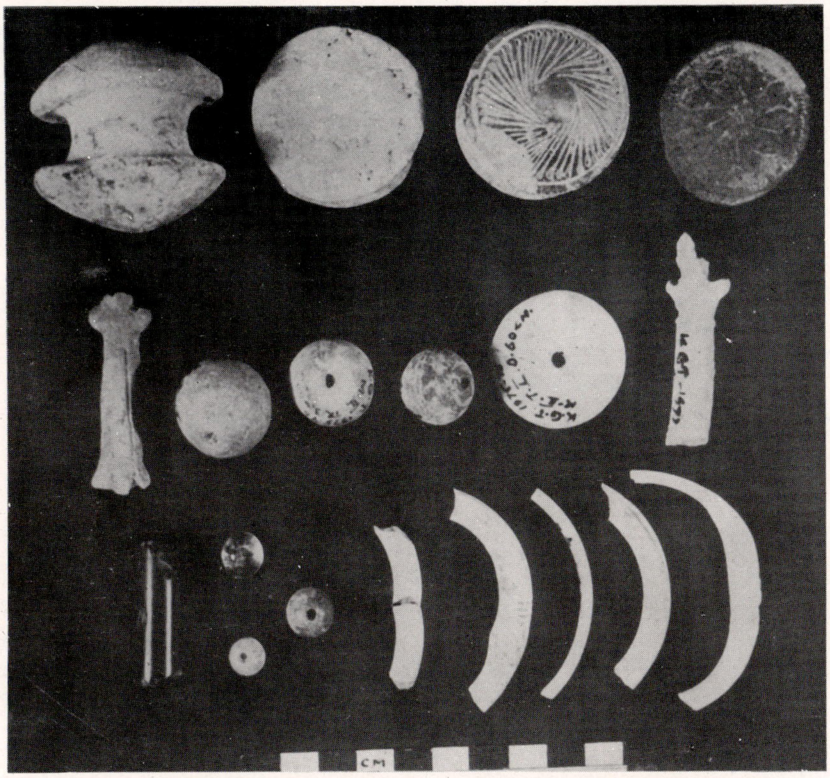

19. Keesaragutta: Shell beads bangles and spools.

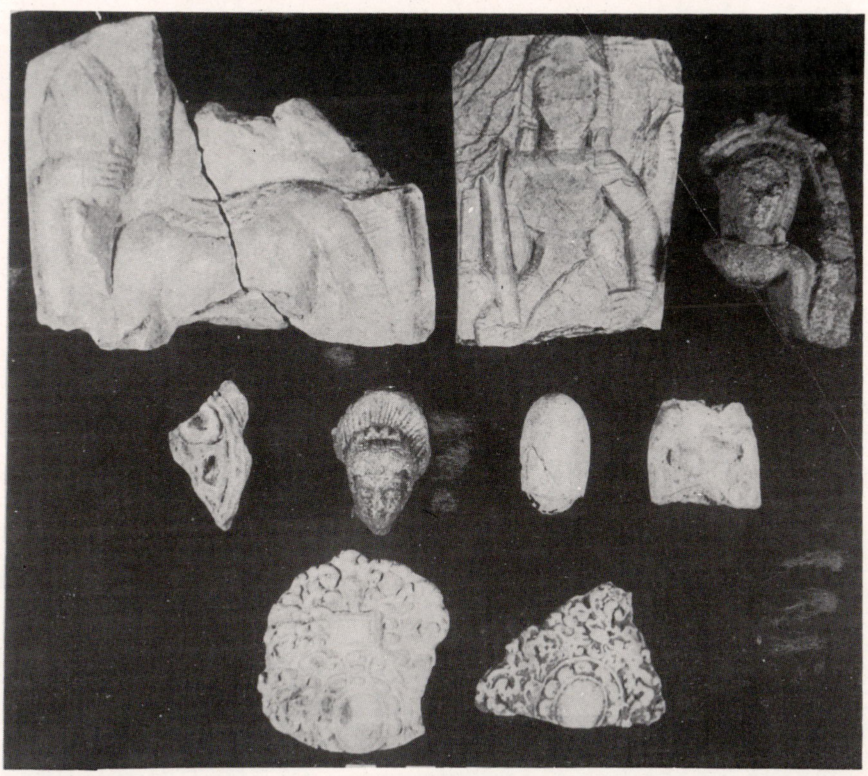

20. Keesaragutta: Stone and terracotta figurines.

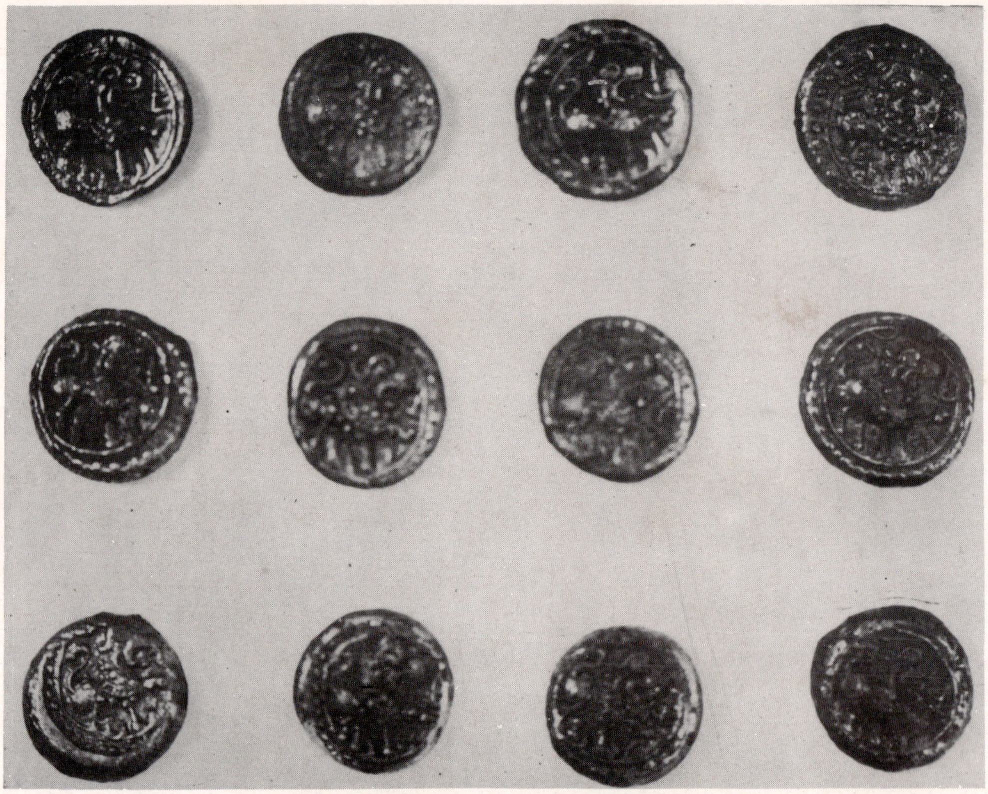

21. Keesaragutta: Vishnukundin coins—obverse.

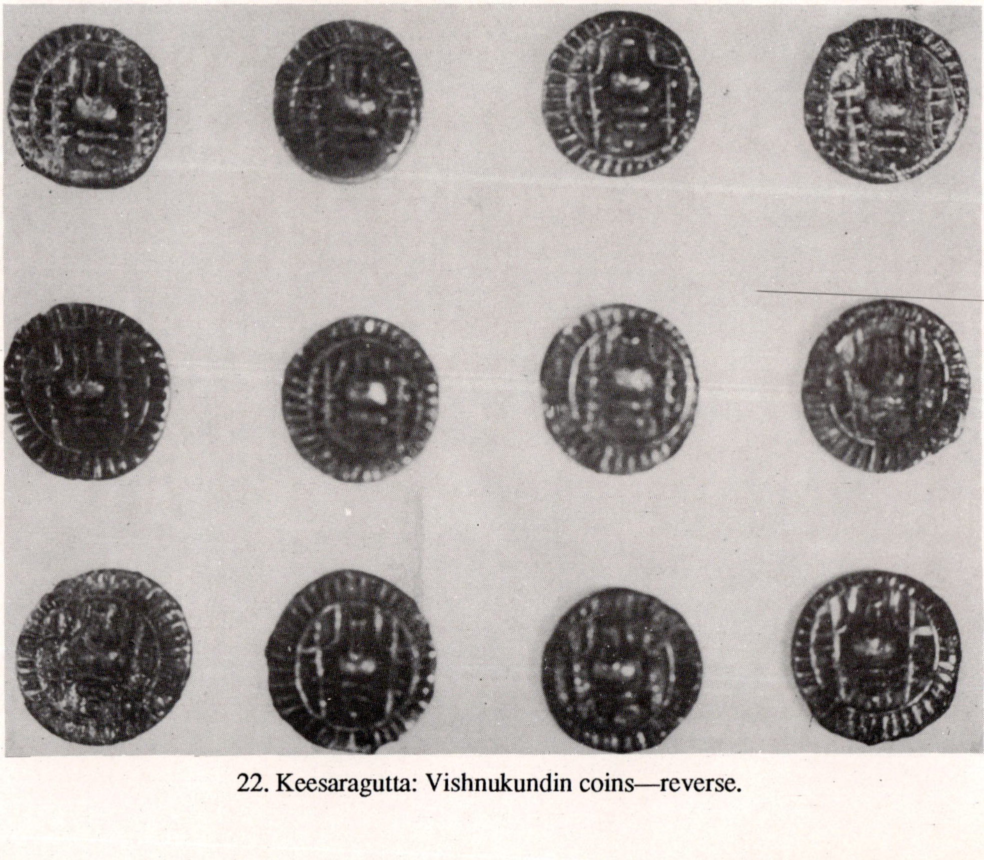

22. Keesaragutta: Vishnukundin coins—reverse.